CW01336329

SOCIAL WORK AS NARRATIVE

Social Work as Narrative
Storytelling and persuasion in professional texts

CHRISTOPHER HALL
Research Fellow
Dartington Social Research Unit

Ashgate
Aldershot • Brookfield USA • Singapore • Sydney

© Christopher Hall 1997

All rights reserved. No part of this publication may be reproduced, stored in a retrieval system, or transmitted in any form or by any means, electronic, mechanical, photocopying, recording or otherwise without the prior permission of the publisher.

Published by
Ashgate Publishing Ltd
Gower House
Croft Road
Aldershot
Hants GU11 3HR
England

Ashgate Publishing Company
Old Post Road
Brookfield
Vermont 05036
USA

British Library Cataloguing in Publication Data
Hall, Christopher
    Social work as narrative : storytelling and persuasion in
    professional texts
    1. Social service 2. Social workers
    I. Title
    361.3 ' 2

Library of Congress Catalog Card Number: 97-76933

ISBN 1 85972 130 3

Printed and bound by Athenaeum Press, Ltd.,
Gateshead, Tyne & Wear.

Contents

Acknowledgements	vii
Introduction	1
1 An alternative approach to social work: accounts, texts and narrative	9
2 Narrative as performance	23
3 Social work texts as stories with readers	45
4 Handling blame and constructing moral character	79
5 Explaining the 'facts' and claiming entitlement	117
6 Retellings: following the social work story	143
7 Reported speech: hearing the words of the client	177
8 Depicting character: reading adequate representations of the client	201
Conclusion	233
Bibliography	251
Author Index	265
Subject Index	269

Acknowledgements

This book is based on my doctoral thesis awarded by Brunel, the University of West London in 1994. Carried out through part-time study, the thesis took a long time to complete and almost as long to re-write for publication. Throughout this period, a large number of friends, family and colleagues have helped with its completion and contributed to the development of the ideas. I wish to thank them all.
My career shift from a social worker to a researcher started at Leicester University School of Social Work, where staff and students provided an invaluable introduction to theoretical argument, especially Pauline Hardiker. At Brunel, staff and students in CRICT and the Department of Human Sciences provided a stimulating environment for developing ideas in new directions. My supervisor, Professor Steve Woolgar, has been a considerable influence, offering unlimited support and critical appraisal—he helped change a worry into a disbelief.
Friends and colleagues have read and commented on earlier drafts (sometimes in a helpful way). In particular, I want to thank Paul Atkinson, Bill Jordan, Bill Munroe, Tom Osborne, Jean Packman, Nigel Parton and Alex Taylor. The ongoing collaboration with Srikant Sarangi and Stef Slembrouck continues to be a major source of stimulation and without the help of Pam Hall, Jill Sharp and Kevin Mount the final manuscript would never have been produced.
Thanks must also be extended to the many social workers who have given up their time and patience to be interviewed, provide access to files and talk about their work. My admiration for their resilience remains. My employers have also provided encouragement, financial support and study leave - a Social Services Department, National Foundation for Educational Research and Dartington Social Research Unit.
Finally, special thanks to Jean Packman, my parents, and to Pam, Alice, Charlotte and Laurence—what can I say but 'sorry'.

Introduction

> Armoured with correctness and righteousness, social workers go out into the world, hunting for what they see as evil. Working constantly amongst the losers of society, it would be surprising if they did not develop a sense of knowing better than the rest of us. As individuals they are well-intentioned and often highly committed to the welfare of their clients. But entrenched behind their ideology and equipped with fearsome legal authority, they have achieved powers which they are plainly unfit to hold.
>
> *Daily Express, July 14, 1993*

Critical media coverage of social work has been widespread over the last twenty years. The Daily Express article above is directed at policies of 'same race' adoption, but it could have been failure to protect children from negligent parents, being 'soft' on juvenile offenders or abuse in children's homes. Social workers are here portrayed as people with particular personal attributes: arrogant and supercilious but at the same time incompetent. The journalist makes the move from the personal to the professional by suggesting that these well intentioned people have become corrupted by their profession. Perhaps the sub-text is that society has somehow entrusted this group of workers with control and responsibilities which they have used irresponsibly and to their own advantage.

On other occasions the media has portrayed social workers as the opposite—woolly minded, easily taken in and indecisive. They have not used their powers appropriately and have been indecisive. As Franklin and Parton (1991) note, social workers are depicted as "inept and passive" as well as "intrusive and authoritarian". Whilst the criticism might not be consistent, its intensity is unabating. Such outrage and its associated moral indignation attacks the centre of social work—its practices, knowledge, values and attitudes. There are not just a few incompetent individuals but how all social workers think and act is challenged.

Scrutiny has not only been by the tabloid press. There has been government review and intense debate by academics. Child abuse, in particular, has come to dominate discussions about social work. In the UK, there were a series of critical inquiries in the 1980s and early 1990s which developed similar themes—too much interference in families (Cleveland 1988, Rochdale 1990, Orkney 1992) and not intervening enough (Beckford 1985, Henry 1987 and Carlile 1987). The Government produced the *Children Act* 1989 which tried to balance intervention and support. Many social services departments set up child protection strategies and guidance to promote 'good practice'. Even though high profile inquiries have not dominated the mid 1990s, a recent Government sponsored research report still considers the balance is not quite right (Department of Health, 1995).

What is it about social work that generates so much controversy and criticism? The power and authority that modern society has vested in professionals is not new nor restricted to social work (Friedson, 1986). Illich refers to the mid-twentieth century as the 'Age of the Disabling Professions'.

> Let us first face the fact that the bodies of specialists that now dominate the creation, adjudication and implementation of needs are a new kind of cartel. They are more deeply entrenched than a Byzantine bureaucracy, more international than a world church, more stable than any labour union, endowed with wider competencies than any shaman, and equipped with a tighter hold over those they claim as victims than any mafia (1992:15)

Social workers, in particular, seem unable to protect themselves against public criticism. They appear more uncertain in their mandate and their claims to knowledge seem less ratified than more established professions. Some note that their work is unknown and unobserved. Barbara Wootton (1959:290) sums up the problem:

> Other professions specify the nature of their cases: in medicine, general practitioners deal with cases of illness, specialists with cases of particular diseases: judges and magistrates deal with fraud, burglary ... but the (social) worker deals with—cases of what?

Pithouse (1987) calls it an 'invisible trade' in order to indicate how social workers spend much of their time in various closed and unobserved encounters—interview rooms, clients' homes, small meetings with colleagues. Unlike other professionals they are not associated with easily identifiable arenas—the courtroom, the surgery or the classroom.

This study does not attempt to answer these big questions of social workers' competence or mandate. It will not attempt to counter media over-simplification nor promote good practice. I will not even suggest some underlying reality about what social work is, noting Gilbert and Mulkay (1984:2) :

> .. sociologists' attempts to tell the story of a particular social setting or to formulate the way in which social life operates are fundamentally unsatisfactory.

Instead, I set a more modest task of exploring how social workers make their work visible and justifiable through their talk and writing. How do they explain their actions and assessments in an atmosphere of criticism and controversy? What sort of language, explanation and analysis do social workers use in order to handle stressful situations and support their decisions?

This is not merely the subjective view of social workers in contrast to some objective version elsewhere. Rather, it is suggested that through the process of everyday explanation social work is created. Drawing on traditions of social construction and discourse theory, we will see how social work is constituted in and through language, how it is performed and made recognisable. Like Gilbert and Mulkay, I do not attempt to reduce the complexities and uncertainties of professional activity to a definitive version of 'what is really happening', but consider the everyday struggle to construct social work, giving opportunities to alternative versions and different voices, sometimes literally. This study draws on and develops a variety of themes which locate professional work in everyday activities—reports, interviews, files, meetings. In particular, social work is not approached through familiar categories like counselling, child protection or advocacy. For a set of performances to be made recognisable as, for example, 'doing family therapy', requires a series of constituting and confirming activities whereby the problems of the family are made visible in the therapy session and reportable to others.

> The process of narratively giving shape and substance to the troubled home is not automatic. It entails the practical interpretative work of linking an abstract, experiential activity—the home—with immediately available concrete signs. (Gubrium, 1992:16)

It is only when the family counsellor is able to demonstrate to his/her colleagues that behaviour in the session displays the family problems that family therapy is being done. In other words, doing social work requires reporting to and persuading important listeners of the reality of the characters, problems and solutions. Social work is seen as constructed in and through the reporting processes of social workers and their audiences. It is constituted by talking and listening, reading and writing social work.

What do social workers do?

Most social workers in the UK are employed by local authority Social Service Departments (SSDs) and organised into local area teams. They are managed by a team manager, with a hierarchy of managers ultimately responsible to local politicians. This study concentrates on the work of social workers concerned with children and families, particularly because child care work is more directly concerned with dimensions of state control and protection than other areas of social work. The mandate for social work with children is based on legislation which regulates intervention to protect children and young people considered to be 'at risk', and to support 'vulnerable families'. The first Children's Officers were appointed to implement the 1948 *Children Act* and, with subsequent legislation, social workers have taken on wideranging responsibilities for the administration of child protection, residential care, fostering and adoption, juvenile justice and family support services.

Social workers spend their time visiting children and families at home, in foster homes, in their office or in other establishments—residential homes, family centres, schools etc. They hold meetings with families, service providers, their managers and other agencies. They make phone calls, write letters and reports. They attend courts and panels. Each social worker is likely to have a 'caseload', a number of families and children for whom they are the designated worker. The social worker is likely to perform a number of tasks which attempt to identify problems and develop strategies to rectify them.

Social workers' work usually centres around counselling, offering support and guidance to help parents look after their children, and co-ordinating the involvement of other supportive and therapeutic services. As a last resort, children may be removed from their families, either with parents' consent or through a court order. When this happens, social workers oversee the services offered to the children and monitor their development. A child's stay in 'care' or 'accommodation' may last a few days whilst parents sort themselves out, several months to enable serious family disputes to be resolved, or there could be a permanent move to an alternative family. Work with children 'in care or accommodation' makes up a large proportion of the work of child care social workers and is the main type of case considered in this study.

Social work as narrative

The study of the language of social work could be approached from several directions but here I will concentrate on themes of narrative and storytelling. This links the study of social work to wideranging debates in the social sciences, linguistics, cultural studies and literary theory. Some commentators make grand claims for narrative. For Barthes (1982:251):

> Narrative is present in myth, legend, fable, tale, novella, epic, history, tragedy, drama, comedy, mime, painting, stained glass windows, cinema, comics, news items, conversation. Moreover, under this almost infinite diversity of forms, narrative is present in every age, in every place, in every society; it begins with the very history of mankind and there nowhere is nor has been a people without narrative... it is simply there like life itself.

Jameson (1981:13) talks of:

> ... the all informing process of narrative, which I take to be the central function or instance of the human mind.

Landau (1984:262) sees narrative in science:

> Seldom do [scientists] recognise that many scientific theories are essentially narratives. The growth of a plant, the progress of a disease, the formation of a beach, the evolution of an organism—any set of events that can be arranged in a sequence and related can also be narrated... Students of literature are so conscious of narrative that some have argued it is storytelling which makes us human.

There are many approaches to narrative, with different versions of what a story is and how it should be investigated. For psychologists, a story is a cognitive construct (Rumelhart 1980, Wilensky 1983); for linguists it is part of the structure of language (Labov, 1972); for literary theorists it is an aesthetic entity (Bal, 1994). In sociology, there is a key distinction between 'grand' and 'little' narratives, that is narrative as an overarching set of explanations as opposed to narrative as locally constructed (see chapter 1). Whilst drawing on a wide range of approaches, the central direction of this study is to approach social work as constructed through the interactional and textual work of storytelling. Writing and reading narrative, hearing and telling stories is the way we communicate with others. People and events are made available by organising them into unfolding linguistic performances. Pithouse and Atkinson (1988:185) also approach social work as narrative:

> In general we take it as axiomatic that the organisation of narrative is a fundamental resource whereby social actors give shape to their per-

sonal experiences, endow them with consequence and value, and render them available to other individuals. Through narrative formats, tellers produce 'accounts' of their troubles, inviting sympathetic response, formulating blame and excuse. They render them dramatic, humorous or sentimental. Stories 'gain in their telling' not simply in the sense that we are prone to exaggerate and dramatise, but also in the sense that without 'the telling' the events and experiences of work and domestic life would lose their meaning.

This approach offers a number of aspects which are explored in this study. Narrative is seen as a way that people package events and experiences into a performance for others. These narrative performances anticipate the audience and guard against adverse reactions and potential criticism, as listeners are instructed to interpret what they hear. Stories persuade, surprise and entertain and in the process, the authority of the storyteller is constituted. Pithouse and Atkinson present narrative as a 'resource', a device, something speakers choose to deploy. In contrast, my approach will see narrative as not only strategic but also unnoticed and unstable. Narrative is available in all aspects of social work communication—written and verbal, description and explanation, everyday and theoretical. We will thus explore social work as narrative in all texts which depict social work: in the claims of the authors, the response of audiences, including the work of the analyst and you, the reader of this text.

Outline of the book

In chapters 1 and 2 theoretical perspectives from discourse and textual analysis and narrative theory are discussed and the implications of such theories for the study of social work examined. Chapters 3 to 8 provide a narrative analysis of a variety of social work documents—research interviews, reports, minutes of meetings, case notes, newspapers and a case conference (see appendix 1). Each chapter develops an aspect of narrative and the role of the reader, looking at what can be gained by approaching social work documents in this way. The discussion centres around the following question: how do rhetorical and narrative features of social work documents construct, instruct and convince (or not convince) critical and competent social work readers? Latour (1987:52) notes the role of the reader in scientific texts:

> The image of the ideal reader built into the text is easy to retrieve. Depending on the author's use of language, you immediately imagine to whom he or she is talking (at least you realise that in most cases he or she is not talking to you!)

Seeking out ideal readers of social work documents enables us to explore how social work attempts to persuade readers and handle potential criticism.

In chapter3, we consider social work documents in terms of two key aspects of narrative: story structure and the role of the reader. We examine whether social work texts have 'story structure' and if this is definitive of narrative. The role of the reader is offered as key to understanding narrative and a variety of reading relations are explored.

Chapters 4, 5 and 6 are linked in that the emphasis is on the 'passive' reader and strategies of persuasion. Chapter 4 looks at social work accounts as moral stories and asks how far the reader is persuaded by deploying moral categories and characterisations. How far is the reader instructed to come to preferred conclusions through appeals to right or wrong, good or bad, innocent or culpable?

Whereas chapter 4 sees the reader as a moral subject, making judgements on the basis of ethics, the theme of Chapter 5 is the construction of facts and entitlement to tell stories; the reader as an empiricist. This explores social work as factual accounts and how a rational reader is attended to. How far is s/he to be convinced on the basis of facts and authority. Chapter 6 continues the theme of chapters 4 and 5, the construction and reception of persuasive stories, but considers changes of depiction and characterisation by following one story through several reading occasions. The question here is how far both instructions to the reader and the strength of the story alter over time and with occasions of the reading.

Chapters 7 and 8 offer a more active reading of social work where opportunities for subversion and criticism are explored. In chapter 7, the voice of the client is finally given a platform; not through direct access, but through the concept of 'the other', the alternative and potentially undermining version available in the reading relations of the story. Chapter 8 questions the categorisation of social work accounting and the way in which flexible and changing depictions of characters and events enable the undermining of formulations. It considers not merely the nature of the appeal to the preferred reader (as in chapter 3), but how retellings of the story on occasions increasingly distant from the events, produce different versions of characters and different appeals to the reader.

Chapter 9 considers the implications of this project for both social work and sociology. How far is the study of narrative an important direction for further investigating other fields of accounting practices? What, in particular, can it offer the growing study of discourse and the professional? For social workers, does this approach to social work as narrative enable a more searching review of everyday activity? Does it liberate or emasculate professional scrutiny of social work practice?

Overall, the study of narrative offers important opportunities for asking questions about social work, professionals and the handling of controversy. I hope to convince readers that social work documents can be rendered more understandable when approached as stories with readers, even if I have to deploy narrative methods to persuade you.

1 An alternative approach to social work: accounts, texts and narrative

There is limited sociological research of social work in comparison with studies of other professions. Research on social work is more usually carried out in social work studies or social policy. Academics in social work studies aim to identify and promote effective social work practice and such research tends to be based on research traditions which treat the reality of social work as unproblematic. Social workers carry out various activities which are easily recognisable and categorisable. Having categorised social work, it can then be evaluated as conforming to effective or less effective social work practice. The data of such empirical research are therefore docile documents—questionnaires, interviews, observation notes etc, which represent the reality of social work beyond the data gathering occasion. In this study, I approach social work as a less certain and bounded enterprise which is constructed through talk and writing. It thus becomes harder to separate the entity of social work from everyday interaction and the research enterprise.

Interview data : facts or texts?

The distinction between social work as facts or texts can be illustrated by considering how data from research interviews are treated. A traditional approach sees research interviews as providing access to the facts of social life, more or less. Researchers asks questions of respondents whose answers are treated as (more or less) accurate reports of events and attitudes. There are concerns about bias, memory or interviewer influence, but provided certain checks are adhered to, replies are seen as offering facts about entities beyond the interview situation (Silverman, 1985:158). For example, Vernon and Fruin (1986) interviewed social workers about how far they planned their work with children in care. From these interviews, they considered that they gained "factual information" about the social work done and decisions made. 'Social work plans' and 'decisions' are treated as unproblematic entities and signified good (or bad) social work practice. Vernon and Fruin delineate three groups where plans did not exist on the basis of comments from the interviewers—"I would hope that...", "I imagine that..." or assessments that the social worker had not "read the situation sufficiently to allow them to predict the likely outcome" (Vernon and Fruin, 1986:119). Interview talk is thus treated as transparent, offering direct access to social work activity outside the interview. It enables the researchers to categorise social workers' activity and offer evaluations about its competence.

Some sociologists are sceptical about the factual status of interview material. They see interview data as so variable and dependent on local and interactional features that the analyst cannot identify a definitive version of facts independent of the interview occasion (Potter and Mulkay, 1985:249). Gilbert and Mulkay (1984:11), for example, interviewed scientists about a bio-chemical controversy but could not find a definitive version of events, with inconsistencies even within the same interview.

> we find that, when we look at any collection of participants' characterisations on a given topic from our data, almost every single account is rendered doubtful by its apparent inconsistency with other equally plausible versions of events ... scientists furnish quite different versions of events within a single recorded interview transcript or single session of a taped conference discussion.

However, interview data can offer an opportunity to explore rhetorical and interactional features produced by interviewer and respondent in interviews. Watson and Weinberg (1982) consider the internal formal sequences of interview talk, whilst Gilbert and Mulkay (1984) look at how speakers use 'accounting repertoires' in interviews. Interviews can tell us something about the world outside the interview, not as facts, but as methods of talk, persuasion and explanation. Potter and Mulkay (1985:269) suggest:

> ...we have to assume that we can, in a more restricted sense, generalise from interviews to naturally occurring situations. For we are assuming that the interactional and interpretative work occurring in interviews resembles to some degree that which takes place outside the interviews.

This then sets up a rather different approach to interview data. The interviews with social workers which form part of the data of this study[1] cannot be seen as testing the accuracy of assessments nor competence of social work, since they consist of interview talk. However, how social work is constructed and justified by the respondent and interviewer in the reporting of social work events and activities offers instances of the active construction of social work. As Potter and Mulkay suggest, such interview talk necessarily draws on descriptive and interpretative resources available on other occasions when social work is talked and written about.

Approaching social work as accounts

This study approaches social work by investigating written and spoken texts which are routinely produced as a part of everyday social work activity. These are occasions on which social workers communicate about their work to others—colleagues, courts, research interviewers.[2] I refer to these documents as 'accounts'. The term 'account' has a number of important connotations. First, 'an account' suggests recounting what has happened, a story, an explanation. Second, 'being called to account' signals justification. Third, a 'statement of account' suggests the pluses and minuses are being balanced. Fourth, 'taking into account' signifies a review of attending factors. Social work accounts describe and justify social work and show professional practice being created through rhetorical and interactional activity.

Accounts and accounting practices have been approached by a number of theorists. For some, an account has a restricted role, referring to those occasions on which interaction is disrupted and an account is required, for example, excuses, justifications or 'saving face' (Scott and Lyman 1968, Semin and Manstead 1983, Heritage 1988). For others, accountability is fundamental to social communication. Giddens (1976:20) notes:

> The organisation of 'accountability' as has been made fully clear in existential phenomenology after Heidegger, is the fundamental condition of social life: the production of 'sense' in communicative acts is, like the production of society which it underpins, a skilled accomplishment.

Garfinkel (1967:1) insists that producing and managing everyday affairs is identical with accountable reporting. Accounting, in the broad sense, includes both repair work and the accountable nature of all reporting. The important point is that social workers in their reports and explanations attend to a range of rhetorical and interactional concerns through which they are able to demonstrate that their work is in accord with responsible, justifiable and defensible professional activity. Garfinkel (1967:186-207) found that medical reports when approached as 'facts' about patients or treatment are inaccurate.

However, if they are read as "a potential therapeutic contract" they begin to make sense. Medical records as accounts do not report facts, but make available displays of justifiable medical work for later inquiries (social work case notes are analysed in chapters 3 and 8). Rhetoric has been an area of study since classical times and the persuasive nature of language is well recognised. For some writers rhetorical work is a form of persuasion which speakers deliberately deploy and which can be improved (Cockcroft and Cockcroft, 1992:1). Here, following Garfinkel, all speech is seen as persuasive and accountable.

Approaching social work as text

The term 'text' is an important theme in recent social and cultural theory. The overall thrust of the 'linguistic turn' is to see social reality as only available through representations of that reality. We do not have access to entities outside the text. Sociology has taken on similar concerns to those of literary theory. There is an interest in how texts are written and read, how social interaction is made possible through conventions of talk; that is, 'how' rather than 'what' questions (Game, 1991:5). Speech and writing of social work thus becomes the object of study without an attempt to discover an external reality.

The everyday use of the term 'text' refers to a book or written document, as distinguished from talk. Here, however, all social work entities—documents, conversations, notes, pictures—are approached as 'texts'. A text is not a self-contained, bounded object, easily separated from production and reception. Rather it is an active entity (Smith, 1993:120), caught in a web of interpretations and social relations, to be read and reacted to.[3] As with Barthes' (1977:155) move from the 'work' to the 'text' in the literary field, so the social work account is no longer seen as a closed entity with definitive meaning, but a site for reading with multiple versions and interpretations. Silverman (1985:148) notes how Anglo-Saxon sociologists have avoided investigating social phenomena as 'texts':

> ...words seem too ephemeral and insubstantial to be the stuff of scientific analysis. Better, then, to leave textual analysis to literary critics and to concentrate on clearly social phenomena—actions and the structures in which they are implicated.

Sociologists have used social entities, like child abuse, as definitive phenomena with which to identify and categorise actions and construct explanatory structures. To approach social entities as texts means to ask questions about how, for example, child abuse is constructed in social interaction and how is it deployed as an explanatory concept. This means going further into the constitution of such entities and observing their use in everyday conversations and writing.

Hanks (1989:95) defines a 'text' as "any configuration of signs that is coherently interpretable by some community of users." Such a definition suggests that a text is a readable, usable entity, made available through a communicative process and within an everyday community of hearers and readers. Interpretation of texts locates analysis in the everyday encounters of a community of users. Unlike literary texts where reading can occur far from the intended or expected reader, social work as 'text' means asking questions about specific occasions of reading and the community of readers; many readings might be available but some are more legitimate than others. The text and the reading occasion interact with one another (Smith, 1993:121)

'Text' is often used interchangeably with 'discourse'. The Foucauldian concept of 'a discourse' as a discursive practice with structural connotations is discussed below. Discourse as the ongoing talk or communication between writer/speaker, reader/hearer and the relations surrounding that encounter are similar to the notion of text already defined above (cp. Dant's definition of discourse, 1991:7). Bauman and Briggs (1990:73) link text and discourse:

> [Entextualization] is the process of rendering discourse extractable, of making a stretch of linguistic production into a unit—a text—that can be lifted out of its interactional setting. A text, then, from this vantage point, is a discourse rendered decontextualizable. Entextualization may well incorporate aspects of context, such that the resultant text carries elements of its history of use within it.

Given this definition, discourse is only available when it is wrestled from the moment of its production and becomes a text. A text is available for reading and analysis, bringing with it elements of its context, history and construction.

Social work as text, then, means approaching the conversations and reports of social workers as rhetorical, interactional and literary entities to be understood through an analysis of the reading practices of different readers. Importantly, the analytic process is treated as a reading occasion.

Approaching social work as narrative and storytelling

Social work as narrative is offered as a framework for encompassing concepts of accountability, reading and textuality. Narrative and storytelling are used synonymously. Theories of narrative are discussed in detail in chapter 2. Here,

I wish to contrast the interactional approach to narrative with the structural approach; that is, narrative as locally produced stories as opposed to narrative as totalising discursive formations. Narrative, like discourse, has been the subject of considerable theoretical debate and is used differently by different writers, even though the arguments often appear similar. The work of Michel Foucault is a focus for many important debates in the human sciences, and, although he does not offer a theory of narrative, his concepts of 'discourse' and 'discursive formations' pose important questions for considering narrative as a social structural feature.

Foucault's concept of discourse can be considered as similar to Lyotard's concern with 'grand recit' or metanarrative. It is a large formation of knowledge and practice which attempts to offer totalising theories of history and society. For Foucault, the archaeologist, a discourse is a locus of autonomous rules which constitute knowledge. Archaeology is the search to uncover the conditions under which it is possible to make a 'statement' ('enounce') on a topic. For example, Foucault saw madness as the product of a discourse of psychopathology, which developed during the nineteenth century.

> Mental illness was constituted by all that was said in all the statements that named it, divided it up, described it, explained it, traced its developments, indicated its various correlations, judged it and possibly gave it speech by articulating, in its name, discourses that were to be taken as its own. (Foucault, 1972:32)

As Dreyfus and Rabinow (1982:61) comment: "such discursive formations produce the object about which they speak." The development and stabilising of the possibility of a knowledge of mental illness was a result of continuous transformations between and within discursive formations.

A Foucauldian approach to narrative as a totalising discourse is evident in a number of studies of how it is possible to conceive of non-Western cultures. Bruner (1986) signals an indebtedness to Foucault in discussing how anthropologists approach an ethnography of Native American culture. He compares the 'dominant story' or 'metanarrative' of how it was possible to talk about the Indian in the 1930s with that of the 1970s, seeing the change from "assimilation" to "resistance and exploitation". He considers that such "narrative schemes provide a science of the imagination" (p.140). The anthropologist is constrained to conceive of the native through the master story. As Bruner (1986:145) says:

> My only claim is that different narratives are foregrounded in the discourse of different historical eras.

Similarly, Said (1978:3) discusses Orientalism as a discourse, the meta-narrative of how it is possible that European culture has been able to manage and produce the Orient "on any occasion when that peculiar entity 'the Orient' is in question."

Such material and cultural relations constitute the rules of formation of objects. Talking about an object is highly constrained by forms of discourse as an underlying code or rules, which are a product of inter- and intra-discursive transformations. This large concept of discourse or narrative is thus an attempt to locate all relations in and through the 'grand narrative', a system of ways of talking which are to be taken seriously. It is not just what is said but who says it and in what circumstances. As Dreyfus and Rabinow illustrate (1982:48):

> For example, 'It is going to rain' is normally an everyday speech act with only local significance, but it can be a serious speech act if uttered by a spokesman for the National Weather Service as a consequence of a meteorological theory.

The consequences for this investigation are that Foucault is not interested in everyday accounting, only in "serious speech acts" (Dreyfus and Rabinow's phrase for 'enounce'). These utterances are divorced from any construction in everyday speech, but are constituted in an autonomous, consistent realm of institutional formation and legitimation. Foucault is concerned with the possibility of discourse, not its practice (Kuipers, 1989:105). Said (1983:186) notes a version of an "overriding society".

> Foucault's thesis is that individual statements or the chances that individual authors can make statements is not really likely. Over and above every opportunity for saying something, there stands a regularising collectivity that Foucault has called a discourse, itself governed by the archive.

Foucault's approach to discourse and narrative does not accord with an interactionist approach to everyday storytelling.[4] Such descriptions are approached only as reductive of the grand narrative. To limit discourse analysis to a level "anterior to the text" (Foucault, 1972:75) ignores the possibility of a fruitful investigation of everyday encounters of reading social work. Fair-clough (1992:57-8) criticises the contention that everyday talk and documents are governed by structures and autonomous rules:

> The questionable assumption is that one can extrapolate from structure to practice, that one can arrive at conclusions about practice without directly analysing real instances of it... In brief, what is missing is any sense that practice has properties of its own which (i) cannot be reduced to the implementation of structures, (ii) imply that how structures figure in practice cannot be assumed, but has to be determined: and (c) ultimately help shape structures.

To approach narrative and narrativity as merely instances of totalising stories is to miss the complexities of local and interactional features of accounting. An analysis of the discourse of social welfare as constituting what can be said about children and families, and by whom, can offer important insights into the historical development of how families are conceived (Stenson 1988, Rose 1990). However, such formulations do not exhaust the everyday manipulation and subversion of structural features. Indeed the possibility of locating practice as an example of structure has been a criticism of the privileged position of the archaeologist. The work of Bakhtin is discussed in chapter 2, but we can sum up the difference with Foucault as an emphasis on interactional/performative as opposed to structural/institutional features. As Rice and Waugh (1989:194) put it:

> Voloshinov/Bakhtin sees, in the social conditions of language use a variety of temporal, provisional and contested fixings of meaning, while Foucault sees, in the configuration of discourse, power and knowledge, the production of surveillance of the social itself.

An investigation of social work accounts as narrative, then, is not easily linked directly to grand narratives of welfare but located in the local and interactional practices of constituting and processing the client.

The link between the local and structural is of course a major theme in recent social theory and cannot be developed here. All texts are "worldly and circumstantial" (Said 1978:23). There is, however, a scepticism about making connections between individual texts and global explanations, particularly the fundamental criticisms of metanarrative or 'grand recit' by Lyotard, when he defines post-modernism as "incredulity toward metanarratives" (1984:xxiv). In promoting local narratives (petit recit), Lyotard offers 'language games' which make use of 'moves', construct 'senders' and 'addressees' and handle the 'referent'. As Jameson notes in the foreword to Lyotard (1984):

> ...this revival of an essentially narrative view of 'truth' and the vitality of small narrative units at work everywhere locally in the present social system are accompanied by something like a global or totalising crisis in the narrative function in general, since the older master narratives of legitimation no longer function in the service of research–nor, by implication anywhere else. (Lyotard, 1984:xix)

Grand narratives are breaking up but this does not lead to the "dissolution of the social bond" (Lyotard, 1984:15). Everywhere little narratives are performed.

In summary, social work is approached in this study as accounts, texts and (little) narratives. This is in contrast to social work as rational, factual or a manifestation of underlying structures. Social work as an account is concerned with occasions when social work is described, reported and explained. The accountable and hence rhetorical character of the talk or writing will be investigated.[5] Treating social work accounts as text signals a concern with talk and writing as interactional entities, available to be read and interpreted on specific occasions by different audiences. The discussion of the distinction between 'little' and 'grand' narratives has been necessary to distinguish the approach here from those with a structural interest. The next chapter explores approaches to 'little' narratives and storytelling.

Author: I'm glad you could all come to this team meeting at the beginning of our performance. I am sure we are all eager to show the reader the work we have done.

Interviewer: Well I don't know where all my work has gone. From that bit on interviews, you seem to be saying that all my interviews were nothing more than cosy chats. Social Worker and I were not talking about anything at all, but merely 'constructing texts'. If you listen to the tapes, you would know what we are talking about. We might not always express ourselves clearly but you would see the social work that was done. When I worked for Social Work Researcher, she was much more appreciative of my interviews and produced some very interesting findings from them.

Social Worker: Yes, I also object to that. I did my best to explain to Interviewer what was happening with my cases–you seem to be saying that it is all show, 'a performance', that there is no substance to my descriptions. Some of these things are very hard to put into words, but if you think they are 'so variable' as Potter and Mulkay (1985) say, then either you are just not listening as would any other reasonable person, or you are being very picky.

Author: I am sorry you feel that way and I did think that the interviews were full of very interesting stuff, that's why I take them seriously and don't want to do them an injustice. I really had no choice but to treat them differently..

Social Work Researcher: I think the implications of the direction you are going are very serious, very worrying. You have made some pretty strong assertions for someone who is being sceptical. I know that you have tried to turn some of them into questions, but that doesn't hide the attempt to undermine, to ridicule. We have worked hard at trying to get our research taken seriously–you have thrown out the possibility of making any general claims, this just isn't scientific. How on earth will you influence policy and practice? No such thing as 'decisions' or 'facts', whatever next? I tell you the policy makers will laugh at this, how on earth can we tell them what is going on out there?

Author: That is exactly my point. This chapter is suggesting a very different way of viewing social work. I can see it is going to be harder than I thought convincing you. Look, I did not realise you would be so upset by this approach, perhaps I have taken too much on. But you've got to admit that all those attempts we made to categorise those interviews were pretty pointless. How many card indexes or coding frames should you attempt before you realise that each research encounter has to be approached for its unique properties, not forcing it into boxes in order to play around with computers. Once accepting that, generalities might emerge in terms of textual features, but not types of cases or good practice. Look, let's see what theories of narrative have to offer in the next chapter.

Social Worker: This talk about it all being 'narrative', you mean it's just a story, a fabrication. I know you are not saying I tell lies, but that what I say is just a load of jargon and professional claptrap, as a judge said to me once.

Author: No no, I am not trying to rubbish your reports; on the contrary, I marvel at the 'artful practices' you display in making links between people and their circumstances.

Social Worker: Thanks, I think I can take that as a compliment. But I have a more serious complaint. I don't think you are taking this subject seriously enough; I mean this dialogue. Don't you realise that children are suffering out there. Surely you are not saying that Jasmine Beckford or Tyra Henry is a 'text' and it is all to do with how she is read. You are just messing around with textual games, when children are dying. You've done the job, some time ago it might have been, but surely you remember all the dilemmas we face?

Interviewer: Yes I was struck by 'the sadness of it all', as the social worker so eloquently put in one interview.

Author: This is a serious complaint and I am not trying to be flippant. I was working in a Social Services Department, when it was rocked by a child abuse tragedy. I am not saying that the child was not killed but I do remember the different reactions from colleagues, the press and the inquiry team. Before the Inquiry everyone was pretty confident there would be no problems, that only good practice would be discovered. Once the Inquiry got under way, the questions ranged from missed letters to Government funding of local authorities, and you are accusing me of not looking at the child's body. I think we need another meeting, don't you? Perhaps we can meet again in chapter 3. Though that last question will come up again; it does worry me.

Foucauldian expert: You have of course misrepresented Michel's position on narrative, you know.

Author: Oh no, not you as well.

Foucauldian expert: He was much more sceptical than you suggest about discursive formations and the possibility of history to understand itself.

Author : Yes, I have rather used his work as contrast device to promote my position on narrative, and contrasts necessarily distort.

Foucauldian expert: Well, by distancing yourself from Foucault, you will miss important opportunities for looking at social work as a site for power relations.

Author: You are probably right, but I just think I'll stick to the interactionist approach. I just feel more ... well... comfortable here. I'm not happy with studies which impose on texts concepts of power from the outside; whose version of power is it? when is power? what constitutes power? But I know that this will be the main criticism of this book. I can hear the critical reviews now. But look, let's see what narrative theory can offer, I think it might be pretty interesting.

All: Will you be looking at some proper data analysis (Social work researcher), interviews (Interviewer) cases (Social Worker) power relations (Foucauldian expert)?

Client (opening the door): Sorry, is this the case conference?

All: No. This is a private meeting. Can you come back later?

NOTES

[1] See appendix 1 for a description of the data gathering in this study.

[2] This is in contrast to research which investigates professional-client interaction. For example, Stenson (1987), Rostila (1994), Stanley (1991).

[3] There has been criticism of discourse analysis for offering a restricted view of the text, as an object of study independent of the observer (Woolgar, 1986). It is therefore important to stress the active process of reading texts by both participants and analysts and to investigate the reflexive moves of the analyst (Fuhrman and Oehler, 1986)

[4] Atkinson (1995:41) considers Foucault's treatment of his subject matter is 'unsociological' as it is "poorly grounded in the detailed analysis of social organisation or everyday practice."

[5] This study concentrates on those occasions when social workers describe their work to others. There is no analysis of social worker-client encounters, although it is not suggested that accountable, textual and storyable features are not available on such occasions. I do not agree with Stanley (1991:124) that studying accounts is less social work that the 'actual' intervention. Atkinson (1995, chap. 3) notes the implications of a "restricted focus" on doctor-patient consultation in medical sociology.

APPENDIX 1
Data, confidentiality and presentation

Being the result of doctorate research, this study has undergone a number of changes of direction. These changes have been associated with both responses to methodological problems and theoretical positions. Many of these problems have centred on the status of the data collected in the initial period of the study, mainly research interviews. These data have, in effect, changed in status during this investigation as different theoretical positions have been deployed. The status of the data is as problematic since social work accounts are now investigated for their reading relations, not their apparent accuracy.

Data have been accumulated rather than collected. Whilst the initial stage of collection was carried out in line with specific approaches of sampling and reliability, the change to a relativist approach led to a recognition that data are easily available within social work settings. It is not necessary to capture social work by careful, 'scientific' methods, which prescribe some information as relevant and other information as irrelevant. This is not to suggest that the data gathering has been arbitrary but that no description of a social work case should be seen as privileged. Even so, having access to reports and interviews of social workers accounting for their work has been possible because of my position as a social worker in a social services department (SSD) and later as a researcher. I have worked for one SSD and carried out research in several others and these data are offered as typical of the cases, conversations and reports of social services departments in the late 1980s and early 1990s.

Type and source of the data

I have collected data through selection procedures (interviews specifically for this project), as a part of other tasks (interviews for other research projects) and other data as I came across them (reports within and around social work encounters). There are four types of data, mainly social workers' accounts of their work with particular cases of children and their families. Most cases involve children who have spent some time in the care of the local authority. First, the initial interviews were randomly selected from all the older children in the care of a social services department. At the time, I was a social worker in the SSD and most of the social workers were well known to me as colleagues. I selected 10 cases and completed 25 such interviews, lasting between half an hour and two and a half hours. Second, as a researcher I have carried out a number of interviews for policy-related research both working within a SSD and for a research unit. Some interviews were concerned with social workers talking about their cases, especially for a policy review exercise which examined decisions to admit younger children into care. These interviews have been added to the data although they were not carried out specifically for this project. There are 28 such interviews lasting between 20 minutes and an hour. All the interviews were 'semi-structured', in Burgess's (1982) terms 'conversation with a purpose'. Questions were not in the form of a schedule but the interview was guided by 'chronological agreements' (explicit and implicit) between interviewer and respondent on how telling the case should be achieved. For example, "I first took the case on when.." or "What were the circumstances before the admission to care.." All the interviews were recorded and transcribed verbatim.

The third type of data are reports, memos and case file entries from the files of some of the cases described in the interviews. It was not originally planned to analyse such material. With the change in theoretical perspective, however, such written texts came to be seen as an important contrast with the conversational material, since strategic and institutional features of telling the story of the case can be explored further. There is also an opportunity to compare textual accomplishment across occasions and settings. Fourth, the accumulation of other material continued with texts from many sources—newspapers, journals, television and radio programmes. All such material is concerned with talk about social workers' cases and all equally occasions of accounting for social work.

Confidentiality

Some of the data are court reports and are confidential. It has been necessary to include confidential information in this analysis because of the importance of the court in these cases. Similarly, the fine-grained analysis requires close scrutiny of documents; the words and phrases used and their relationship to one another.

The *Children Act,* 1989 section 97 (2) says:
> No person shall publish any material which is intended, or likely, to identify—
> any child as being involved in any proceedings before a magistrates' court in which any power under this Act may be exercised by the court with respect to that or any child; or
> an address or school as being that of a child involved in any such proceedings.

It is not the concern of this study to be seen to describe 'real' social work cases since I am not evaluating social work practice. However, it is important that the words and stories did appear in social work documents and the linguistic conventions and styles of argument are typical and authentic. Therefore, in order to disguise the identity of the children, families and social workers, key features of all documents used in this study have been altered, sometimes radically—names, ages, gender, characteristics are changed and features of cases are mixed together. In other words, they are an amalgam of features and no longer 'real' cases. However, the words and stories did appear in social work documents. Some readers may feel that the stories are altered by these changes.

Other publications about social work do quote freely from social work documents (including court material) and are concerned to display 'real' cases (Hardiker and Barker 1981, Dingwall et al 1983, Spencer 1988). Furthermore, these data are between 5 and 10 years old and, at the last visit to the departments, all the social workers had left, the cases were all closed and finding some case files was difficult.

Data presentation

The data are analysed by drawing on a variety of methods associated with discourse analysis, conversation analysis, literary theory and sociolinguistics. There is controversy over the relative merits of the various approaches to textual analysis which will not be discussed here (See, for example, Levinson 1983, Gilbert and Mulkay 1983, Wooffitt 1992). Instead, themes and concepts are deployed as the transcripts are investigated for their narrative and rhetorical accomplishment.

The data are presented either as fragments of texts or as entire documents. The interviews are approached both through selecting specific exchanges or utterances and larger segments of talk. This is discussed throughout the thesis as the relative importance of hearing whole stories and rhetorical formulations is considered. There is not a detailed transcription of data similar to the methods of conversation analysis. Rather, the words of speakers are presented without punctuation, but with repetition, pauses denoted by (-) and continuers by 'erm'. There is limited use of emboldening of emphasised speech. Given the length of the interviews, none is presented in full, since the transcriptions are on average fifteen pages long.

2 Narrative as performance

Having identified social work documents as 'little' narratives, we now develop the concept of storytelling as an interactional, strategic and rhetorical performance. In this chapter I will explore theoretical approaches to narrative from ethnomethodology, literary theory, sociolinguistics and anthropology, which will form the basis for a textual analysis of social work accounts.[1] An interactional approach to narrative will be contrasted with those approaches which see narratives as autonomous or formal, that is, as entities independent of reading and interpretation. This is an important distinction since it directs a search for an understanding of narrative to either the structures of texts or the dialogue between writers and readers.

To see narrative as a performance follows from our view of social work accounts as interactional and active, not static and docile documents. Texts take on meaning only in and through their performance and reception. For example, a social work report is only a piece of paper when locked in a filing cabinet; it has no meaning in itself. It is only when it is read and reacted to that meaning, interpretation and significance become available. Grint and Woolgar (1995:291) consider this the general problem of the nature of text.

> Do texts possess intrinsic meanings and do these meanings then have effects on readers (e.g. by causing a particular interpretation)? Or do such meanings arise only in and through the active interpretive work performed by the reader?

The latter question leads to notions of readers and audiences, of occasions of reading and alternative interpretations. Performance refers to formal occasions of performing a text, like the theatre or public readings, but also to all occasions on which texts are read in a context and interpretations made. For McLean (1988:1) reading literary texts is performance:

> The basic problems of narrative can, in the first instance, be better understood in relation to oral narration... the teller-hearer nexus inherent in all narrative.

Social work texts constitute performance when a judge reads a court report, members of a case conference consider a social worker's recommendations or a researcher analyses an interview. Performance means reading for a purpose and from a position.

Text in context, however, is not straightforward, since what is taken as 'the context' presents problems as to the appropriate dimensions. Ethnography offers versions of the appropriate background to consider when reading texts, for example, interactants' attributes, knowledge and relationships, the institutional and organisational features of the setting. But how should such factors be compared and when is the search for explanation complete—structural relations, class relations, economic structure? Conversation analysts go to the other extreme, refusing to look beyond the participants' talk for explanation since they consider that the text includes its own context.

Studies of performance draw on both an appreciation of the text and the context of reading. As Bauman and Briggs (1990:69) note:

> Performance analysis has become simultaneously more textually and more contextually focused in recent years. In order to avoid reifying "the context" it is necessary to study the textual details that illuminate the manner in which participants are collectively constructing the world around them. On the other hand, attempts to identify the meaning of texts, performances or entire genres in terms of purely symbolic, context-free content disregard the multiplicity of indexical connections that enable verbal art to transform, not simply reflect social life.

In this chapter we examine approaches to narrative which do not impose explanations on the text from the outside. However, context is taken as part of the reading activity, not only available in participants' talk, but invoked in reading through notions of audience.

Conversational stories

Whilst Lyotard's direction to consider local narratives is clear, this is based on scepticism of grand narratives rather than sympathy with a detailed analysis of everyday storytelling. Postmodernists like Pratt (1986:32) propose to go "amongst the people and let then speak for themselves", but their anti-empiricist, anti-theoretical focus is not easily linked to available theories of conversational storytelling (Rosenau, 1992:85). Furthermore, few approaches to conversational storytelling are concerned with performance and audience.

Two important approaches, speech act theory and conversation analysis lead to rather different views of conversational narratives. Austin (1962) developed speech act theory in order to study language as social action, performative utterances which do things, for example, 'I name this ship'. In distinguishing the active nature of language, speech act theorists have been concerned with delineating necessary and sufficient conditions for various types of speech act. Schegloff (in Sacks, 1992:xxvi) notes the difference between Searle, a speech act theorist, and Sacks, a conversation analyst, in analysing an 'invitation'. Whereas Searle attempts to distinguish conditions, Sacks is interested in "practices and methods." For Sacks, a possible instance of an 'invitation' has two parts: a partial definition which then provides for the actual use on this occasion. The important difference is not the conditions for the act nor the rules of performance, but the interactional work necessary to bring off the act—to raise the possibility of an invitation and then attend to this particular incidence. That it is a 'possible' invitation can only be recognised by charting the outcome of the response. This difference between the necessary conditions of speech act theory and the interaction of conversation analysis distinguishes Labov and Sacks's approaches to narrative.

Labov and story structure

Labov is an important writer on conversational narratives. His aim is to understand what is going on in a particular stretch of conversation: to "lay bare as much of the scaffolding of conversational interaction as we can" (Labov and Fanshel, 1978:26). A narrative is one type of speech act through which the structure of a conversation can be recognised; others are requests, challenges, assertions. A story can:

> ...function as equivalent to such single speech as response, putting off a request, challenge and so forth (1978:105).

A speaker abides by 'obligatory' rules to use speech acts and the listener must respond appropriately for the act to be successful. The analytical questions for Labov are: is this a narrative or another speech act for displaying experiences, and what are the essential features of narrative structure? Labov and Waletsky (1967:20) define a narrative as:

> one method of recapitulating past experiences by matching a verbal sequence of clauses to the sequence of events which actually happened.

A narrative is structured to relate what happened and why it is worth telling. It has a temporal form outlining the events, but also an evaluative clause to answer the 'so what' question. For a fully formed narrative, Labov and Waletsky offer six elements: an abstract which prefaces the point or topic; an orientation which sets the scene and provides the background; a complicating action which lays out the problem to be solved; an evaluation which comments on the problem; a resolution solving the problem and a coda to signal the end of the story.[2]

Delineating story structure has been the basis of much narrative analysis, although there are theoretical differences over what constitutes the definitive characteristics.[3] A story is a mental construct, a linguistic feature, a literary genre. Labov's model is of interest since empirical studies have shown that reading stories does seem to require that complications are set up and resolved. For example, Stewart (1991) observed how in case study methods used in management training, the material presented to students has a truncated narrative structure, leaving the student to solve the problem, to answer the 'so what' question. However, what does story structure constitute? Is it a set of necessary conditions which reside in the text, independent of the reader? Alternatively, is recognition of story structure a reader's task, an audience response? A theoretical definition of story structure does not ensure analytic privilege of story recognition; rather it suggests the search for story structure is a 'reader-as-analyst' task, a lay theory.

Labov's elements can be approached less as necessary conditions or obligatory rules for the identification of a story and more as possible interactional accomplishments and tasks in writer/reader communication. Labov hints at the role of the reader more than others interested in story structure, but his reader and writer are formal constructs with fixed roles. A number of writers have criticised Labov, questioning whether his elements are clearly identifiable or necessary for successfully hearing a story (Polanyi, 1985). Shuman (1986:50) considers that the evaluative question with which the storyteller is faced may not be 'so what?' but rather 'who says?'; a challenge of the entitlement to recount, not interest. This is clearly an important aspect of the accountability of the storyteller. Culler (1980:36) asks whether story structure is of interest or the persuasiveness of the telling, suggesting this is ultimately a reader's task:

> The question of whether any given story is being told primarily in order to report a sequence of events or in order to tell a tellable story is of course difficult to decide, but the ethical and referential lure of stories makes listeners want to decide (is that the way it really happened or is he just trying to impress me?). Labov avoids this question.

In summary, Labov's model of story structure is not helpful if seen as an abstracted theoretical formation of necessary conditions, an extended speech act. If story structure is approached as a possible interactional accomplishment for achieving accountability, then Labov's features are a useful starting point. It is here that the work of Sacks can be developed.

Sacks and conversational stories

Sacks investigates stories in conversation but is not concerned with necessary conditions. Stories are approached as interactional constructs on the occasions and through the methods that they are attended to by speakers and hearers. Stories exist when participants react to them as stories. It is not what they are but 'how does it matter'; not what a story is but what a story does. As with the earlier discussion of an 'invitation', Sacks is interested in a 'possible' or 'candidate story', its emergence as a story being dependent on its production and reception in conversation.

> Does it matter that a story is produced to be recognised and that it is recognised by its production? With that, we are in a position to examine—not stories but candidate stories, to see whether it appears that it matters. And we look for some way to find that it might matter. What sort of facts about candidate stories can be found, in terms of which a demonstration of the relevance of that the thing is a story can be done? And what I'm offering as such a fact is that stories take more than an utterance to produce. (1992:223)

Sacks considers that the production of stories involves making the ordinary unusual. Scenes do not simply present themselves. Speakers and hearers look at events for their 'storyable' and hence 'reportable' features, and find a story from the many possible representations of experiences.

Sacks notes different ways of handling this interactional problem. They can be presented through the events and experiences of the storyteller, a 'witness' (1992:242). Alternatively, a reporter is likely to use a course-of-action characterisation from within the story events. For either approach, the storyteller has to tell the story through an unfolding puzzle, which leads the hearer through the maze of potential tellings. Sacks (1972:340) notes how any possible description can be developed into a possible story:

> It happens to be correct, for Western literature, that if some piece of talk is a possible description it is also, and thereby, a possible story or story part.

It is this work at making the descriptions of events and experiences into stories which involves the use of storytelling devices and story structures. Story structure is not intrinsic to the story but is a feature of the joint work of hearer and speaker. Goodwin (1984:245) demonstrates how participants use story structure as a constitutive feature of the events in which they are engaged:

[this analysis], by showing how the story provides for a field of action for a range of different types of participants and how these participants analyse and make use of the emerging structure of the story, is thus relevant to some general questions about story organisation that have been raised by workers in a number of fields.

Whilst story structure for Sacks and Goodwin is a product of interactional work, some of the features of story they suggest are similar to Labov's model. Sacks discusses beginnings and endings which are similar to Labov's abstract and coda, but he sees 'openings' as strategic moves to disrupt the normal turn taking sequence of conversation. The problem faced by a storyteller is to continue for more than a single utterance and to prevent a potential next speaker from starting to speak. Story prefaces offer instructions to the hearer to allow the storyteller to hold the floor for more than a single utterance. Sacks (1992:226) notes ways in which permission is sought and granted. For example:

> There are sequences with an initial utterance such as 'I have something terrible to tell you' followed by some other party saying 'say some more' via such specific obvious technical things that can be done as 'what?' which returns the floor to the last speaker with an instruction to say some more.

Whilst Sacks does not suggest that stories have a 'point', he considers a story is completed when the subject of the story preface has been provided:

> Just taking the type of preface I have given you, 'I have something terrible to tell you', then in stories that have characterising adjectives like 'terrible', the business of such a term is not just to arouse interest but to instruct hearers to use terms to monitor the story—when they've heard something that it could name, the story is over. (1992:228)

As with Labov's model, for the hearer to remain interested, the story must be heard to provide a complicating and then resolving feature which was promised at the beginning. For Sacks, such features are not intrinsic to the story, but interactionally linked to the occasion of telling. Also in contrast to Labov, Sacks sees utterances not as chronologically related to the events of the story, but demonstrating the storyteller finding a tellable story from within the mass of possible representations.

Ultimately, there are few differences between the story structures which Labov and Sacks offer—both suggest a beginning, an ending and a story complication or interest being satisfied. The important difference concerns the interactional nature of the story. For Labov, story structure is a framework 'outside' the interaction which an analyst can identify. For Sacks, a story is available through communicational cues between any teller and hearer to enable story recognition and reaction. This distinction is important since any occasion of hearing a story by hearer or analyst means following the unfolding interactional features presented and reacted to by hearers.

What are the implications of Sacks' interactional, 'possible' stories for approaching social work accounts as stories? Sacks only discusses conversational stories and locates them in the turn-taking sequence of everyday conversation. A story is an extended turn. Social work accounts are not all produced within conversation. In this study we have available research interviews, reports and case files entries as well as conversation. Research interviews do not necessarily abide by a turn taking sequence (Silverman, 1973), nor do conventions of research protocol match conversational storytelling.[4] In written social work documents, the reader is not identifiable in the next turn. To recognise stories only in the explicit reaction of next turn is thus to limit the potential of hearing stories. As we will see with the work of Bakhtin, narrative as performance involves considering both the 'already spoken' and 'not yet spoken'. Storytellers, listeners and later readers monitor narrative performance through contextual cues, anticipation and previous utterances on the topic.

The narrative features of all social work accounts might be usefully considered for the way in which Sacks attends to the role of the reader/hearer, but not restricted to the next turn. Similarly, story structure is approached as potential interactional features available in such performances. We can now consider how literary texts are approached as interactional and through the occasions of their performance.

Literary texts and narrative performance

As with the study of conversational stories, literary theorists have debated whether there are specific properties which distinguish a literary narrative, referred to as 'literariness' (Rice and Waugh, 1989:17). Literary theory has recognised that by approaching the literary work as a 'text', interpretations can change with the reading occasion, as Barthes (1977: 157) says: "the Text is experienced only in an activity of production". The reader does not merely receive the story but evaluates it and the storyteller's accomplishment. This debate is discussed in the distinction between autonomous and interactional stories as illustrated in the dialogue between Chatman (1978, 1980) and Herrnstein Smith (1978, 1980).

Autonomous versus interactional stories

Chatman (1978) offers a structuralist approach to narrative which considers that there is a basic story structure underlying any narrative. He acknowledges the distinction between story and discourse, that is, the events of the narrative and how they are told in a particular version.[5] The basic story is autonomous, independent of its surface manifestations. The narrative in a film or book reproduces the basic story, but the discourse changes with different techniques and devices to represent it. Chatman concludes that:

> The transportability of the story is the strongest reason for arguing that narratives are indeed structures independent of any medium. (1978:20)

A similar structural approach has been applied to non-literary writing.[6] Unlike the concept of story structure in Labov, this contention is not that a story **has** a structure, rather narrative **is** a structure, a cultural entity independent of its use or construction. Any storytelling occasion is a surface manifestation of an underlying cultural entity.

In contrast to a formalist/structuralist approach, Herrnstein Smith offers an 'interactionist approach' to narratives and, in doing so, questions the idea of a separate literary narrative. She rejects the distinction between story and discourse, considering that a basic story would be 'unknowable' (1980:216). She concludes:

> No narrative version can be independent of a particular teller and occasion of telling and, therefore, that we may assume that every narrative version has been constructed in accord with some set of purposes or interests (1980:219).

Any reading or interpretation of a narrative is a product of contexts and interests; no version can be privileged above any other.

> Whenever we start to cut back, peel off, strip away, lay bare and so forth, we always do so in accord with certain assumptions and purposes which, in turn, create hierarchies of relevance and centrality (1980:221).

All narratives and versions of narratives are a product of occasions of telling and reading, with no version more basic. Multiple versions can be constructed for every given narrative, each one reflecting the purposes of the storyteller and audience. The analyst, as much as the storyteller or reader, is involved in producing metanarratives. The work of Bakhtin develops such reader-text-context interaction into a complex theory of communication and dialogue.

Bakhtin: narrative and dialogue

The work of Mikhail Bakhtin (and his colleagues Voloshinov and Medvedev) can help develop these questions.[7] His work provides a complex theory of dialogue, which locates narrative within a wide view of language use, communication and performance. A number of his main themes are outlined here and taken up in later chapters.

Bakhtin is interested in what Morson and Emerson (1990:15) call 'prosaics' as opposed to poetics, a theory of literature that unlike formalism, privileges prose over poetry. He emphasises the study of the everyday and the ordinary, with non-literary language seen as equally artistic and creative. As Morson and Emerson (1990:23) comment:

> For Bakhtin, Voloshinov and Medvedev, the everyday is a sphere of constant activity, the source of all social change and individual creativity. The prosaic is the truly interesting and the ordinary is what is truly noteworthy.

Dialogue is treated in the widest sense in that social existence cannot be separated from communication, "To be means to communicate" (Bakhtin, 1984: 287). It is not dialogue in the sense of turn-taking, but the complex interplay of speakers, hearers, occasions of speaking, and the many potential voices that can be invoked in relation to a topic.

His work offers a number of advantages. First, it offers an approach which is situated between societal constraint and individual creativity, considering both the occasion of performance and the history of language use. For Bakhtin, there is a continual interplay between the use of language, 'the utterance', and previous and potential use.

> The living utterance, having taken meaning and shape at a particular historical moment in a socially specific environment, cannot fail to brush up against thousands of living dialogic threads, woven by socio-ideological consciousness around the given object of an utterance; it cannot fail to become an active participant in social dialogue (1981:276).

Utterances are 'overpopulated' with the 'already spoken about'. Bakhtin sees all speech as reported speech in that previous uses are always available to be invoked. In every encounter, a new utterance is created as speakers reflexively monitor their stories and readers decode, evaluate and prepare responses.

> The word is interindividual. Everything that is said, expressed, is located outside the 'soul' of the speaker and does not belong to him. The word cannot be assigned to a single speaker. The author (speaker) has his own inalienable right to the word, but the listener also has his rights and those whose voices are heard in the word before the author comes upon it also have their rights (Bakhtin, 1986:121-2).

Second, a feature of Bakhtin's concept of language use is the constraint of 'speech genre'; cultural conventions of what constitutes adequate communication. Speech genres are given a wide canvas and can refer both to locally produced forms as well as "scientific statements and all literary genres from the proverb to the multivolume novel" (Bakhtin, 1986:61).

> Each separate utterance is individual, of course, but each sphere in which language is used develops its own relatively stable types of these utterances. These may be called speech genres. The wealth and diversity of speech genres are boundless because the various possibilities of human activity are inexhaustible, and because each sphere of activity contains an entire repertoire of speech genres that differentiate and grow as the particular sphere develops, and becomes more complex (Bakhtin, 1986:60).

Such a view of creativity and constraint in the performance of accounting appears ideally suited to this investigation. It focuses on the local construction of events and entities but, unlike conversation analysis, it anticipates future ambitions and past uses.

Third, Bakhtin is concerned with the unfinalised nature of entities. As Morson and Emerson (1990:30) comment: "Wholeness is always a matter of work. It is not a gift but a project." There is a continual interplay between forces which attempt to control fixed meaning and order, and those which seek to disrupt it; what Bakhtin calls 'centripetal' (or official) and 'centrifugal' (or unofficial) forces. A concern with instability sharply separates Bakhtin from formal or structural approaches which see events and entities as the product of an underlying system. For Bakhtin, there is no such system apart from momentary stability in the struggle of competing languages or 'heteroglossia'.

> Every concrete utterance of a speaking subject serves as a point where centrifugal as well as centripetal forces are brought to bear. The processes of centralisation and decentralisation, of unification and disunification, intersect in the utterance; the utterance not only answers the requirements of its own language as an individualised embodiment of a speech act, but it answers the requirements of heteroglossia as well; it is in fact an active participation in such speech diversity (Bakhtin, 1981:270).

The construction and reception of texts thus involves constantly attempting to stabilise meaning and, in the act of such construction, entities and their meaning are re-invented and altered.

The work of Bakhtin is complex and wideranging. It suggests an interactional approach to narrative but one which recognises past stories and future evaluation. As with the discussion of conversational stories, the search for narrativity in literary texts focuses on the performance of the story and the process of reading. It also requires a different approach from traditional approaches to analysing narratives.

Plot, character and point of view

Literary theory has concentrated on analysing narratives in terms of plot, character and point of view. Whilst these remain important aspects of narrative analysis, an interactionist approach requires some revision. Plot has tended to dominate with characters often seen as merely products of the plot (Chatman, 1978:111).[8] Formalist methods are in danger of imbuing techniques with explanatory significance available only to the researcher, with the 'average reader' merely a recipient (Bal, 1994:6). Bakhtin is critical of analysis which sees plot as the author's grand plan, within which characters are fitted. Instead he considers plot the unanticipated outcome of dialogue of characters.

> Its goal (plot) is to place a person in various situations that expose and provoke him, to bring people together and make them collide in conflict—in such a way, however, that they do not remain within this area of plot-related contact but exceed its bounds (1984:276-7).

Not based on a finalised plot or predestined plan, plot and character work through reader interaction. As Morson and Emerson (1990:249) put it, readers are "dialogic partners of the characters and author... it is impossible to be just an 'eyewitness'."[9]

Plot provides the reader with a framework for organising and connecting events and experiences. Stories can be recounted in many ways, and the storyteller has to find a route into the events which enables the performance to be heard as 'storyable' (Sacks, 1992:230). S/he displays only those features of events and experiences which support the 'point', glossing over the 'noise' of real life (Carr, 1986:123). Not only must the reader be persuaded to follow this route, the story requires authorisation. As Smith (1993:24-5) notes:

> ...an endemic problem [for the storyteller] must always be how a given version is authorised as that version which can be treated by others as what has happened. Accordingly an important set of procedures concern who is allocated the privilege of definition and how other possible versions or sources of possible disjunctive information are ruled out.

In analysing historical narratives, White (1987:173) shows how 'emplot-ment' changes a fragment or chronicle into a narrative. For a sequence of events to become a narrative, events must be "'configured' ('grasped together') in a such way as to represent 'symbolic discourse'". White (1980:9) contrasts the historical narrative with the chronicle:

> The chronicle, by contrast, often seems to wish to tell a story, aspires to narrativity, but typically fails to achieve it. More specifically, the chronicle usually is marked by a failure to achieve narrative closure. It starts to tell a story but breaks off in the chronicler's own present; it leaves things unresolved or rather leaves them unresolved in a story-like way.

Such a view of plot changes the discussion from merely an organising function to a legitimating function.[9] Plot is not an *a priori* structure but an authorising interaction between storyteller and audience. This requires an investigation of the instructions and pathways which are provided to guide the reader through the story (Smith, 1993:23). How are events and entities woven together, 'emplotted' and, in particular, how are preferred audiences constructed and dispreferred avenues closed off?

Character and character depiction in social work accounts will be developed in chapters 4, 5 and 8 and are of central concern to this study. Whilst recent literary theory has developed more complex approaches to character, some have imported concepts of psychology, for example 'traits of personality' in Chatman (1978:121). Notions of 'the subject' as "a position within language" (Foucault, 1972), and Bakhtin's 'unfinalisability' of characters suggest analysis should concentrate on how character is constructed and reacted to, without using psychological constructs to legitimate or categorise characters. Some novelists resist the construction of consistent character depictions; for example, Eco comments:

> In the pages to follow I shall not indulge in descriptions of persons... as nothing is more fleeting than external form, which withers and alters like the flowers of the field at the appearance of autumn. (1983:14)

For these writers, it is no longer possible to see emplotment as a source of creative intentionality, but a part of the free play of unfinalised characters and events, open to continuing (re)interpretation. For this study, the investigation of characters which are open to subversion from within the account as well as from outside is similar to the problem of social workers faced with depicting 'real' characters who may resist their portrayal.

Point of view is developed as interactionally negotiated by Herrnstein Smith's concept of narrative version. She considers the narrative act as a version, "accounts told from a particular or partial perspective" (1980:215). Similarities between versions of the 'same' story are dependent on similarities in:

> ...the verbal acts of particular narrators performed in response to— and thus shaped and constrained by—sets of multiple interacting conditions. (1980:226)

The sociology of science has considered the partiality of alternative accounts of scientific controversies without locating a definitive version (Gilbert and Mulkay, 1984). In attempting to write a history of the discovery of pulsars, Woolgar (1976:397) found that in reading summary accounts, there were a number of differences and gaps. More fundamentally, they were already histories and, furthermore, Woolgar was involved in "logical reconstruction" (1976:400). To read an account is to construct a local, perspectival reading; a 'text-event'.

To use concepts from literary theory to analyse non-literary texts requires adjustment and revision, but many writers are looking to the narrativity of all social interaction in which the 'literariness' of everyday life is central.

Functions and effects of storytelling

So far I have considered the construction and recognition of stories—what a story looks like and how is it available to be read as 'storyable'. A wider and more difficult question is what is the purpose of a particular story. What does the storyteller achieve with his/her narrative? What does the hearer/reader take from hearing it? This is not an investigation of motives or intentions as prior to the encounter (Sharrock and Watson, 1984), but considers the effects of storytelling performances. Confronting this question differentiates reading social work accounts from reading literary texts, which are associated with entertaining, desire, 'the pleasure of the text' (Barthes, 1976). Social work accounts are written and read through legal and administrative occasions. A reason for the document might be stated at some point, a request for a particular resource, a recommendation of court disposal. However, many local and global functions and effects might be attended to by the teller, listener and analyst.

One way of approaching social work accounts is to investigate the extent to which it performs community, how is it heard as social work? How are relations established between a particular account and concepts and conventions available in and recognisable as social work? This is not to suggest a discrete professional language but to investigate how words, utterances and concepts display the "taste of a profession" (Bakhtin, 1981:293).

Displaying professional competence

The term 'competence' in linguistics has been associated with Chomsky's (1965) distinction between a speaker's knowledge of language (competence) and the use of language (performance). Such a distinction has been criticised as separating features which are in fact inextricably linked and constantly interact with each other (Cicourel, 1973:44). 'Social competence' according to Harré and Secord (1972) refers to the stock of social knowledge which enables actors to respond to social situations in appropriate ways. Professional competence might be considered in a similar way, but not as a fixed set of social recipes, rather as rhetorical formulations which perform and display the social work community. A competent professional story can be investigated by both hearer and analyst to see how far it both displays and creates shared understandings, prescriptions for action and sentiments about what constitutes competent social work talk.

Sociolinguistics has developed notions of coherence and cohesion to investigate the way accounts hang together as stories. Cohesion refers to the way clauses in text are linked to each other, one clause read as understandable in relation to a previous one. Coherence is a similar concept referring to the connectedness of larger segments of text. The importance of a shared understanding for communicating a text is emphasised and according to Schiffrin (1987:22) the work of making such connections is reflexive:

> ...not only are [hearers] constrained by the larger interpretational frames in which they are situated, but they actually create interpretive contexts through which a speaker's underlying communicative intention can be inferred.

Hearers examine utterances in order to interpret the 'totality' of a message, not merely the communicative cues, and in doing so enable context and interpretation to be made available. The link between textual coherence and a competent storytelling is complex. Some writers develop concepts of 'schema', which attempt to interpolate from textual coherence a speaker's overall intention in telling a story (Agar and Hobbs, 1985). Such approaches, however, appear concerned with the storyteller's intentions and how they are textually achieved. Competence is rather a matter of reflexive display and reader response, attended to by both hearer and teller, not merely inferred by an analyst.

Demonstrating professional competence through storytelling may be a way of linking functions of storytelling directly to the communicative task of the storyteller and hearer and their shared inspection of professional talk. Competence in telling and hearing professionally acceptable stories both displays the speaker and hearer as in line with professional norms and at the same time constructs and reconstructs conventions of professional adequacy.

Entitlement to tell stories

The function of storytelling can be located in displays of entitlement to tell stories, to provide within the story methods of creating legitimacy to speak, to be listened to and taken seriously. In historiography, there is a debate about how historical narratives are concerned to display legitimation through moral construction or fact building. White (1980:24) sees narrative as essentially concerned with moralising:

> The demand for closure in the historical story is a demand, I suggest, for moral meaning, a demand that sequences of real events be assessed as to their significance as elements of a moral drama.

Mink (1978), on the other hand, sees narrative as a "cognitive instrument", standing outside and above events, taking them in at a glance, external to the storyteller. Moral and fact construction have been discussed at length in conversation analysis and the sociology of scientific knowledge and offer a way of approaching many of the narrative features so far discussed (see chapters 4 and 5). Furthermore, entitlement (Shuman, 1986) can link facts and morals in the interactional display of both authority to tell the story and legitimacy to make moral assessments.

Occupational narrative

Narrative has been utilised in studies of occupational texts (Manning 1986, Pithouse and Atkinson 1988). It is not suggested that social work accounting should be approached as a distinct occupational discourse, different from other readings of narrative. As Manning (1986:297) comments, police stories are "a framed bit of culture". Even so, in order to be heard as performing community, we can ask how connections are made between an account and social workers' occupational genres. How is the reader/hearer instructed that the account is occupationally legitimate and shared? How do instructions for the reader vary with reading in institutional contexts? (see chapter 3).

Deploying and invoking shared understandings in reading occupational accounts has been investigated by a number of writers. Manning (1986) studies how the police reduce complex incidents to "mini narratives" to enable simple processing and reconstruction. Performing community in such 'organisational texts' makes use of crude narrative structures–plot, character and action. Manning (1986:298) notes how occupational context is invoked:

> Context is, if nothing else, assumed knowledge; it is what is absent from speech but signalled by it.

Garfinkel (1967:199) notes how medical records are concerned with demonstrating that treatment has been "in accord with expectations of sanctionable performances by clinicians and patients." The requirement to display 'medico-legal responsibility' outweighs a concern for accuracy. Later readers are able to reconstruct action as "documented representations" of an underlying doctor-patient contract.

Strong and Dingwall (1983) discuss displays of accounting through appeals to a range of organisational licenses, mandates, charters and missions. Having to reconstruct everyday activity in terms of charters:

> ...restricts the range of legitimisable discourse through which organisationally relevant action may be identified, analysed and discussed by members (1983:109).

Strong and Dingwall consider how far charters constrain occupational action through formal ceremonies. Of more interest for this study is how charters are invoked in social work accounts, for example, how is departmental policy or legal statute displayed in reports?

Pithouse and Atkinson see organisation talk as interactionally constructed through skilled narrative display, a "kaleidoscope of occupational and personal views of proper domestic arrangements" (1988:195). This is an analysis of collegial accounting in social work supervision. Here social workers look to one another for local legitimation in establishing a 'narrative contract' between teller and hearer.

Reflexivity: the analyst's storytelling

At the beginning of this chapter it was noted that a text does not have an intrinsic meaning but only comes into being through reading. Such a predicament also applies to the analyst's reading occasion. To claim a mandate, competence and entitlement to read social work accounts and write an academic text also applies to this study as a storyable account. Reflexivity is a key issue in the human sciences, although with a variety of positions (e.g. Foucault 1970, Clifford and Marcus 1986, Woolgar and Ashmore 1988, Bourdieu 1992). In general terms, it means self reflection, a turning back on oneself as an analyst. If we recognise all texts as social constructs, so the theories, concepts and claims of social scientists are equally seen as rhetorical and strategic activities. As Lawson (1985:9) comments:

> Our concepts are no longer regarded as transparent—either in reflecting the world or conveying ideas. As a result all our claims about language and the world—and implicitly all our claims in general—are reflexive in a manner which cannot be avoided. For to recognise the importance of language is to do so within language. To argue that the character of the world is in part due to the concepts employed is to employ those concepts.

Rather than a problem to be overcome, Woolgar and Ashmore (1988:2) see reflexivity as offering new ways of addressing questions of knowledge. To investigate our own claims may help us understand the claims of our research subjects and to approach social work as storytelling may have something to say about storytelling by sociologists. Mulkay (1985) and Woolgar and Ashmore (1988) investigate the analytic enterprise using alternative literary forms (dialogues, plays, voices) which disrupt the conventions of academic writing.

Historical studies, in particular, have approached narrative as a problem, a source of falsification. To analyse the past means imposing literary techniques on 'the facts'. As MacIntyre (1984:214) comments "to present human life in the form of a narrative is always to falsify it." Norman (1991:121) sees historical narrative as "interpretative violence". Other historians do not see it as a problem but an opportunity for asking questions about the representation. For White, representations of the real and the imaginary have much in common. 'Real' events can only be represented through narrative forms. Barthes (1981:7) considers that "the narration of past events" has been subjected to the "sanction of historical science" and "bound to the underlying standard of the 'real'." He asks:

> ...does this form of narrative really differ in some specific trait, in some indubitably distinctive feature from the imaginary narrative, as we find in the epic, the novel and the drama?

Historical representations of 'real' events cannot be separated from the narrative forms used to display them. Woolgar (1983:246) offers a similar comment on social scientific analysis:

> We presume a reality independent of our accounting practices, even though it is not possible to demonstrate this independence; each of our attempts to 'tell' reality inevitably involves the use of accounting practices.

Garfinkel's discussion of the documentary method of interpretation is an important way that both analysts and research subjects can be seen to make claims by linking events to explanations about those events.

> The method consists of treating an actual appearance as 'the document of,' as 'pointing to,' as 'standing on behalf of' a presupposed underlying pattern. Not only is the underlying pattern derived from its individual documentary evidences, but the individual documentary evidences, in their turn, are interpreted on the basis of 'what is known' about the underlying pattern. Each is used to elaborate the other (1967:78).

Other methods of investigating claims making through storytelling by both the analyst and social workers are discussed throughout this study. To legitimate the telling of a story is to attend to the situated features of the performance of that story, both the social worker's and the analyst's. Any comment on the practices of social work storytelling is equally applicable to the analyst's storytelling, including his/her construction of legitimacy.

This chapter has considered how theories of narrative can inform an investigation of social work accounts as texts which are available to be read as stories. There have been four key features—stories as performances, stories as literary texts, stories as displaying rhetorical functions and stories as reflexive enterprises.

First, the review of theories of stories as structure or performance has favoured an interactional investigation but one in which the past, present and potential occasions of reading are available. Stories as recognisable through definitive structures, as suggested by Labov or literary theorists, are more appropriately examined as an interactional task. Features of story structures are not outside the occasion of the performance but may be attended to by speakers and hearers in the process of the storytelling. The implications for this study are that the structure of social work documents may be laid out in terms of institutional conventions (a standard court report or memorandum), but the story then enters into a variety of readings based around the interactional production and reception of a social work account.

Second, the discussion of the literary text and narrative method has suggested that features of literary analysis can be applied to social work accounting. Heard as stories, social work accounts can be investigated for their handling of plot, character and point of view. This raises important questions about whether character is made available through reporting events, or plot is determined by character. Furthermore, are characters able to question and subvert their construction? Whilst literary theory offers interesting questions about narrative and reading relations, it is recognised that there are major differences in reading social work accounts. In particular, the role, occasions and power of social work readings offer the potential for immediate and direct challenge and subversion. How far is the social work account able to present a defended, finalised version of the client or is it open to the free play of alternative readings?

Third, it has been suggested that social work accounting can be heard to fulfil a number of local interactional and rhetorical functions. How far can social work accounting be heard as performing community? In what way do accounts function to display competence and entitlement of writers and readers? How do social work accounts link local entities with occupational concerns, mandates and prerequisites? The implications of these questions are that this investigation should attend to the reader of the accounts, who is being addressed and how they are constructed and persuaded?

Fourth, acknowledging multiple readings directs us to a reflexive investigation. The analyst's claims about social work as narrative are also caught in a web of multiple readings. How the social worker substantiates his/her accounts may help with our own storytelling. This review is itself a rhetorical enterprise, attempting to convince the reader that the author has put forward a convincing argument that social work can (even should) be approached as accounts, text and narrative. A succession of allies have been marshalled in the form of famous names and reference made to 70 texts. Preferred versions of the way forward have been contrasted with dispreferred versions. An attempt has been made to recruit the reader by participative devices, like 'we have seen', suggesting that the reader is a part of the enterprise. Such displays by the writer offer some of the storytelling features which can now be applied to social work accounts. At the same time, it is suggested that not any version will do or rather that only certain readers are welcome.

Fundamentally, the ubiquity of narrative has been emphasised, albeit through varied and conflicting approaches and definitions. Herrnstein Smith (1980:232) questions whether narrative can be seen as a distinctive discursive act.

> Almost any verbal utterance will be laced with more or less minimal narratives, ranging from fragmentary reports and abortive anecdotes to those more distinctly framed and conventionally marked tellings that we are inclined to call 'tales' or 'stories'. Indeed, narrative discourse is, at one extreme, hardly distinguishable from description or simply assertion. That is 'telling someone that something has happened' can, under certain circumstances, be so close to 'saying that something is (or is not) the case' that it is questionable if we can draw any logically rigorous distinction between them or, more generally, if any absolute distinction can be drawn between narrative discourse and any other form of verbal behaviour.

Narrativity is available potentially in all discursive performances—conversational, documentary, scientific and literary. Other writers have recognised narrativity in historical texts (Mink 1978, White 1980), scientific texts (Myers, 1990), legal texts (Bennett and Feldman, 1981) and organisational texts (Phillips, 1995). As Butler (1990:13) notes:

> All, then, is narrative, the literary and the non-literary alike. Even those stories intended, say by a speaker in deadly earnest, to be accurate representations of something that has just happened fall into the narrative patterns created by the inelectable semantic potential of words and sentences.

Whilst remaining aware of the danger of being overwhelmed by narrative (Barthes, 1982:252) one possible solution is to locate ourselves in the role of readers and critics. Several of the theories discussed posed questions in terms of readers and reading relations as ways of approaching narrative and narrativity. Sacks (1992:228) considers that 'potential' stories are located in how speakers and hearers attend to the story. Lyotard (1984:24) is interested in the 'addressee', Bakhtin (1984:18) in the 'participant'. For Barthes (1977) the author is now dead, readers are no longer consumers of texts but producers. For Culler (1980:36), it is the listener who decides. Smith (1993: 23) looks to instructions to readers, Garfinkel (1967:200) approaches occupational texts as made available for later readers. A reflexive response also suggests reading relations are a way of attending to how the analyst and social worker attempt to control readers. At the same time, not any reading of texts will do. The next chapter applies concepts of narrative and reader to the analysis of social work texts.

NOTES

[1] In this study, narrative and storytelling are used synonymously. However the word narrative has a root suggesting a more expert type of storyteller. As White (1980:5) notes:

> The words 'narrative', 'narration' and so on derive via the Latin 'quarus' ('knowing', 'acquainted with', 'expert', 'skilful' and so forth) and 'narro' ('relate', 'tell') from the Sanskrit root 'gua' ('know').

Story, on the other hand, suggests an entertaining rather than an expert account. The balance between entertaining and convincing and between the imagery and the factual are key tensions throughout this study.

[2] A number of writers have made use of Labov and Waletsky's formulation of narrative, for example, van Dijk (1987) and Polanyi (1985). Stewart (1991:126) links the elements of a narrative to Aristotle's beginning (abstract, orientation), middle (complication, evaluation and resolution) and end (coda) and considers that :

> The lifelong experience of stories that comes from participating in the traditions of his or her culture leads a reader to expect these elements and to perceive as incomplete any story that lacks them.

[3] Prince (1973) and Todorov (1977) identify story structure in the change from one state of affairs to another. Propp (1928) and Rumelhart (1980) treat stories as purely structural objects with a grammar similar to a sentence. Wilensky (1982) develops a schema based on the organisation of the 'point' of story. For many of these writers, the narrative is a psychological notion, a way of organising memory and thought processes (Bruner, 1991:4).

[4] Research interviews are more appropriately seen as examples of 'invited stories' (Watson and Weinberg 1982:62) where the interviewee is given the floor through methods of questioning and encouragement, but the interviewer sets the agenda for the relevance of the story in the invitation and through back channelling.

[5] The formalist approach to narrative is well established in literary theory and forms the basis of what is termed 'narratology' (Bal, 1994)

[6] Bird and Darenne (1988:67) consider that news stories are a "triumph of formulaic narrative construction" in that they reproduce the structures of the "larger symbolic system of news" (1988:69)

[7] There is a dispute as to whether Bakhtin wrote the works attributed to Voloshinov and Medvedev. It is not proposed to comment on this debate and the writers will be acknowledged separately. The prime interest in such uncertainty is that contested and unstable versions of text and narrative apply to Bakhtin's identity as well as his theory.

[8] Todorov (1977:68-70) makes an interesting distinction between psychological and a-psychological narratives.

[9] There is a major debate in history about the authority of the historical narrative in achieving the status of an historical text (White 1987, Carr 1986). For us, authority is everyday and interactional as well as an academic achievement. The authority of the narrative is discussed in Chapter 5.

3 Social work texts as stories with readers

In this chapter, social work accounts are analysed in terms of two key concepts from the review of narrative theory: story structure and the role of the reader. The first part of the chapter examines three social work documents for features of story structure and story recognition. In chapter 2, it was suggested that delineating story structure was insufficient for developing an adequate notion of the performance of narrative. However, its recognition was suggested as an interactional task for both analysts and hearers. We can thus ask if social work accounts display elements of story structure but also if participants and readers react to them as stories. The second part of the chapter investigates how stories are interactionally accomplished by constructing readers and the same social work accounts will be re-examined. The overall question is whether identifying narrative features improves our understanding of how social work texts are organised and how readers are persuaded by the force of the narrative.

The social work accounts examined in this chapter consist of three documents concerning social services contact with one family—part of an interview between the researcher and the social worker working with the family,[1] a court report on the family written by the same social worker and entries from the social work case file. These kinds of documents are typical of those which constitute the daily activity of social workers.[2] In addition, the three texts are linked since they address the 'same' set of circumstances—social services reaction to a child abuse allegation. The analysis concentrates on a part of the interview, the court report and case notes are too long to consider in full. The family consists of a mother and her children, with the father, who is the alleged perpetrator of the abuse, living outside the family but nearby.

Social work accounts as stories

In analysing social work accounts as stories we can ask a number of questions. How useful is it to distinguish how texts are structured? Do participants attend to them as stories? How far does each version of the 'same' story depend upon local and interactional features? Whilst theories of narrative discussed in chapter 2 have different definitions of what constitutes a story, several outlined similar components of story structure—an opening orientation, a complication, a resolution and an evaluation or comment. These features are investigated here for their interactional significance rather than their definitional authenticity. How far does hearing a story contribute to the interactional accomplishment of the social work account.

The research interview

An extract from a research interview appears as appendix 3.1.[3] Whilst the text might be read as co-participants attending to an occasion of a research interview, the interest here is to what extent they are also collaborating in the production and reception of a story. Mishler (1986:69) notes how research interviews might be achieved through telling stories:

> Telling stories is far from unusual in everyday conversation and it is apparently no more unusual for interviewees to respond to questions [in research interviews] with narratives if they are given some room to speak.

Opening

In the opening utterances, the participants have some difficulty agreeing on the appropriate format. The social worker locates the starting point of these events as the date of the children's admission to care; it is the outcome which is to be explained. The truncated and contested nature of 'floor seeking' (Sacks, 1992:681) in the initial utterances (lines 1-39) can be heard to create an unsettling set of exchanges—the interviewer is attempting to ask questions and receive answers and the social worker is trying to introduce characters and events. The interviewer can be heard to undermine potential storytelling by cutting across the social worker's utterances to ask informational questions—race, gender, age—thereby interrupting any bid for an extended turn. For example, a strong bid for telling a story can be observed at line 15 "now the children ..." which is interrupted by the interviewer, line 16 "sorry sorry race". The social worker can be heard to stop trying to tell a story and to revert to a question and answer format—line 21 "go on".[4] To take Labov and Waletsky's definition of a story, the opening of the interview is not structured by narrative clauses nor is there a recognisable story preface (Sacks, 1992:226). There is rather a contested set of exchanges with different positions about the nature of the encounter.

The interviewer can be heard to acquiesce at line 22 and the social worker accepts this as a story invitation. A chronological starting point to the story is offered as the initial intervention by the department to make the children wards of court (line 25). A further bid for an extended utterance can be heard in the instruction to provide "a bit of background" (line 37), which the interviewer acknowledges. Not only can this be heard as a story preface, but it suggests that understanding what happened requires a 'background', a story. Despite the initial uncertain nature of this exchange, a bid for an extended utterance, hearable as a story, has been interactionally accomplished through chronological markers and 'floor seeking'.

Orientation

The 'background' offers a description of particular features of family behaviour which can be heard as the problem which brought about social services involvement. It makes available a moral categorisation of the case and describes a particular state of affairs. The mother is young with three children. She has entered a pattern of moving home because of the violence of the father (line 46). The family is specifically constructed as a mother with her children (line 40). The constant reference to "the father of the children" (line 41) can be heard to underscore any basis for a relationship between herself and the man in the story. He is not, in the social worker's narrative, a part of the family. This preferred family set-up establishes an initial state of affairs and offers a chronological and categorical starting point—they used to be like this. The initial state of affairs and preferred family set-up is the focus of a set of interventions (lines 51 to 88), to "get her settled" (line 84) and sort out the children's behaviour (line 86). The benefits of this state of affairs is demonstrated by a series of upgraded descriptions of the social work interventions: the family are not just re-housed but "a 5 bedroom house in a (sought after) area" (line 69); not just pre-school day care but "a community package" (line 80) and the safety of "an injunction against [father] to stay away" (line 72). A potentially satisfactory state of affairs can be heard.

Complication

A complication now occurs and a new state of affairs emerges. This change is marked with an approximate date (line 88) and the injury to the eldest child can be heard to signal a breakdown in the former state of affairs. It means the father is on the scene and hence there is a breakdown of the preferred family set-up and the co-operation of the mother. The 'da da da da da' (line

91) is an important comment as it can be heard to herald a domino effect of all the consequences that follow from father's presence in the family. It also acts as a pivot between the two states of affairs, signalling the obvious implications, which are not necessary to spell out. To emphasise the breakdown, reported speech is used to show that the mother does not really seem to take it all seriously and was being deceitful (line 93). The very foundation of the preferred state of affairs has been reversed.

Resolution (with a twist)

The breakdown can be heard to justify the strongest action available to the social worker–to remove the children against the mother's will (line 99). However, the judge did not go along with the social worker's "side of the story" and the children returned home (line 106). That her formulation is described as a 'story', a version, rather unsettles the display (line 104). It is a story but also a version, of which there may be several–the social worker's, the mother's and also now the judge's.

Evaluation

The interviewer is now able to intervene, following a slight pause. The story is not over, but the resolution was unexpected ("oh", line 107). An explanation is required for the apparent failure of the social worker's story and justification is made available in terms of timing and future safety which the judge did not accept. The story is completed by the closing comment, line 121 "that's it in a nutshell really", which interviewer acknowledges "ok".

This account displays features of story structure suggested in chapter 2. The story has been interactionally accomplished since the interviewer responds to key narrative points–floor seeking, surprise, ending. In particular, a complication has located events and characters through a change between two states of affairs; a preferred set of characteristics is replaced by a dis-preferred set. A series of events and behaviours has been linked together in a plot. Furthermore the speaker describes it as a 'story' in the sense of a version of events. As Sacks suggests, a 'potential' story has been interactionally produced with both participants attending to its production. This conversational social work text has thus displayed a number of features of story structure. How far can a story be heard in a written account?

The court document

The affidavit is a sworn statement by the social worker which was presented at the Court to justify the removal of the children and request that they remain in care.[5] Whilst it may not be surprising for an unstructured research interview to be seen as similar to conversational storytelling, a court document is unlikely to be denoted by participants as a story or a version of events. Although describing the 'same' events, the affidavit presents major differences in structure and content from the interview. There is no detailed 'background information'. It concentrates instead on two encounters between the social worker and the mother. Given such differences, can the affidavit be read as a story and how is story structure achieved?

Opening

The bid for 'floor seeking' by the social worker cannot be negotiated through turn taking sequences as in the interview. The affidavit displays an introduction of standard legal protocol—name, address, institution, qualification of social worker—which can be heard as seeking entitlement to present the report. An opening is made available by outlining the purpose of the document:

> I make this affidavit to apprise the Court of relevant developments which have occurred since the matter was last before the Court ... None of the Minors are currently residing with their mother for reasons set out below.

The situation to be explained to the court is that the children are no longer at home. A similar explanation is provided in the interview as to why the children were admitted to care. Such an opening can be heard to function as a story preface, a state of affairs to be explained. The outcome is offered at the beginning, available to be heard as a problem to which the report will offer a solution.

Orientation

A preferred state of affairs is described, but not in the form of a description of family relations as in the interview. The report describes a visit by the social worker to the mother, after the incident was reported to social services by the hospital, but before it was 'confirmed' as 'non-accidental injury'. This can be read as setting up a contrast between the mother's behaviour before and after the social worker knew 'the facts' two days later. The mother is heard to dismiss any claim by the hospital that the father was involved in the incident and, given her general manner, the social worker believes her:

> Mrs B was calm and collected and told me "There must be a mistake. They must have been mixing D up with another kid". I asked her if she had seen [father of children] recently and she assured me that she had not ... I felt inclined to believe her due to her calm and co-operative manner.

A state of affairs and preferred family set-up similar to that in the interview is undisturbed and is recognisable in the "calm and co-operative" mother. The normality of relations is confirmed by a description of a conversation about day care arrangements.

Complication

Two days later "information is received" about the 'facts' of the injury and a new state of affairs exists. The hospital confirmed that the mother had made reference to the father being involved in the incident and the police arrest him. The decision to go ahead with the admission into care is stated in a short and matter-of-fact way:

> In the light of the above information [from the hospital and the police] Ms. L, my team manager, interviewed Ms B as a result of which [the children] were removed from their mother.

The description of the removal continues in some detail and the character of the mother can now be heard as in contrast to the earlier visit. In the later description, she is depicted as "agitated", "distressed", "hysterical and threatening", "throwing objects around" and "flung herself on the floor". In contrast to the mother being out of control, the social worker is pictured as responding to the children—"reassuring", "cuddling" and answering their questions in the car on the journey to the children's home.

These contrasts can be heard to perform three tasks. First, the calm, co-operative mother is discovered through subsequent information to be "dishonest" and deceitful, putting in doubt her apparent co-operation. Second, in her moment of hysteria she is never heard responding to her children, her behaviour sounds almost indulgent; she can only be heard as causing distress to the children. Third, the social worker is heard as calm and reassuring, thinking first of the children's welfare.

Resolution and evaluation

The conclusion is available as an evaluation of the consequences of the present moral state of play between the social services and the mother:

> I share the concerns outlined [in other affidavit]. In addition it is a matter of grave concern that [mother] lied to me concerning her involvement with [father]. It is my view that [mother] needs a great deal of support which I have been endeavouring with others to offer her. I do feel that honesty is an essential ingredient in our relationship.

Such an appeal can be heard to display the difficulty of co-operation with this mother rather than the needs of and danger to the children—the injury is not mentioned in the conclusion. The social worker's discussion of "future long term plans" is available as an appeal to the judge that the future is safer with social services in charge and they should stay in care.

Is this affidavit a story? Narrative features are available to be recognised in terms of a story structure—orientation, complication and resolution. A move between two states of affairs is suggested by Prince (1973). There are also similarities between the affidavit and the interview fragment in terms of contrasts between preferred and dispreferred states of affairs. Since it has been suggested that narrative features are only available in the reading of an account, such an occasion requires both instructions from the storyteller and appropriate responses from the reader. Attention to textual features must be accomplished by the reader in order for a text to be read as a story. It is not a story outside the occasion of reading, nor is there a story structure intrinsic to the text.

For the reader to respond to the narrativity of the reading occasion, the affidavit has required following a series of textual instructions and taking part in shared and ratified readings of the social work community. For example, that social services taking on future planning for these children is a 'resolution' to the 'complication' requires being part of the community of competent readers of social work accounts. Other readers, for example the parents, may not accept such logic. A considerable amount of interpretive work has already been accomplished if this text is read as a good report. Stories and storytelling are joint productions, whether there is a listener present or not. It is to the detailed and complex reading relations whereby the reader is drawn into a shared and ratified reading that this study should now turn. Before such an investigation, it is worth asking similar questions of the story structure of the case notes.

Case notes

Case notes are a series of entries in a file, recording visits, phone calls, reports and letters on a family, completed on various occasions by different social workers. How can they be considered a story given their disjointed completion? White (1980:13) notes that an annal, a historical document consisting of a list of dates with events, is a potential story since:

> Nonetheless there must be a story since there is surely a plot—if by plot we mean a structure of relationships by which the events contained in the account are endowed with a meaning by being identified as parts of an integrated whole.

Are entries in a case file oriented to or constitutive of an 'integrated whole'? Social workers consider such file entries as particularly important in child abuse cases, since like a policeman's notebook, they could be used as evidence in a future court hearing, therefore accuracy of dates and comments is crucial (cf. Garfinkel, 1967:198 on the accuracy of medical records). Here is an important entry about the child abuse incident:

13/9. Phone call from [children's home manager]. They had received a letter from Dr. H describing an interview with [mother] the previous Sunday and the examination of [child's injury]. He was very concerned about [father] being at the home and the injury to [child]. I phoned [manager of hospital social work team] and asked him to get information for me as hospital still hadn't properly informed us of the incident. Dr.H phoned me and repeated the information given in the letter to [children's home]. There could be no doubt that [mother] had described the incident as accidental caused by her husband. I asked whether the injury was consistent with the explanation especially being a fall downstairs. He said [the injury] could only be caused by excessive force and a severe blow. I said I would be informing the police as I said I thought it should be investigated and he agreed.

Does such an entry make available a story? Elements of a story structure can be identified: Opening—phone call and concern by 'key player'. Complication—confirm new state of affairs, child was injured by the father and is in danger. Resolution—inform the police. There are, however, major differences from the other stories.[6] First, there is no detailed orientation, the initial state of affairs is assumed, taken as read. Also the resolution offers no comment or evaluative statement; the reader is expected to draw the appropriate conclusion from the display of information. By both the Prince and Labov definitions this is not a story.

However, attention to the reading relations of this text enables this entry to be read as a story. Case files are read for their overall justification of concern and action requiring a "competent readership" (Garfinkel, 1967:199). By entering the institutional reading relations of case files, such an entry makes narrativity available in reading the case file as a whole. Indeed it is essential that this entry contributes to a larger narrative which is available to be invoked. The 'entitled' reading situation, as Garfinkel suggests, is for later readers to reconstruct an overall "therapeutic contract" of justifiable assessment and action. This entry can be read as attending to and contributing to two incomplete narratives, neither of which is explicitly discussed, but both are required to be available. There is the original story, what happened on the day that the child was injured. There is also attention to an ongoing story, what should social services do next? Neither of these stories is explicitly stated but both are available in the performance of the reading relations of the community of competent social work readers. In this way, as White (1980:13) notes of the annal, case file entries can be heard to contribute to a sense of plot and, as such, are available to be read as stories.

The orientation-complication-resolution structure is likely to be available in many accounts, given the rhetorical structure of the formulation (see Toulmin, 1958 discussed in chapter 4). However, the identification of, and links between, such features requires following the instructions of the text and performing social work community. A further feature of the foregoing discussion of story structure is the extent to which accounts of the 'same' set of events offer major differences in content, form and style. The link to an autonomous story independent of these accounts seems difficult to substantiate. Each text is dependent on local and interactional features which orientate that text towards particular occasions and specific audiences. That the storyable features had to be looked for, suggests that approaching a text as storyable depends on active reading, not fixed story structures. Whilst the narratologist might discover a story structure, the judge might discover evidence and a social worker discover professional competence. Roles, relations and occasions of reading would appear to be key to narrative. It is now proposed to investigate the reading of these texts as stories or storyable, located not 'in' the structure of the text, but made available by the interaction between the writer, reader, the text and occasion of reading.

Interviewer: It is so embarrassing. Did I really lead Social Worker so blatantly. It seems like she told me the sort of social work practice that I wanted to hear. All those instructions, not very subtle ones either, which forced her to explain things in the way I approved. Especially that one at line 37 where I appeared to reward her for telling me the 'bit of background'. And I was so inconsistent; at the beginning I was stopping her talking with all disruptive questions just to get the basics together. I wonder what I said to set up the interview in such an uncontrolled way, I can't remember now but that beginning was a mess. I obviously need to announce things better in future, get the basic information first, then it can flow better and I need not interrupt ... oh dear! perhaps I should look for another job.

Author: Hang on now, I am not suggesting that your interviewing is deficient, inappropriate or even atypical. Remember Mishler (1986) notes how interviewers can't help hearing storytelling, the main problem is when they try to suppress them. I appreciate your 'unprofessional' approach to 'interviewer detachment', my point is that all accounting is interactional even if there is no explicit hearer. Indeed in the next section we are going to look at a variety of readers and hearers; some present, others not.

Narratologist: You might be happy with Interviewer but you seem to have brought me to this meeting under false pretences. I thought you were looking at the way social workers tell stories and you wanted my help identifying whether they are stories or not. You now seem to be saying that they are not stories with structures, points and all the other properties we have discovered, but only there in their reading. I can't see the difference.

Author: This is important and something I find rather hard to sort out myself. What I think some of your colleagues are saying is that stories don't exist in themselves, they have to be read. How do you know that 'War and Peace' is not a shopping list or perhaps more appropriately a battle plan or copy from a war correspondent? You know by picking up cues and your knowledge of writing and reading conventions.

Narratologist: Yes, that's what our work has been about, locating such features in the story.

Author: Well, are they 'in' the text or only discoverable in the reading? Suppose someone read the text with different conventions of what is a novel or battle plan, couldn't they make a mistake. More precisely, does a 'resolution' necessarily resolve a 'complication' for every reader? Some readers may remain unconvinced. I bet the mother or her solicitor would read those texts differently.

Narratologist: Some readers can make mistakes, especially with some of these newer novels. I get lost sometimes.

Author: Not so much mistakes as deviating from the reading instructions. So you agree, a story is only available in its reading. Now we hope to see how reading conventions work, if I can get on.

Sceptic: Are the instructions 'in' the text then?

Author: I didn't invite you to this meeting. What do you mean?

Sceptic: Is any meaning available in a text–story structure, instructions to readers, performing community. They are all textual constructions. Is any reading better than any other? I quite like the idea of 'War and Peace' as a shopping list.

Author: Oh dear, I don't want to get so nihilistic but I accept your point. Look, let's agree that anyone can read anything into anything else, given the appropriate reading relations. However if we try to find how certain readings are made available and more appropriate than others, then can we get at some sort of stability?

Sceptic: I doubt it.

Author: Look, I will keep saying that certain readings are 'made available', 'can be heard', 'it can be suggested that' indicating that you will probably find others. I just hope that the reader will find mine convincing, persuasive; I'll try to use all the rhetorical and narrative techniques of the social workers.

Social Worker: I am pleased that you are going to use my persuasion as a guide, I just wish the judge had done so in this case. And you still haven't said anything helpful about child abuse, especially now we have come across some.

Author: No, I am sorry we must talk more about that. But Sceptic had got me worried about something else.

Social Worker: Your petty navel gazing is irrelevant compared with children's pain.

The theory of the reader

This section reviews theoretical discussions on the role of reader. It is not possible for the analyst to re-enter particular encounters where texts are performed—to sit in the court where the report is read or observe a social worker consulting case notes. Even if this were possible, it is not clear that the judge would explain his/her reactions to the report or if such a description would explain how it was read. It is not suggested that studying reading performances restricts analysis to specific occasions. Rather, a social work account is performed whenever it is read, including sociological analysis. Such performances draw the reader into a web of reading relations, making connections between entities and events and attempting to persuade, entertain and privilege preferred interpretations. Identifying the reader of a text is not straightforward.[7] Our task is to ask if certain readings and readers can be heard as attended to more than others. Are particular features available which instruct us as to how the text is to be read and by whom?

The role of the reader

The 'death of the author' (Barthes, 1977) in literary theory has questioned the search for textual meaning in the intentions of the writer/speaker. It suggests instead that the novel creates a space for multiple interpretations, with a possible momentary stability located in the role of the reader. 'Writerly texts' (Barthes, 1975:4) have a reader who is "no longer a consumer, but a producer of the text." Other writers have noted the opportunities for readers to re-write non-fiction texts (Roe, 1994:24).

Social work accounts are active texts with different audiences and potentially critical readers. Social work reports are usually handed to the judge or passed round at the case conference to be read in silence. On such occasions writers and readers might comment on the report, using it as a starting point for discussing the case. The reaction is not usually mere consumption nor agreement; the judge or case conference may ignore, applaud or criticise the report. Readers feel free to agree or disagree with parts of the report and in particular, to comment on the connections between facts, conclusions and recommendations. Case notes and research interviews are more often performed as private, individual readings, with less opportunity for direct critical response. The private reader is likely to search for consistency of message or a specific piece of information, but such reading occasions entail a range of interests, for example, to check dates, assess client response, evaluate social work competence. None of these interests is mere reception.

Literary theorists have studied the role of reader. It has been debated whether reading a novel involves the interpretation of messages and codes already potentially available 'in' the novel, or whether interpretations are related to the reading occasion and the activity of the reader. Iser (1989:77) considers that the reader concretises a potential text, making interpretations and filling in gaps that are already 'in' the text.

> The convergence of text and reader brings the literary work into existence, and this convergence can never be precisely pinpointed, but must always remain virtual, as it is not to be identified either with the reality of the text or with the individual disposition of the reader.

In the reading process, however, the reader has her/his expectations questioned and re-formulated, as s/he seeks coherence on the basis of sense making. Reading 'awakens' processes in the reader, "... a process out of which emerges the actual content of the text itself." (Iser, 1989:78). Although the reader does not passively receive the text, for Iser s/he still moves towards an understanding of the "ultimate meaning" (p.79) of the text. The text and the reader are both pre-existing entities which interact with one another.

For Fish (1980) there is no ultimate meaning of a text, only that which is conferred on it by the reader. Everything about the text is a product of interpretation, there are no factual 'givens'. The only reason there are not many different interpretations of a text is that readers share some conventions of what constitutes an appropriate reading. Fish calls 'interpretive communities' the academic conventions for interpreting literary texts.

> Interpretive communities are made up of those who share interpretive strategies not for reading (in the conventional sense) but for writing texts, for constituting their properties and assigning intentions ... (this) explains why there are disagreements and why they can be debated in a principled way: not because of a stability in texts, but because of a stability in the make up of interpretive communities and therefore in the opposing positions they make possible. Of course this position is always temporary (unlike the longed for and timeless stability of the text). (p.171)

Fish's interpretive community has been criticised (for example, Shepherd, 1989:97). It suggests a 'cosy' debating shop of academics and does not resemble the potential conflict of reading texts in, for example, a court or case conference. It does, however, suggest the possibility of attempts at stability of interpretation based on constructing appeals to conventions of mutuality. This is not merely reading texts by a community of interpreters, but the active construction of community conventions in the performance of the text.

Dialogic texts

A dialogic approach to analysing texts is linked to the work of Bakhtin and acknowledges the interactive but also evaluative nature of language. Texts are read and assessed from socio-ideological positions, hence reading is located in performing community, anticipating answers and appealing to share reading conventions. Bakhtin (1981:280) notes the dialogic nature of all texts:

> Every word is directed towards an answer and cannot escape the profound influence of the answering word that it anticipates.

The text and the reader anticipate and construct one another. The reader makes interpretations influenced by aspects of reading occasions and her/his attachment to reading conventions. At the same time, the text is constituted through a range of stylistic conventions and communicative instructions of how to read entities and events. For Bakhtin, such activity is not the gentle persuasion of the interpretive community but the clash of language and genre. It is not a simple determinism by either the text or the context, but an interaction of the two. Words have histories and conventions of use, contexts have to be constructed and mutually established. Whilst texts and contexts are caught in competing dialogic relations, at the same time they are able to carve out a stability, a style.

> Style organically contains within itself indices that reach outside itself, a correspondence of its own elements and the elements of an alien context. The internal politics of style (how elements are put together) is determined by its external politics (its relationship to alien discourse). Discourse lives, as it were, on the boundary between its own context and another alien context. (1981:284)

Bakhtin calls this 'internal dialogisation'. Texts and contexts create stability through their relations with one another and through the style or genre of the speech community.

> ... we speak in diverse genres without suspecting that they exist. Even in the most free, unconstrained conversation, we cast our speech in definite generic forms, sometimes rigid and trite ones, sometimes more flexible and creative ones ... We are given these speech genres in almost the same way that we are given our native language. (1986: 78)

For Bakhtin, then, texts are cut across by a wide range of contexts and styles, which set up a continual dialogue with audiences over fixed and changing interpretations. Words and phrases carry with them past uses and generic conventions which readers and writers manipulate, appropriate and re-write.

The ratified reader

How does a text privilege some interpretations rather than others? A number of writers identify the preferred reader of the text through conventions of reading and attributes of readers which are made available. What sort of reader is drawn in and persuaded? Iser (1974) talks of the 'implied reader', a potential audience to which the text is addressed. Goffman (1981:132) distinguishes between those who overhear, bystanders, listeners who are ratified hearers but not specifically addressed, and those who are ratified and addressed. Garfinkel (1967:201) considers that medical records are constructed for an 'entitled reader':

> The entitlement refers to the fact that the full relevance of his position and involvement comes into play in justifying the expectancy that he has proper business with the expressions, that he will understand them and will put them to good use ... The possibility of understanding is based on a shared, practical and entitled understanding of common tasks between writer and reader.

The 'entitled' or 'ratified reader' is someone familiar with and persuaded by the reading conventions of social work; s/he hears the values, mandates and working knowledge of social work. It is a reader who will make the logical step from complication to resolution, from concern to action. S/he will accept that a warrant justifies a claim and hears the cues and instructions of the text. The 'ratified reader' is an important concept throughout this study.

There is another potential reader available at the reading occasion; some sort of guardian of standards or judge of legitimate action, before whom the account must eventually be justified. Bakhtin (1986:126) suggests a 'superaddressee':

> Any utterance always has an addressee whose responsive understanding the author of the speech work seeks and surpasses. This is the second party. But in addition to this addressee (the second party), the author of the utterance, with a greater or lesser awareness, presupposes a higher *superaddressee* (third), whose absolutely just responsive understanding is presumed, either into some metaphysical distance or a distant historical time ... Each dialogue takes place as if against the background of the responsive understanding of an invisibly present third party who stands above all the participants in the dialogue...(the superaddressee) is a constitutive aspect of the whole utterance.

Mecke (1990:209) considers that a 'superaddressee' is an "a priori condition of communication". Goodwin (1990) notes amongst adolescents a story could be told to one person but directed at another, what she calls an "absent audience". Unlike the ratified reader, who is constituted by the reading conventions and cannot disagree, the superaddressee is approached more cautiously, yet to be convinced. In social work this might be an understanding judge or some guardian of professional standards whose judgement really counts (Morson and Emerson, 1990:135).

It is an important theme of this study that contested meanings and preferred interpretations of social work texts can be identified through reading relations. It is proposed to investigate reader construction by returning to the social work documents discussed earlier. This analysis investigates the preferred, ratified reader. A study of alien voices and alternative readings which disrupt the text, 'the other', are explored in chapters 7 and 8.

The reader in social work texts

In the first part of this chapter we examined the 'Broken Nose' case for its story structure. Here we are interested in how the text offers instructions through appeals to shared reading conventions of competent social work readers. Some of the methods for achieving story structure also delineate the reader. For example, preferred and dispreferred versions of family life enabled the 'orientation' to become the 'complication' in the interview story. Such a contrast also instructs the reader how to understand family relations through use of the word 'dad' in the court report. For the mother and her children, 'dads' can legitimately punish children:

> (Child) asked "Why are you taking us away from our mummy"? and later "You put our dad in prison ... it's OK for dads to smack children". He later made reference to the fact that his father was entitled to hit him because "he's my dad".

Whilst this dispreferred view of family relations is not explicitly challenged, a few lines later the strength of the child's protest is devalued and his formulation of family relations undermined:

> After [child] had made his point of view he calmed down and then I was able to explain to him why he was being taken to a children's home.

This unacceptable version of 'dad' is heard to undermine the mother's case, as the child is seen to acquiesce. The report also contains a similar use of the concept of Mum needing Dad's support, which is read as unacceptable as it is negated by his violence.

> At one point [child] remarked "She needs daddy to support her". I agreed that his mother needed a lot of support but explained that his

father had been violent towards his mother and this had meant that they had to move home on many occasions.

The constitution of acceptable and unacceptable family relations is achieved by establishing how the conventional use of the word 'dad' does not apply to this family, thereby legitimating the removal of the children. The reader has been instructed to see abnormal family relations in conventions of inappropriate punishment and support, recognisable by competent social work readers.

Constructing the reader/hearer in the interview

The construction of the 'ratified reader' and 'superaddressee' in the interview is investigated in three ways: the set of categories manipulated by the speaker and hearer; the contrast between preferred and dispreferred behaviours and states of affairs; and the use of specific instructions to bind speaker and listener into an interpretive social work community.

The use of categories and concepts to perform social work

A wide range of categories and phrases are available here which can be heard as social work talk : 'care and control', 'this area', 'contracts'. They are phrases which have a specific use in social work which would not be similarly used elsewhere. However, whilst such utterances display a knowledge of social work terminology, they are not enough to construct a legitimate social work reader.[8] It is the competent manipulation of such categories and concepts that brings off a successful account and enrols the reader.

It was noted in the discussion of the story structure of the interview that chronological boundaries were made available which framed the story. They also frame social work. The social worker responds to the interviewer's request for information about this case by announcing the date and length of the stay in the children's home (line 1). Such a response acknowledges the orientation of the interview task and confirms the event requiring explanation, to which everything that follows will be addressed.[9] An adequate explanation is required: a 'proper puzzle' to the outcome, a stay in a children's home (Smith, 1993:30). When the children leave the children's home, the hearer will know the task is complete, a 'terminal action' (Sacks, 1972:342). When the storytelling has been negotiated (line 22), a chronological boundary locates the beginning of the story as the initial social work intervention, which outlines the legal basis of the case: it is a social work case because the children were made wards of court (line 25). These boundary markers, then, instruct the hearer how to recognise the beginning, ending and point of the story but also the boundaries to social work.[10]

Another feature which can be heard to establish shared social work conventions also deploys legal categories. At line 52, putting "a stop to" undesirable states of affairs is elaborated to "putting a legal framework around it". This is developed into a justification "for the children" which is extended with the phrase: "y'know in the best interests of the children". This latter concept is widely used in social work literature and legislation as legitimating social work intervention (Jacobs, 1982). Here, extending the justification "for the children" with "y'know" in the middle can be heard to link this occasion to wider social work concepts. At the same time, it instructs the listener to share in the performance of social work community. Schiffrin (1987:282) notes the frequent occurrence of "y'know" with reported speech and here "in the best interests of the children" can be heard as reported speech from authoritative social work sources. Bakhtin (1981:342) notes that authoritative discourse is filled with sacred words or phrases, distant from the present utterance of the speaker. The utterance at line 54, then, can be heard to provide both sacred legitimation and create a shared understanding with hearers. Once such words are used, they bind speaker and hearer together in worlds removed from the here and now, and can be heard to provide for an approach to the superaddressee.

Contrasts

By developing the notion of contrasts, we can examine how the two states of affairs do more than merely offer a chronological story structure. As with the contrasting versions of 'dad' the preferred and dispreferred states of affairs set up notions of acceptable and unacceptable behaviour, and hence enrol the listener into the community of social work readers. Story structure which is more than 'in' the story can be heard as a formulation for enrolling the moral order of the 'ratified reader'.

The contrasts in this account do not lay out a rule and specify its infringement in a direct way as Smith (1993:34) suggests. The enrolment of the reader in the interview relies on the obvious nature of inferences, without instructions as to what is acceptable and unacceptable. For example, the problem of instability in the family is not set up by an explicit contrast but by picking one feature of the family to illustrate deviance.

> ... and for instance C who's seven has moved in his lifetime about 30 times (-) (lines 43-4)

The deviant feature of this family is illustrated rather than explicitly indicated. The hearer is expected to make the link that a seven year old should not move home so frequently and hence deviant family circumstances can be identified. The upgraded nature of the description, "in his lifetime" moved "about 30 times", followed by a pause, can be heard to offer the reader an opportunity to acknowledge the deviance.

A more elaborate set of contrasts than Smith's rule breaking is available as the story structure moves between the two states of affairs. Each statement can be heard to contribute to the overall contrast between the state of affairs before and after the broken nose incident. Beginning with the seven year old's moves, the first state of affairs depicts the father's violence (line 46), the sudden moves of home (line 47), the social work intervention (line 49), the legal framework (line 52) and the disturbed behaviour of the children (line 58). The appropriate social services response is outlined (lines 68-86). The second and contrasting state of affairs does not indicate changes in the mother or children's behaviour as more deviant. It is mother's non-cooperation with social services in maintaining the preferred family set up without father which signals the breakdown in the previous state of affairs. How can this be heard to justify taking the children away from home?

The listener is again enrolled as a ratified social work hearer since the justification of stronger social work intervention is in terms of non-co-operation rather than deviance or child abuse per se. A competent social work hearer would be clearly aware of the obvious consequences of non-co-operation.[11]

> ...this meant alarm bells y' know father's on the scene da da da da... (line 91)

With "y' know" and "da da da da da", the speaker instructs the listener to make obvious inferences. The reappearance of the father as constituting a new dispreferred state of affairs needs no elaboration. Both the "alarm bells" and the "da da da da da" are powerful instructions to the listener. A figurative formulation can be heard to sum up the drama of the change better than a list which contrasts the preferred state of affairs (lines 68-88). The sound of "alarm bells" can be heard as a metaphor for the call to action of the fire brigade, all aware of the crisis with no uncertainty or hesitation. The "da da da da" figure, as mentioned earlier, can be heard as a 'domino' effect; the appearance of the father is enough information to demonstrate that all the elements of the first state of affairs have collapsed. It too can be heard as a figurative communication, as one effect disturbs the next with rapid succession, with little ability to intervene.

The contrasting of states of affairs can be heard to construct a competent hearer/reader who is expected to follow the story without needing specific instructions about deviant and normal behaviour. By binding the reader into obvious inferences, any criticism challenges the community of ratified social work hearers.

Binding instructions

Two specific features can be heard to bind the listener to the community of ratified hearers: "y'know" and "we". It has already been noted that "y'know" at lines 54 and 91, as well as "da da da da da" can be heard to specify instructions to the reader. "Y'know" also appears at lines 56 and 58. Schiffrin (1987:284) considers that "y'know" in narratives can be heard as a story evaluation:

> "Y'know" enlists the hearer's participation as an audience to the storytelling by drawing the hearer's attention to material which is important for his/her understanding of why the story is being told ... it marks meta-knowledge about shared (either speaker/hearer or general) knowledge. That is, once speakers produce in their hearers recognition that a story is about something with which they themselves are familiar—something which is shared knowledge—then much of the informational and interactional dilemma facing the storyteller is resolved.

The two sections where "y'know" appears are available as summaries of states of affairs—the first where the overall problem of the family is being outlined and the second where the new state of affairs is indicated. They can be heard, as Schiffrin (1987:283) suggests, as 'pivotal points' in the story. The first use (lines 54-58) displays a list of three "y'know"s, which Jefferson (1990) sees as a particularly strong method of tying together entities in a formulation. Here "in the best interests", "some legal framework" and "their behaviour" ties together three crucial aspects for justifying social work. A competent listener can hear a full display of social work justification—the professional, legal and personal. The second use, as has already been suggested, coupled with "da da da da da" instructs the listener that the event of the broken nose indicates a dispreferred situation. In both these uses of "y'know", the obvious nature of social work inference is displayed. The logic of a social work justification is outlined, but not expanded since to a competent hearer it is clear. "Y'know" is therefore heard as a strong inclusive feature to the ratified hearer.

As was noted earlier, the dialogue begins with negotiation over the use of active/passive voice and entitlement. Social services is portrayed as active but the storyteller still does not associate himself with the organisation.

line 49 social services having worked quite hard...
line 51 social services decided that they...
line 55 they went back to court...

The use of 'they' separates the storyteller from these actions, although in the next line he reverts to 'us'.

line 56 it gave us some legal framework to work with E ...

The change to 'us' is linked to the description of the everyday "work with E". There is a gradual change of use from the impersonal to the personal pronoun as the "background" is filled out and the story unfolds.

Following the adoption of the personal plural pronoun, the collective nature of action and evaluation remains throughout the rest of the account. For example:

> line 68 we got hold of a property in ...
> line 79 we were trying to work ...
> line 92 we talked to E ...
> line 95 we felt that ...
> line 97 we went to court ...
> line 99 we expected mum ...
> line 111 we were sort of seriously saying that ...
> line 117 we needed time to think about it ...

The collective nature of action even relates to circumstances in which one person in the group was engaged–line 92 "we talked to E". According to the case notes, it was the team manager who interviewed E on this occasion. At line 105, "our side of the story" was put to the court by the storyteller, but it can be heard that it was the social services' view of the case that he was presenting. The use of 'we' is thus deployed in all actions described, implying community based support for all that was done; one person may have carried it out but they were all acting on behalf of the collective.

The continual use of 'we' in describing both action and evaluation can be heard to enrol the shared community of social services. Goffman (1981:144-5) notes alternative roles of a speaker:

> Sometimes one has in mind that a 'principal' (in the legalistic sense) is involved, that is, someone whose position is established by the words that are spoken, someone whose beliefs have been told, someone who is committed to what they say. Note that one deals in this case not so much with a body or mind as with a person active in some particular social identity or role, some special capacity as a member of a group, office ... some socially based source of self identification. Often this will mean that the individual speaks, explicitly or implicitly, in the name of 'we', not 'I'.

To speak on behalf of such a community is both to establish the community and to seek legitimation from it. The individual speaker is bound to the collective with its apparent agreement.

Does the use of 'we' also include the hearer? Has the storytelling enrolled the interviewer as a ratified reader? The features discussed above–use of "y'know", contrasts, and community based categories–could establish the interviewer as a community member, but the specific uses of 'we' do not include the interviewer. 'We' can be heard as a contrast to 'them' at line 104–'her side of the story'. The interviewer distances himself from the collective at lines 107 and 109 by referring to the social services' actions as "you'd" and "your sort of hope at court", where he could have said 'we'd' and 'our'.[12] This can be heard to create some uncertainty in the relationship between interviewer and social worker. The judge has not accepted social services' formulation and the children have been sent home. The social services collective has been undermined. Is the interviewer now deserting the social services collective view, opening up the possibility of a critical response? In the next few lines (111-121), the large number of instances of 'we' appears to emphasise the gap between speaker and hearer, as the 'we' collective can be heard as united but unsuccessful. The possibility of the undermining nature of storytelling is developed further in chapter 8.

This analysis has highlighted the possibility of shifting formulations of readings, as the roles of the ratified reader and superaddressee are negotiated. The reader/hearer has been constructed through a variety of binding instructions, contrasts and categories as a ratified member of the community of social services readers. However, success in establishing consistent roles and readings appears to have been challenged by the superaddressee, the judge. The hearer/reader is in danger of adopting a critical stance and deserting the social work collective. It is now proposed to investigate whether similar constructions can be identified in the court report.

The reader in the court report

The court report writer does not have an opportunity to invoke shared agreements through binding instructions like "y'know" nor can the performance of community appeal only to social work conventions. How then can the court report be heard to instruct and construct the ratified reader and superaddressee?

Instructions to the reader

The layout and structure of the court report explicitly displays this document for a particular purpose to be heard in a special arena with an identified audience. It has a standard legal format on the first page and the status of the document is gravely introduced as 'an oath' with named 'plaintiffs' and 'defendants'. However this formal introduction is only apparent on the first page and thereafter the language uses a wide range of legal, occupational and colloquial talk.[13] The reader is heard as the judge and the court. S/he is explicitly addressed on a number of occasions, with specific instructions to look at other documents, consider particular information and, at the end, carry out specific action. There is the customary display of deference towards the judge in such instructions:

> I crave leave to refer ...
> I make this affidavit to apprise the Court ...
> I shall refer to the Minors herein by their first names ...
> I respectfully request this Honourable court to make the following Orders...

The opening and ending can be heard as standard protocol and set up the document for a specific reader and reading occasion. Whilst a written document, these instructions anticipate the reading situation and point the ratified reader in particular directions.

Contrasts and the superaddressee

It was noted earlier how this document can be read as narrative through the contrast of two depictions of the mother—as co-operative and trustworthy before the information was received from the hospital and police, and hysterical and dishonest after the father's arrest. The earlier analysis of story structure highlighted the use of contrasts through character depiction; here the contrast is investigated for how the reader is constructed and enrolled, and the superaddressee approached.

The reader is transported into two key encounters, both carefully set up and graphically illustrated with reported speech. A meeting between the social worker and mother before the information is confirmed by the hospital can be heard as an amicable and wide-ranging exchange. Mother is told of social services' concern and she denies contact with the father. Two methods can be observed. First, an indirect approach: she is given the opportunity to tell her version of the incident and is then challenged by pointing out that the hospital said something different:

> I talked to Mrs. B and D about how the incident had occurred. They both told me that D and [his brother] had been fighting on the stairs when D had fallen, thereby causing the injury to his nose. I explained to Mrs. B that we had received information to indicate that she (i.e. Mrs B) had told the hospital that the incident had occurred in a different way as described above.

Second, there is a direct question:

> I asked her if she had seen [father] recently and she assured me that she had not. She stated that the last time she had seen him was ...

In between these questions is direct speech:

"There must be a mistake. They must have been mixing up D with another kid."

This section can be heard to function as a dialogue. The social worker describes her own utterances and reports the mother's. To the ratified reader, the Judge, and on this reading occasion, the court hearing, this report can be heard to operate like a cross examination (cf. Atkinson and Drew, 1979). The social worker, like a barrister, asks an indirect question, offering the mother the opportunity to tell the truthful/preferred version. This is then confronted with contrasting, objectively verifiable information from the hospital. The direct question is made available to await later condemnation by objectively verifiable facts from the police. The difference here from 'real' cross examination is that the replies are also provided by the cross examiner.

The second encounter, the removal of the children by the social services with police assistance, reports the mother's words and behaviour in considerable detail. The reported speech charts her mounting hysterical behaviour:

> She had been clearly agitated when the Police spoke to her, but on seeing me she became extremely distressed and shouted "Get her out of the house".
>
> Meanwhile [mother] had run into the sitting room and was holding on to the pushchair in which [child] was sitting. She shouted "No no no, tell me what I've done".

Again this can be read as cross examination, only now the social worker has 'taken the stand' to relate the incident as a first hand observer. The decision to remove the children is not explained; there was 'no alternative' because dialogue with the mother was impossible. The social services can be seen as rational in contrast to the 'hysterical' mother.

By mimicking and anticipating cross examination in court, the judge is addressed as the ratified reader, but the superaddressee is the defending barrister. The defendant's own words can be heard as condemning, presenting points which the defence will be forced to confront. Did mother really behave in such a manner? Did she say such things? At the same time, the contrasting characters of social worker and mother set up depictions of reliable and unreliable witnesses.

The reader of case file entries

In locating the ratified reader of social work case notes, we develop Garfinkel's discussion of medical files as displaying a 'therapeutic contract', through a "conversation with an unknown audience" (1967:200). The concept of the ratified reader is suggested by Garfinkel's 'entitled reader' who reads from "the perspective of active medico-legal involvement" (1967:201).

Several readers and reading situations might be imagined for child abuse case notes. First, a colleague looks for facts or assessment when the social worker is not available. Second, as mentioned earlier, case notes may be used in court reports and, on occasion, the social worker may be required to read them in court as evidence. Certain court officials may examine files (notably the guardian *ad litem*).[14] Third, the social worker her/himself may use them as a note book for recording opinions and events, which may be used in future documents and discussions. All such readers can be conceived as having different reading interests—a single piece of information, a point of view, or an overall plot. There are still other potential readers—senior officers when resources are requested or reviews completed, the clients themselves, researchers, inspectors etc. Such readers are less likely to be ratified or addressed, but they may constitute the superaddressee. Given this potentially wide range of readers and reading situations, who is the ratified reader and is there a superaddressee?

Mere facts

Case file entries could be imagined to be 'mere facts', stating events and conversations, untainted by opinion or evaluation. They might be offered as raw material for readers to make their own assessment of events and characters. However, it will be observed that 'mere facts' can be seen to be doing work. For example:

> 18/9. Phoned Health Visitor. Gave up-to-date information. She said [mother] had come in yesterday to the clinic but stayed 2 minutes and stormed off—reason unknown. Agreed to keep in touch. She asked if a case conference will be called. I said not at present. Needed to move quickly, then a case conference. Will do this through the High Court.
>
> 19/9. Team manager phoned [children's home] to inform them of our plans and confirm that [oldest child] will stay there.
>
> 19/9. Phoned Family Centre, informed them of current situation and plans.

Whilst all these entries report phone calls to other professionals, they can be heard to do more than note events. They demonstrate that current action and evaluation is taking place in consultation with other professionals. The community of professionals is demonstrated as in active operation. The first entry, in particular, signals the inclusion of the health professional, an important ally from another welfare institution. This entry does not merely recruit her support, but displays the social worker's attention to the joint nature of intervention and the shared experience of mother's unreasonable behaviour.

> 17/9. Message from Team Manager. [Father] remanded in custody until 27/9. Need to discuss plans with [Area Manager] then [mother] before going to court.

Here, 'mere' information has consequences and sets up instructions to ratified readers, addressed to the social worker herself and colleagues. At the same time, the careful weighing of strategy is displayed. Mere facts can be heard to perform community by demonstrating to readers an adherence to conventions of legitimate social work activity, notably constructing the welfare network and strategic action.

Points of view

Whilst the entries of phone calls above demonstrate other professionals being enrolled, other entries can be heard to recruit the 'point of view' of other professionals. For example:

> 19/9 Team manager phoned Legal Department. Spoke to Solicitor—advised to get a warrant to remove the children from home. This means that we need to go to High Court today to request a warrant. This would mean that if necessary the police would have the power to break or force entry. It was felt best for Team Manager to go to High Court due to her being the person who spoke to [mother] on the 18/9 and which contact we have based as our reasons for taking the children into care.

As well as reporting phone calls, consequences are identified and action outlined. The Legal Department can be heard to take the concerns of the social workers and turn them into a legal strategy. The action is no longer merely social work concern but legal process. Throughout the file entries around this incident, medical, legal and police advice can be heard to be recruited to the social work formulation, whereas family centre, day nursery, children's home, school are informed.

In the earlier entries, professionals are heard to be recruited and translated into the social work strategy; later however, such forces can be seen to desert:

> 19/9. Police informed me that (Police Doctor) was not prepared to give an opinion as to how the break on child's nose occurred. He has asked a forensic pathologist to give his opinion. (Police) made it clear that information regarding the break was dependent on this otherwise they have no evidence. They are not certain yet as to whether the nose was deliberately broken by [father].

> 26/9. Judge decided that children should return home ... Just before going into court we'd heard [father's] charges were dropped. Decision for children going home was based on this knowledge ...

It suggested that points of view, which are recruited to persuade the reader of the strength of the account using the network of professionals, can also be used as an excuse when things go wrong. Colleagues who read such entries are likely to sympathise as other professionals are heard to let the social worker down.

Plot

It was noted earlier that White (1980:13) suggested that events and dates of an annal can be read as a plot. Given our concern to investigate reading relations, is it appropriate to consider plot structure? For a social work reader, the reading of a plot is available in the sense of direction of the action. A 'rational decision making' investigation can be heard as the social workers are seen receiving information, interpreting its significance and taking action. This is made available particularly in the activities of the social worker, Team Manager, Area Manager (Team Manager's boss) and a Principal Social Worker (a headquarters post responsible for tricky cases). These intra-organisational characters are depicted as strategists, others only contribute. For example:

> 18/9. Met with (Principal Social worker, Team Manager and self; 1) Decided to find out [mother's] view about the accident, 2) Her view of [father] and him seeing the children, 3) Why she's not been honest with us and could she be honest with us about [father] in the future in order to have a workable relationship.
>
> 18/9 [mother not accept points above] ... she said she could not talk to [social worker] and didn't want any more mealy mouthed social workers interfering, just bribing her with carpets, washing machines etc ... In my view [mother] is not prepared to accept any role in protecting the children from [father] and indeed felt SSD [social services department] were to blame for the fact that [father] was locked up. At this point I suggested she see her solicitor ...
>
> 19/9 Discussed with Area Manager, Team manager and myself. Decision to take the children in care today. Reasons: 1) [Mother's] clear statement that she will not work with social services in any way, 2) Her view that [father] has a right to see the children and apparent need to have him around, 3) Dishonesty and the need for [mother] to be honest if there is any chance of working together.

At each stage the social workers can be heard gathering and interpreting events and characters. Despite recruiting other points of view indicated earlier, facts can be seen as turned into interpretations and action.

Different readings of the case file entries, however, could locate other plots especially given the benefit of hindsight. After the failure of the court case, could a social services reader identify what went wrong? Was the information inadequate to warrant the action? Were procedures followed correctly? The careful instructions of facts, points of view and rational decision-making can be heard as attending to such potential accusations, especially the explicit links made between information and decisions in the 18/9 and 19/9 entries. The entries 19/9 and 26/9 can be heard to blame the police.

However, other readers might read a different plot; did social services act too hastily? From the 13/9 entry (displayed earlier), removing the children can be heard as inevitable. Was acting on the hospital doctor's point of view mistaken, given the later police doctor's refusal to support that opinion? The process of decision making after that was very careful, or was it? Who knows what conclusions the scrutiny of later readers might lead to. Could the information have been put to High Court before taking the children away, were they in such imminent danger? Is an accidental broken nose in father-son play so serious? Should children not see their father ever? On the other hand, were the police inept with their evidence and the judge mistaken?

Critical readers could question minor mistakes of strategy, they could also undermine the social worker's formulation of the whole case. But critical readers are not from the community of ratified social work readers, they are superaddressees and harder to predict. Critical readers may construct a wide range of interpretations given their interests and positioning.[15] In this case, social services were unsuccessful in recruiting the judge by professional persuasion and any number of later readers could criticise.

This chapter has discussed two important approaches to reading social work accounts. First, social work accounts make available features of story structure, suggested by theories of narrative. However, by rejecting the notion that such features are 'in' the text, the approach to narrative as performance has focused on the reader. Second, the construction of the reader, the performance of a shared community of ratified social work readers, multiple audiences and approaches to the superaddressee are offered as important concepts.

The construction of the reader in social work texts is seen as more complex than is suggested in scientific texts (Latour 1987, Law 1986, Rip 1986). A variety of readers have been identified, some ratified and approachable, others distant and critical. Attempts to recruit readers have focused on ratified social work audiences. Medical and legal concepts were also appropriated although they were soon seen to fade away. The superaddressee, approachable with the support of the ratified reader, is suggested as a way that readers and writers make links between local and more exalted reading occasions.

The implications for the rest of this study are that social work accounts can be successfully investigated as narrative. In particular, the construction of the reader offers an opportunity to investigate how social work accounts make available a wide range of instructions and features in attending to such concerns. Social work accounts can be heard to anticipate, persuade but not always convince later readers. In the following chapters, the construction of the reader, reading occasions and relations are treated as important features of textual interpretation. Different attributes of the text-reader dialogue are investigated, starting with the handling of moral concerns.

NOTES

[1] At any one time, a number of social workers may be seeing a family; however, one social worker is usually seen at the 'key worker' or 'allocated social worker' who is considered to have an overall view of the work taking place.

[2] See appendix 1 concerning the accumulation and presentation of data.

[3] This interview was a part of a review of admissions to care of younger children, see appendix 1. It is also used in a rather different analysis in Hall, Sarangi and Slembrouck (1997 b).

[4] In another research interview, the social worker interrupted the interviewer's initial questions to demand the floor "I'll talk..." and proceeds to talk uninterrupted for about 12 minutes, indicating the interactional force of 'floor seeking' (see chapter 4)

[5] As mentioned in appendix 1, the concern over court material has meant that the affidavit is not displayed.

[6] Apart from a different structure, there are important differences in content from the other texts. The case notes display a more uncertain picture of the identification of abuse, with social services appearing to play an active role in problem definition. The information did not come unambiguously from the hospital as the 13/9 entry displays. The social worker had to seek it out. In a later entry of 19/9, uncertainty re-emerges as the Doctor 'is not prepared to give an opinion as to how the [injury] occurred' to the police.

[7] There are different views as to whether the 'reader/hearer' is a straightforward concept. Law (1986) and Rip (1986) discuss the reader of scientific articles, grant applications and patents and have no difficulty in locating the attributes and expectations of readers. However Goffman (1981 chapter 3) criticises traditional notions of speaker, hearer and conversation as too "crude" He considered there are complex "participation statuses" and "production formats" within different "footings".

[8] I recently observed a discussion amongst social workers where there was great amusement in the way a 15 year old used social work terms to complain about his treatment, e.g. "You have not considered my best interests."

[9] Not all interviews started with details of the stay in the children's home. Some began with a description of family circumstances or main characters. The admission

to care was portrayed as one event amongst many, whereas in this case it was a key event. Perhaps this an example of plot related or character related stories (see chapter 5, low risk stories and serious situations).

[10] Atkinson (1995:97) notes the importance of chronological markers based on previous medical interventions when reporting a medical case.

[11] Dingwall et al (1983:92-6) note the importance of 'parental incorrigibility' in child abuse cases, but they relate this to decision-making. Here it is suggested that such formulations of characters are less a factor of making decisions as rhetorical devices for bringing off adequate stories.

[12] This is one of the interview where the interviewer worked for the same department and was well known to the social worker (see appendix 1).

[13] Jonsson and Linell (1991:430) describe police reports for court as:
a hybrid mode of expression, mixing bureaucratic forms (that would never appear in spoken dialogue) with colloquialisms which are most often drawn from the actual interviews (when the suspect is interviewed by the police).

[14] In other case files, possibly less serious cases, entries were frequently completed in only a cursory fashion, with visits and telephone calls not noted but summaries of contact completed.

[15] Goodwin and Goodwin (1997) note how in the (first) Rodney King trial, the jurors were persuaded to see the defendant lying on the floor as a potential threat by entering into and accepting the police's formulation of the appropriate use of batons in handling suspects. They had accepted the reading conventions of everyday police work.

APPENDIX 3.1
Research interview: The broken nose case

Int: Interviewer
SW: Social worker
(2)   pause in seconds
(-)   pause under 2 seconds
...   utterance interrupted or speaking at the same time
[child] proper name used

The interviewer has described the aim of the research study as a concern with the admission to care of younger children, and has identified how this case fits into the study. After some initial uncertainty about the status of the children's home, this extract starts with the social worker's first complete turn. The family is mother, E, with four children at home, A, B and C, and another child D is living in a children's home.

SW: right so they were placed in [children's home] on the nineteenth of november and they stayed there till the twenty seventh of november and the one that's under five is A (-) and erm how old is he (-) have you got his date of birth
Int: no but roughly...
SW: erm he's two and a half (-) ok
Int: right ok and the ...
SW: oh there's another one B and B is just four ok that's roughly (-) erm
Int: and sorry did they come into care how many came into care at that time
SW: three
Int: three of them so how old was the other one
SW: er seven
Int: right ok (-) right
SW: now the children..
Int: sorry ... sorry sorry race
SW: race (-) wh.. erm (-) black (-) mixed race
Int: right (-) and gender
SW: boys
Int: all boys three boys right sorry
SW: go on
Int: no I'd rather you talk

SW: ok

Int: it's just that...

SW: erm(-) th these children were made wards of court in february (-) erm in 25 february 19__ and erm and with interim care and control to [local authority] (4) and erm (-) the decision at that time was to leave the children with the mother although we had interim care and control erm they were to be placed at home with mum (2) erm (3)

Int: can I just interrupt(-) how long had you been involved with the case before

SW: I got involved in february

Int: in february right

SW: cos it was it's a case that was known to this area [another social worker] was involved with the family before (-) right (-) erm (3) I suppose I'll have to give you a bit of background actually to explain this

Int: yes

SW: the family erm E [mother] is a young mum who's lived with the father of these children for about eight years there is an older older child but he's actually at [children's home] so these three are with mum and (-) for instance C who's seven has moved in his lifetime about 30 times (2) the reason that that's happened is that mum erm has kept returning to to the father of these children who who at times can be very violent towards her and when that happens and he suddenly turns she's off with the children she's always protected them she takes them away (-) now (2) in february she did this again having with social services having worked quite hard at having contracts with both her and the father of these children the thing blew up again social services decided that they had to put some sort of stop to this some sort of legal framework...

Int: ...hm hm..

SW: ...around it for the children y'know in the best interests of the children so that's why they went back they went to court which meant then   erm (-) y'know it gave us some legal framework to work with E to say look you cannot keep moving around these children are you know their behaviour is showing us this that and the other ....

Int: ...where does she go where does she stay....

SW: ...showing signs of disturbance.... Well what she did was to go to bed and breakfast in erm [area] and then another bed and breakfast in [area]

Int: oh she just books herself in

SW: well no [local authority] put her in homeless families

Int: oh I see

SW: she went down to homeless families violence they put her into B and B and then erm finally we got hold of a property in [area] so she's in a 5 bedroom house in [area] so the whole family moved over to there without the father (-)

Int: right

SW: the courts put an injunction against him to stay away from the family and under no conditions could he see either E or the children (2) then what happened was

Int: sorry when was this?

SW: this was in february it was all ...part of the same time ok

Int: ...the same time ok

SW: so E knew quite clearly he had to stay away and that she had to stop moving around and to work work with us and we were trying to work sort of promote some sort of community package with the idea of a family centre which is fixed up with [name of centre] day nurseries getting the two eldest children into special schools because they were no longer going to be able to from the assessments be able to sort of stay in mainstream school try and get her settled because I mean moving about was one of the biggest things and the children were all over the place quite insecure (-) then so E was supposedly keeping to that contract and having no contact with the father (-) and then erm in november the beginning of november the eldest child who was there at weekends broke his nose he went to [hospital] and he told the hospital that his father had done it this meant alarm bells y'know father's on the scene da da da da da so because of that erm and because we talked to E and she seemed to think well it's ok for for dad to see the children I'm not really bothered erm and because of that attitude the fact that she hadn't been honest with us (-) we felt that the children's sort of long term future was at risk and that and that they were at risk because he was around and he could turn up at any moment so we went to court and got an injunction to actually go and collect those children from the home because we expected mum to not let us have them erm and that's why that's why they came into care...

Int: ....right

SW: erm and then we went back to court for a fuller hearing because you would have got it in half an hour this this injunction to go and collect the children (-) and so E was able to then put her side of the story and we put our side of the story and the judge decided the children should go back home

Int: oh (-) cause you'd not wanted that

SW: no

Int: what what would have been your sort of hope at court that you'd been asking for

SW: well we were we were sort of seriously saying that erm we hadn't I 110 mean basically we were saying look we haven't had a chance to really think about erm the future for these children it's all happened so quickly but what we do recognise at the moment the children are not safe at home because of the father being on the scene and because of what has happened to the eldest child and that we needed time to think about it

Int: right

SW ..and in the meanwhile we wanted the children to stay in care and then come back to court the court wouldn't grant us that so the children went home (-) erm (2) and that's it in nutshell really

Int: ok (-)
120

4 Handling blame and constructing moral character

> I think you will know what abuse is when you hear about it. (social worker 1992, overheard talking to a teacher who had suggested that child abuse was culturally specific)

> There is no objective behaviour we can automatically recognise as child abuse. (Gelles, 1975:364)

Having established that social work accounts make use of, perhaps depend on, narrative features which set up relations with readers, we can explore further the interactional, rhetorical and literary nature of these relations. This chapter considers how the reader might be persuaded by moral rhetoric. In chapter 5 the topic is factual rhetoric.

Morals and morality are familiar concepts in sociology. There are, however, contrasting versions of the moral dimension. An interactional approach focuses on 'moral construction' and 'moral character'. It suggests a concern with processes and formulations rather than externally constraining moral rules or normative structures. The study of moral construction explores how far accounts allocate blame and responsibility, whereas investigating moral character considers how people and entities are depicted using concepts of good/bad, deserving/undeserving, blameless/culpable. To the sociological investigation of moral construction must be added a literary concern with character portrayal: how traits and attributes of characters are made available in narrative. It also suggests a concern with constructing the reader and community of competent hearers. Moral characterisations of actors and entities are dependent on available moral formulations. The deserving client, the inadequate parent, the child abuser are moral categories which enable characters in social work accounts to be described and categorised through definitions available within, and constitutive of, the community of competent social work readers.

In this chapter, there is first a discussion of theoretical approaches to moral construction. This is followed by an analysis of social work accounts which considers moral construction through deploying ascriptions of blame and responsibility to characters and entities. The data studied are reports from a social work journal and part of a research interview. This chapter also raises important questions about the moral basis of child abuse.

Theoretical approaches to moral construction

Moral concerns pervade theoretical and everyday accounting. Definitions of right/wrong, acceptable/unacceptable and appropriate/inappropriate behaviour, especially in the area of family relations, posit deeply held moral formulations, with vehement accusations and denials.[1] The social worker quoted at the beginning of this chapter sees child abuse as clear and objective, unlike the social scientist. What, then, are the consequences of suggesting that child abuse is morally constructed, relative to a society and a time, even dependent upon the moral activity of professionals?

Moral rules or moral processes?

Put simply, there are two major sociological approaches to morals and morality: 'top-down' and 'bottom-up', what Heritage (1984:83) calls 'regulative' and 'constitutive'. The former approach, associated with Durkheim, sees morals as externally constraining the activity of actors, internalised through socialisation. Society is the transcendental source of moral action, marking out proper behaviour and guiding action (Tiryakian, 1979:210). As Poggi (1990:170) puts it, for Durkheim morality involves:

> ...institutionally sanctioned obligation... a subject's conscious acceptance of and willingness to surrender to the intrinsic superiority of claims higher than his/her own.

The 'constitutive' approach, associated with Garfinkel and Blum and McHugh (1971), sees morality as the product of ongoing interaction. The moral nature of reality is accomplished by actors continually accommodating and accounting for the responses of others. Moral formulations are interactionally deployed to make sense of and produce a shared moral world. Morals are not a priori, pre-figuring the actor's choice of action, what Garfinkel calls the 'judgmental dope' (1967:68). They are rather situationally constituted and negotiated evaluations, where the moral basis of a shared understanding is sought. Garfinkel (1967:50) calls this 'trust', "a person's compliance with the expectancies of the attitude of daily life as a morality". Garfinkel demonstrates both the fragile nature of social interaction and the extreme moral sanction when common sense expectations are transgressed.[2] Speakers expect entitlement to co-operative communication which is morally sanctionable (Garfinkel, 1967:42).

In this study, we are interested in how these two aspects of morality, the societal and the local, come together. How do social work accounts handle the moral outrage of contentious issues, for example child abuse, by deployed moral construction and characterisation? Social workers use moral formulations both to establish characters and depict action as sanctionable. At the same time, they recruit and instruct hearers and readers through shared moral conventions: what we all know about child abuse. There are dire rhetorical and interactional consequences if the reader is not appropriately enlisted.

Child abuse as a moral category

Child abuse is seen by many writers as morally determined, not separated from definitions of right and wrong. A moral category is the basis for operational and scientific definitions.

> ...what is abusive is already constituted through a discourse outside science. Child protectionists have fixed the moral and political parameters of the debate. Especially in the case of sexual abuse the definitions employed by the child protectionists are transferred into scientific research on the basis of their moral authority. (Clegg, 1994:31)

Moreover, what constitutes child abuse is constantly changing. Pfohl (1977) and Parton (1985) consider that there has always been 'child beating' but certain developments in political and professional appropriation enabled its recent conceptualisation as 'child abuse'. The category child abuse has been extended (Hacking, 1991:259). A Department of Health report 'Child Protection: Messages from Research' (1995:14-18) discusses the changing threshold of what constitutes child abuse. However, as Parton (1996:7) notes, this report presents an uncertain version of social constructionism. He suggests that in the report:

> ...there are certain objective underlying conditions which necessarily and objectively constitute child abuse but which are lost or obscured by their social construction.

The version of morality and social construction deployed is critical. If morality is seen as societally determined, although changeable, then there will be fairly uniform versions of what child abuse is and how it should be handled, at any one time.[3] If, however, all social phenomena are seen as morally constructed, then what constitutes child abuse is a product of complex institutional negotiation. The moral work of 'the child protectionist' is seen as much in the activity of social workers, police and doctors, as the "radical feminist or socially conservative pressure group" (Clegg, 1994:31). Definitions of child abuse are debated at higher levels of professional and political activity, but there is a loose relationship between such definitions and their flexible use in the everyday interprofessional arenas. Parton (1996:7) directs us to study 'child protection *work*':

> Child abuse for organisational accounting purposes is not simply in the eye of the beholder, a subjective definition, it is an inter-subjective phenomenon whose meaning and import can only be understood in the culture and organisational context in which it is not simply constructed but constituted.

Social workers as moral assessors

Moral assessment is central to the processing of public officials. Delinquents (Cicourel, 1976), welfare claimants (Zimmerman, 1969), even river polluters (Hawkins, 1983) are characterised and categorised by public officials through conceptions of moral worth and culpability. Decisions about services offered or sanctions imposed are not based merely on the facts of the case but expectations of typical characters—a depraved youth, a deserving claimant, a negligent factory owner.

This approach is also applied to child abuse (Gelles 1975, Parton 1985, Dingwall et al. 1983). There is an interest in how social workers' assessments of child abusers involve complex moral formulations and typical characterisations. Such formulations might be influenced by changing definitions in the wider professional and political arena. For example, Dingwall et al.'s (1983) discussion of social workers in the late 1970s as operating a 'rule of optimism' which neutralised possible allegations, can be contrasted with concepts of 'dangerous families' (Dale et al., 1986) typical of the 1980s. However, social workers' accounts of child abuse are likely to deploy a wide variety of general and specific moral formulations aimed at specific audiences and occasions.

Handling blame and responsibility

Moral construction has been located in processes of allocating blame and responsibility (Watson 1978, Atkinson and Drew 1979, Cuff 1980, Potter and Wetherell 1987, Silverman 1987). These writers look at how accounting in the form of excuses, disclaimers and justifications is used to allocate and mitigate blame. Blame can be both allocated to those outside the conversation (Watson, 1978) or handled within sequences of charge and rebuttal (Atkinson and Drew, 1979). Much of this work has focused on the sequential nature of blame in naturally occurring conversation.

Blame allocation is, however, more than a defence against direct accusations in conversation. Atkinson and Drew (1979:137) note how on some occasions, blame in cross examination in court is anticipated and countered, such that the rebuttal comes before the charge. Witnesses anticipate questions and criticism, having rebuttals already prepared. Heritage's (1988:130) complaint-apology sequence (A: why don't you come and see me sometimes. B: I'm sorry. I've been terribly tied up lately) can be heard as reassuring the hearer that a competent and acceptable story of 'being busy' is unspoken but available to counter the complaint. Thus storytelling not only produces moral tales but can make use of blame allocation to resist criticism and thereby assert the speaker's moral authority.

> The teller, in producing an account of what is happening in the world, is also unavoidably producing materials which make available possible findings about his characterological and moral appearance as displayed in his talk. (Cuff, 1980:35)

Silverman (1987) notes how the parents of teenagers with diabetes managed blame for monitoring their child's blood-sugar levels by balancing their parental responsibility with trusting the autonomy of the teenager. He sees this as a result of granting the teenage patient 'theoreticity' and moral responsibility: the teenagers are capable of rational thought and if they fail it is they who are to blame.

The study of social work accounts, then, can explore a number of aspects of moral construction and characterisation. It offers a site to study how wider moral questions are handled through local moral narratives. We can consider how characters are depicted, how blame and responsibility is allocated and how events become reportable in terms of wider moral debates.

Reporting child abuse in a social work journal

Media reporting has become an important arena for debating child abuse. Appendix 4.1 presents eleven reports from a social work journal and one from a national newspaper of child abuse tragedies. It is not suggested that these examples are typical of child protection cases. They are some of the few cases that hit the headlines since in all but one report a child has died. They appeared in the journal in 1989 and 1990 shortly after a series of highly publicised cases. Given their audience, these reports might offer the sort of explanations envisaged as reportable and hearable by social workers.[4] They are in contrast to local and national press coverage and can be heard as a professional and balanced response to other reporting.

Whilst the national press constructed negative stereotypes of social workers during this period (Franklin and Parton, 1991), these journal reports offer different versions, sometimes in direct contrast to national coverage. Two reports respond directly to the alternative version. In report 4, the headline and the introduction make it clear that a version offered by the Minister is dismissed by the Inquiry Report. In report 1 (para. 11), the Director of Social Services describes press criticisms of the social workers as "unfortunate". The frequent reporting of such cases in this period might be seen as making available explanations which social workers can rehearse for any future public exposure of their case. It is offering rebuttals to potential blamings making available a social work accounting repertoire (Gilbert and Mulkay, 1984).

Headlines

The framing of a text by its heading has been noted by Woolgar (1980:251) as providing a guide to the reader of how to understand what follows, as well as summarising the message. In six of the reports, the issue of blame is the focus of the headline, the four others report the process of inquiries (report 2, 4, 9 and 10). The response to a potential blaming is immediately set out as either critical of the social workers or exonerating them. Those which resist blame are unequivocal in their instruction—report 5 "Death could not have been prevented" and report 6 "Boy's death no fault of social workers". Where social work culpability is reported, it can be heard as the lesser charge of making mistakes or poor judgement—report 8 "Avon director admits mistakes were made", report 3 "SSD was mistaken", report 1 "Judgements flawed says child death review". These are in contrast to headings like the Times (18/12/87) "Tyra Henry Inquiry says social workers to blame over murder". One method of handling blame is therefore to accept one (technical) aspect of the charge without necessarily admitting full responsibility. In over half the reports, the initial instruction to the reader can be heard as attempting to handle actual and potential blame.

Point of view

Given the widespread criticism in other media reporting, who is heard as the 'trusted teller of the tale' in these reports? (Smith, 1993:22). It was suggested in chapter 2, that the point of view is an important aspect of framing a story. It is also linked to the process of constructing the ratified reader and performing the social work community, discussed in chapter 3.

Two preferred 'points of view' can be heard in most of the reports—the reporting Inquiry Team or the response of the Director of Social Services. Inquiry Teams consist of commentators who are both 'objective' and 'informed'. There are not only social work, police and health representatives but in the case of independent inquiries they are chaired by lawyers—reports 2, 3 and 4. Hence, they can appear as legitimate critics and in contrast to the 'sensational' press. The Director is the receiver of the Report, the ratified reader, and speaks for the social services. S/he invariably accepts the Inquiry Team's conclusions and the Department's share of blame, for example, report 1 paragraph 10 "fairly balanced in its criticism". S/he can be heard to outline how things have been changed or will be changed in response to the findings. In report 6, the photograph of one Director shows a face of compassion (is that a tear in his eye?). The overall structure of most of these reports is similar. They offer the conclusions of the Inquiry team, using direct speech, some details of the case, followed by the response of the Director of Social Services. Findings generally criticise structures and procedures (reports 1,2,3,7 and 10), with individual staff portrayed as having "the best intentions" (report 1, paragraph 2), "conscientious" (report 2, paragraph 9), "offering regular support" (reports 5, paragraph 1). On occasion they made "flawed judgements" (report 1, paragraph 1), "failing to make accurate assessments" (report 7, paragraph 2) and made "mistakes" (report 8, paragraph 1):

> The report does not criticise any of the individuals involved, but states it was the system which broke down "letting down those who worked within it" (report 3, paragraph 6)

This strong defence of the individual worker can be heard to depict them as also victims of an inadequate system.

Overall, the two explicit points of view in these reports, the Inquiry Team's and the Director's, can be heard to support one another in providing authoritative endorsement for the integrity of social work, though with provisos. Systems need adjustment, individuals make mistakes but individual workers are all right, the profession is not in crisis. This is in contrast to, for example, the Daily Telegraph (18/12/87), where social workers are considered "incompetent and insufficiently professional" and more recently "one hundred errors of welfare team in Orkney child sex inquiry" (Today, 27/10/92).

Linking characters and events

Referring to Inquiry Reports and the Director is not the only defence. The reports construct child abuse and defend social work, the two apparently dependent on one another. Three major entities can be identified in the reports—a dead or injured child, the child abuser or murderer; and the professionals and their procedures. The reports (and social work in general) can be read as attempting to link these entities in a way which is competent and reportable, what White (1987:173) calls 'emplotment'. The first entity is an indisputable fact, the body. It has been processed by doctors, police and courts, and the task now is to explain it:

> Sukina... was beaten to death by her father after she was unable to spell her name. (report 1, paragraph 7)
>
> The boy was suffocated with a pillow by his mother... (report 6, paragraph 2)
>
> Liam died from 16 spinal fractures at the hands of his father. (report 4, paragraph 2)

The report emphasises that the outcome was unquestionably caused by the murderer but now attends to the question of how it is possible that such an outrage occurred. It is a task of moral (re)construction. With the legal proceedings over, the focus shifts from the act of the abuse/murder to the surrounding circumstances and, in particular, to the activity of the professionals.[5] Through the sequential process of reporting, child abuse becomes less a criminal matter and more a social service matter. How do the reports deflect blame away from the social services?

The predisposition

Explanation, and hence blaming, is achieved by describing circumstances and attributes of the murderer/perpetrator. There are situational features around the time of the murder:

> [the murder occurred] following a row between the woman and her ex-boyfriend. (report 6, paragraph 2)
>
> [the murderer] who was acutely depressed and also trying to kill herself... (report 5, paragraph 2)

Moving further away from the scene of the murder, aspects of the background and character of the perpetrator are made available:

> The court heard that Palmer was 16 and in council care... (report 2, paragraph 10)

Explanations in terms of the character and circumstances of the perpetrator suggest the search for a predisposition to child abuse. The abuse/murder can be located through such features, recognition of which might have prevented the incident. However, this sets up the possibility of a charge of culpability for not preventing by not recognising such a predisposition. A further account is thus made available to rebut any such charge. In report 6, the mitigation of "no SSD involvement" (paragraph 3) and "no evidence that her care of the child had been anything other than satisfactory" (paragraph 4) demonstrate there was no social worker access to any predisposition. In report 2, the decision to allow the young man in care to set up with his girlfriend is backed by an account of "trying to work with the adolescent" (paragraph 14). In report 9, "no criticism" is linked directly to "keeping in regular touch" (paragraph 4).

On the other hand, report 5 locates possible social worker access to a predisposition since "the woman was receiving considerable social work support at the time" (paragraph 1). The strong headline and opening state categorically that the social services department "could not have predicted nor prevented the tragedy" (paragraph 1) and these are the conclusions of two reports, one of which is independent (paragraph 2). Furthermore, that the woman was "acutely depressed" (paragraph 2) may be heard as suggesting that the department did all it could and could not be blamed for not trying, although it was unsuccessful. The reduced culpability of the woman because of her severe depression was expressed in an earlier report on the same case (report 10, paragraph 2). If the formulation—very depressed, needed and received social support but still social workers did not predict—has not convinced the reader, blame is further deflected as there was no criticism:

> It was felt that the family needed help and support. Neither prosecution nor defence had criticised the SWD, he [the deputy director] said. (report 10, paragraph 6)

It is thus suggested that one way that these reports can be heard to emplot characters and events and at the same time rebut any charge of culpability, is to construct child abuse in terms of a predisposition, to which the social workers did not have access or which they were powerless to prevent. Other reports do not offer such formulations and the character of the perpetrators is viewed less sympathetically.

The pattern

As well as a predisposition to child abuse, a further feature available for the social workers and other professionals (and readers) to identify is a pattern of abuse. Reports offer previous incidents of abuse which constitute a potentially observable pattern of abuse having occurred before. Having set up such a formulation, a rebuttal is made available as to why the pattern was not observed and acted on. A defence is offered in several levels related to the extent of previous social services contact.

The first level excuse is that social workers had no access to the pattern as there was no contact with social services:

> The committee's report on the case said there had been no SSD involvement with the mother. (report 6, paragraph 3)

If social services were not involved with the case, how could they be held accountable.

At a second level, there was social work contact but no evidence of child abuse. This level is less forthright in its excuse and implies an external constraint on potential action because of, for example, the law:

> "We are satisfied that at no time was there evidence which would have allowed the department to have instituted legal proceedings." (report 2, paragraph 10)

Similarly in report 8, despite information on the family's problems, it was "not sufficient to take [the child] into care" (paragraph 13). This can be heard to suggest that the social workers knew there were problems but were constrained from responding because of the evidence needed to take court action. In contrast, report 3 portrays lack of information (as opposed to evidence) as a blaming:

> The report finds that a decision made at a case conference to return the child to its home was based on "inadequate information and a superficial assessment of the case". (paragraph 4)

Cuff (1980:35) notes how the same construction can be turned round from an excuse and used as a blame. Lack of information or evidence of the pattern appears to be constructed on the basis of differing conceptions of social work activity—a social worker reacts to information received or seeks out information to adequately inform decisions.

A third level excuse of not having access to the pattern is that the information was interpreted differently. Information of incidents, which are now suspected as child abuse, was at that stage not seen as abuse. In report 4, possible previous abuse was considered "accidental" (paragraph 12). In report 8, despite a broken limb, "medical opinion was that abuse had not occurred" (paragraph 10). Again, this formulation can be inverted and used as a blame. In report 7:

> Medical and SSD staff saw his earlier injuries as the result of "poor parenting" and no one was willing to confirm abuse, the health authority report claims. (paragraph 5)

The incorrect interpretation of instances as not being part of the pattern can be made available for an excuse and a blaming.

Other reports are less explicit about access to the pattern or predisposition but still make assertions that the death could not have been prevented. In report 3, this is linked to "inadequate procedures and overstretched resources" (paragraph 6). In report 1, although "indicators" were unrecognised and there was "an unwarranted optimism" (paragraph 4)—the blame, still the death could not have been "anticipated and therefore prevented" (paragraph 5)—the excuse. Blame and excuse can be heard as linked together, with degrees of each—some blame ('mistakes') and yet an overall excuse.

The ability to observe, interpret correctly and act on a pattern or predisposition of child abuse makes use of the 'documentary method of interpretation' (Garfinkel, 1967). There are incidents of injuries (the documents) that social workers and other professionals have access to, which point to child abuse (the underlying pattern). Dingwall et al. (1983:80) note a 'prospective-retrospective' feature, past events now fit into the pattern and hence provide an assessment of the abuser's moral character:

> This means that past events can be re-analysed to fit the actor's present status, as evidence, for instance, that a parent was 'really' an abuser all along, and to organise the unfolding present as yet further confirmation of the correctness of this ascription.

The use of the documentary method in social work reporting not only links instances to an underlying pattern, but also the enables the attribution of blame (indeed moral outrage) when such a link is unrecognised. The pattern and the predisposition become important and contested features of reporting and accounting for child abuse. Their manipulation might be hearable as a rebuttal to a possible 'superaddressee', the Beckford Report, which concludes:

> On any conceivable version of events under inquiry the death of Jasmine Beckford on 5 July 1984 was both a predictable and preventable homicide. (1985:287)

The overall balance sheet of blamings and excuses, mistakes and competent (although unsuccessful) social work activity enables a normalising social work story to be heard. Reporting child abuse is depicted as a balancing act and a balanced view, and as neutralising the other press reporting. Report 11 from the national press covers similar material to the social work press report about the same incident (report 12), outlining and quoting the court and police comments. However, the last paragraph does not appear in the journal report and can be heard as a blaming without any social work account:

> [the social worker] said he had not had much experience of such cases but that he had said this to his superiors.

The moral character of the perpetrator/murderer

It has been suggested that the reporting of child abuse can be heard to allocate and mitigate to two opposing entities: the perpetrator or murderer, their circumstances and attributes, and the social workers, their organisations and related professionals. The two entities are not only related but are constitutive of one another. The circumstances and personal history of the perpetrator can be constructed on the basis of social workers' activities, and the handling of blame and responsibility by social workers is tied up with constructing perpetrators. How is the depiction of the moral character of the perpetrator/murderer linked to handling potential blame and justifying social work activity?

Some of the reports, like those in the national press, describe details of the murder and suggest a construction of the perpetrators as 'monsters' (Dingwall et al., 1983:87). This can be heard as in contrast to the construction of moral character of 'the predisposed', which makes available a sympathetic excuse for the abuse—depression, history in care. Monsters, on the other hand, are not offered such excuses. They are not constructed using pejorative terms, as in the national press, but by reporting particularly lurid details of the offence. In reports 1, 4 and 8, such details are provided and significantly the nature of social work support is not discussed. Perhaps if child abusers are monsters, they are seen as less likely to be receptive to (or deserve) social work help. In contrast, the predisposed characters in reports 2, 5 and 6 are described through their use of and access to social work services which also reduces blame of the social workers. The reader feels sorry for them and their predicament, the predisposition is not their fault and blame is mitigated. In a later version of report 5 (report 10 paragraph 5), it is suggested that the social workers considered the sentence too severe.

We have thus seen that the attribution of blame to the perpetrator and the construction of their moral character is inextricably tied up with demonstrating the competent operation or mistakes of the child protection and social work support systems. The moral character of the perpetrator/murderer can be constructed on the basis of 'the predisposition' and 'the pattern' which suggests social work help or surveillance. There are available a number of potential links between, on the one hand, the less blameworthy, the predisposition and the offer of social work help, and, on the other hand, the monster, the pattern and surveillance. In either case, the social worker is not to blame. In the first set of relations, there were too many problems, and in the second, just uncontrollable monsters. It is not suggested that these formulations are stable but are available as resources and relations to be deployed flexibly in shifted stories.

In summary, it is suggested that reports in a social work journal are strategic documents aimed at the self preservation of social work. They can be read as in contrast to (and perhaps rebutting) charges about the integrity of social work reported in the national press. Such reports mitigate and allocate blame by building moral constructions of and relations between child abuse, child abusers and social work activity, each of which constitutes the other. Inquiry Reports are complex and wide-ranging documents, yet they acknowledge that allocating blame is their predominant concern. The Beckford Report (1985:287) concludes that "The blame must be shared by all the services..." Others resist it. A press release for a later Inquiry ends:

> We would like to emphasise that our evaluation and the analysis of the case, showed no indication that any one individual was responsible for the outcome. Critical decisions were made corporately. To attempt to apportion blame would both ignore the facts and deny the reality of the complexities of this particular case. It was not the social workers, health visitors, doctors, teachers or nursery staff who were responsible for Sukina's death–but her father. (19/4/91)

This section appears in bold type. By directly highlighting the only appropriate allocation of blame, any charge is countered with an ironic contrast between the professionals and the perpetrator/murderer. Blame is central but relativised.

Barkin (1984:30) see news reports as representing cultural values through storytelling which is full of morals associated with folk tales:

> There must be villains and heroes in every paper, and the storylines must conform to the usage of suspense, conflict, the defeat of evil and the triumph of good that have guided the good sense and artistry of the past storytellers and controlled their audience's ability to respond.

And yet the social work journal reports contain few such storyable features. Whilst there are villains, the heroes are uncertain. The temporal features are confusing, the story structure is disturbed and there is little suspense. Perhaps they operate by reassuring readers that competent professional stories are available and waiting to be heard from the social workers involved or from the Inquiry Team. The ratified reader is invited to look further but will be able to (re)confirm the integrity of social work. We will now turn to one such potential, competent story from a research interview.

Constructing moral character in a research interview: the 'failure to thrive' case

This analysis considers the beginning of a research interview concerning a case of 'failure to thrive'. The social worker provides a long, uninterrupted monologue telling the story of the case, the first part of which appears as appendix 4.2.[6] The boundaries of the story presentation are marked with a beginning, the social worker demanding the floor with an instruction not to be interrupted (line 7 "well look I'll speak"),[7] and finishes with "that's the position at the moment and that in summary is the case" (line 181-2) some ten minutes after this extract. We investigate blame allocation by concentrating on the construction of the moral character of the mother and the professional. How is the depiction of the mother able to be read as constructing a moral order of child abuse and at the same time as handling potential criticism? It is first necessary to consider features discussed in the previous section in this chapter and in chapter 3.

Point of view in a research interview: institutional voices

From the initial invitation by the interviewer (line 1), the social worker can be heard to tell the case from his point of view, beginning with being allocated the case (line 7). Unlike the 'broken nose' case in chapter 3, where storytelling was delayed, here "the circumstances were... " (line 11) is immediately offered. Like that interview, there is a temporal detour backwards from the allocation to the first social services contact (line 7 to 48). The re-emphasis of "I was allocated... "(line 48) can be heard to re-establish the point of view of the storyteller as 'camera eye' (Chatman, 1978:154), where action is in the presence of this social worker.

In contrast to the highly collective nature of the chapter 3 case, which contributed to the construction of a community of competent hearers, here there is a continual alternation between 'I' and 'we':

> ...I had called a further case conference and the case conference accepted my recommendation that we should go forward with care proceedings and that we should seek a supervision order... (line 72-5)

> ... we tried to discuss this with mother but she wouldn't hear of it and regrettably I was forced into a situation where not only had I... (line 154-6)

The 'we' refers less to social work colleagues and more to a variety of other professionals, including doctors, health visitors and nurses. In the examples above, the 'I' can be heard as more active, with the 'we' in a supporting role. The reader can hear a united front of professionals who share the social worker's concerns and provide him with a mandate. The importance of enrolling entities and recruiting allies has been developed by Callon et al.

> (an actor world) associates heterogeneous entities. It defines their identity, the roles they play, the nature of the bonds that unite them, their respective sizes and the history in which they participate. (1986:24)

They describe processes of simplification, association and translation as entities are enrolled into the actor world. Here, a wide range of entities can be heard to be reduced to simple roles and linked into the plot, or 'emplotment' (White, 1987:173)—doctors, health visitors, family members, foster parents, police, judges, scales, charts, court orders and procedures, illness, violent behaviour, case conferences.

There is, in particular, a split between medical and social entities enrolled in the account (Dingwall et al., 1983:31). The point of view of the doctors and their instruments is offered as the basis for the concern and the definitions of the condition:

> ...on being taken there er the hospital felt that this was a clear picture of a failure to thrive the child was as I recall off the top of my head I think it was two and a half kilos under weight was very dehydrated and in fact had the situation been left further longer the child would have died ... (line 27-31)

> ...the GP who felt further concerned and the baby was taken to [hospital] where it was admitted and a diagnosis was made of a very er clear failure to thrive in that... (line 135-7)

To this medical evidence and opinion is added a social analysis as the attributes of the family members depict social problems.

Juxtaposing institutional voices can be heard as stronger than the point of view of a single narrator, despite the emphasised use of 'I'. The display of medical and social entities and attributes forms a link to wider discourses in the Foucauldian sense, institutional voices which bring with them authority and legitimacy. It is not merely particular doctors or weights that are being enrolled, but the language of authoritative allies. The reader is being encouraged to hear respected and powerful voices beyond the words stated.

The pattern and the predisposition

For 'failure to thrive', a pattern is an essential resource for instructing the reader/hearer that this case is an example of the condition. Such cases make up only a small proportion of cases officially registered as child abuse (Creighton and Noyes, 1989). With no obvious physical signs or child's disclosure, weights, measurements, charts and feeding regimes provide the evidence. 'The pattern' is thus required. It is possible to construct 'failure to thrive' as not an issue of child abuse, but of 'normal' developmental delay or a 'small child'.[8] This could cause uncertainty, especially in attributing culpability for the condition—is it merely slow development with no one to blame or is it negligent care?

In this case, the social worker can be heard to construct 'failure to thrive' as child abuse through both 'the pattern' of the weights and scales, but also attributes of the parents, 'the predisposition'. Initially, this is in terms of their age, unstable housing and family relationships (lines 13-18). To this is added criminal activity (line 70) and then considerable detail on a pattern of non-co-operation and violence. By constructing a 'pattern' of underweight and a 'predisposition' to deviance and incorrigibility, the social worker can be seen to link failure to thrive and child abuse. In order to investigate how the mother is constructed, we first consider the sequential handling of blame in a rhetorical pattern.

A three stage feature

A rhetorical figure, the three stage feature, can be seen in this talk.[9] It is a repetitive motif which can be heard to allocate blame to the mother and justify action. A three stage approach to performance and argumentation has been noted by a number of writers (Jefferson 1990, Heritage and Greatbach 1986). The three stage feature outlined here is slightly different from a list and nearer to the structure of a claim, as outlined by Toulmin (1958:97). He draws a distinction between:

> ...the claim or conclusion whose merits we are seeking to establish (C) and the facts we appeal to as a foundation for the claim—what I shall refer to as our data (D).

The link between the two in his model is a 'warrant' (W):

> which can act as a bridge, and authorises the sort of step to which our particular argument commits us. (1958:98)

Schematically, his model is:

$$D \xrightarrow{\text{since } W} \text{so } C$$

This model has been used by a number of studies to demonstrate the structure of an argument (Best 1987, Herndl et al. 1991). In this interview a pattern can be heard based on moral warrants depicted as 'outrage'. So the three stage feature can be heard as data–moral outrage–justification. This is available between lines 32 and 35:

> Data: the mother er the the staff found the mother very very difficult very hostile uncooperative er
>
> Outrage: and the the situation er caused so much anxiety
>
> Justification: that [an emergency court order] was taken and the child kept in hospital.

Also at lines 45 and 49:
> Data: there was an incident however involving this worker when he was assaulted he was kicked and punched
>
> Outrage: and it really was a very serious matter on the basis that this worker would find it extremely difficult to proceed
>
> Justification: I was allocated.

Similarly at lines 58 to 63:
> Data: we were in some difficulty because we felt that we couldn't arrange access in in the foster home as we normally would so what happened was that access had to be arranged in the area office
>
> Outrage: which was a horrendous task
>
> Justification: to overcome this and to enable me to assess this family's ability to care for his child we involved the family welfare association.

Such a motif can be heard first to describe a difficult situation, the data. The warrant directly instructs the reader as to its very serious nature. The necessary action is then inevitable and justified. The warrant is further achieved through a range of vocal pauses and emphasis which add dramatic tension to the performance of the story.

This three stage feature can be linked to other rhetorical features, 'last resorts' and 'extreme case formulations'. 'Last resorts' are dispreferred options when all normal first resort responses have been tried and failed to contain the trouble.

> In a last resort situation, then, the impending response does not simply rank at the top of the list of possible options; it is the sole course of action remaining. (Emerson, 1987:5)

A feature of the last resort is that the decision to carry out a particular action is straightforward and obvious; there is no discretion for the decision maker.[10]

In the 'failure to thrive' case, at each appearance of the three stage feature, intervention is heard as a 'last resort', as an inevitable and dispreferred outcome. There are first resort responses, for example, the assessment at line 68 and the supervision order at line 75. Such interventions, however, are heard as short lived successes as three stage features can be heard to structure the account as an inevitable move to the ultimate 'last resort'–the removal of the children with a police order at line 157. At line 98-105 the exhaustion of options is displayed:

> Data: it got to the point that by sort of January February nineteen— that none of us were actually able to work with the family at all and be... because they weren't allowing us in too and as I said they just stopped co-operating er

> Outrage: (-) our concern was that here we have a statutory supervision order er and we were not able to work on it at all we were not able to supervise
>
> Justification: we attempted to hold case conferences where we could review this situation...

As Potter and Wetherell (1987:91) note: "the greater the constraint the less the blame". Extreme constraint is demonstrated here by for example "... and regrettably I was forced into a situation ..." (line 155) or "I had no er alternative but ..." (line 160). There are other 'last resort' interventions: at line 35 an emergency court order, allocation of this social worker (line 48), access in the office (line 60), liaise through the agencies (line 123), each can be heard as dispreferred but no choice. The difference with Emerson's formulation of 'last resorts' is that he suggests a clear tariff from preferred options through more coercive action to the 'last resort'. Here, the tariff is less clear and the 'last resort' option is not necessarily more coercive. It is rather the only and dispreferred option, whether more intrusive or not. 'Last resorts' are thus seen as rhetorical formulations and not specific interventions. On occasion doing nothing (or very little, line 123) is a 'last resort', as it is all that is available.

The three stage feature also implies an 'extreme case formulation' (Pomerantz, 1986). This can be heard as similar to 'last resorts', but it is the upgraded manner of the expression which creates the extreme case, compared with the nature of the action in 'last resorts'. The use of upgraded terms is a feature in legitimating claims, however the 'extreme case formulation' is associated by Pomerantz with situations of "complaining, accusing, justifying and defending" (p.219). It is thus appropriate in developing the notions of blame allocation and moral outrage, Pomerantz refers to it as "an adversarial or defensive stance" (p.220). She considers that:

> Interactants use Extreme Case Formulations when they anticipate or expect their co-interactants to undermine their claims and when they are in adversarial situations. In being prepared for others to scale down her alleged losses, the plaintiff formulates them as maximum cases. (p.222)

Extreme case formulations are more than upgraded terms like 'everyone knows' or 'we were completely ineffective', but are part of developing complex defences against accusations and blame. In this account, the extreme case can be heard as associated with the warrant and hence is pivotal in justifying action. Expressions in stage two of the feature, the warrant, are noted above— "it was really a very serious matter" (line 47), "caused so much anxiety" (line 34), "a horrendous task" (line 61), and "not able to work on it at all we were not able to supervise" (line 102-3). This last example adds emphasis with the repeated negative. There is also an example of stage one of the feature 'data' as an extreme case, using complex upgrading: "very very hostile very difficult unco-operative" (line 33) adding to its strength with a three part list.

The warrant thus makes use of extreme case formulations to emphasise moral outrage. Furthermore, it is available as a direct instruction to the reader to take these circumstances very seriously, to increase our sense of alarm. The warrant directly involves the reader/hearer, acting as an instructive pause between a list of events and facts, and the explication of subsequent action. It shouts at the hearer to take note and enrols him/her in the move to the next stage of the story.

These examples of 'extreme case formulations' and 'last resorts' can be heard in a research interview where the speaker is unlikely to have claims undermined nor to be required to defend them from criticism. This suggests that this feature might be more than a situational telling of the account, but may be available in other tellings of this case. It may have been constructed for a variety of audiences, some of which are likely to be adversarial or to undermine claims—the mother's barrister, the chair of the case conference. Blamings appear to have been well rehearsed.

The moral contrasts of character

In chapter 8, the concept of character in social work stories is developed further; here we investigate how contrasts display the moral character of the mother and the social worker. In the 'failure to thrive' case, the main characters are the mother and the social worker with others less significant and attached to one or other side of this divide. A clear division can be heard between the two—one culpable, the other competent; one violent and irrational, the other flexible and tolerant; one a villain, the other a hero. The villain appears overwhelmingly culpable, rarely reasonable, and the hero always flexible, never mistaken. There are contrasts with other actors and contrasts with normal behaviour. Both can be heard as demonstrating the irrational and deviant nature of the mother.

The character of the mother is contrasted with that of many other reasonable people. She is uncooperative with a wide range of other actors and entities. Thus with nurses (line 33), a chair of a case conference (line 38), two black social workers (lines 40-45), two sets of foster parents (line 53-57), the family welfare association worker (line 119), the GP and health visitor (line 123) and the case conference (line 145); she is respectively "very very difficult, very hostile, uncooperative" (line 33), "physically assaulted" (line 38), "very difficult" and "assaulted" (lines 42 and 46), "hostile" and "frightening" (lines 54 and 56) nearly "physically assaulted" (line 120), "not co-operating" (line 124) and "went off in a temper" (line 145-6). Whilst there is no direct instruction to the listener that this behaviour is unreasonable, the contrast is achieved by the tender or innocent nature of the actor whom she abuses—nurses, foster parents, social workers—compared to her violent behaviour. Furthermore, the sheer number of actors with whom she is aggressive is overwhelming. Each telling of an incident not only stresses a pattern, but further confirms the obviousness of the categorisation of the villain, the 'documentary method' is pushed almost to capacity.

Contrasts with normal behaviour are displayed by violent reactions and non-co-operation which are heard as inappropriate to the circumstances. The mother continually fails to meet the expectations of normal client behaviour by breaking agreements (line 89), just stopped co-operating (line 100-1), not turning up at case conferences (line 105), failing to keep hospital appointments (line 133-4), not allowing access to a child under supervision (line 150). Such contrasts with normal client behaviour can be heard as preventing the delivery of normal social work. Not only is co-operation rejected but surveillance is also refused.

Normal behaviour is most explicitly contrasted in two examples. First, the proof of failure to thrive in lines 137 to 144 is demonstrated by the child's failure to gain weight when at home compared with increasing weight in hospital under a "normal regime" (line 143), hence depicted the mother's handling and feeding (line 144) as deficient. Second, the depiction of the grandparents later in the interview, portrays them as in stark contrast to their daughter. They are "very co-operative and no problem" and:

> oof no problem they're happy and they've always been very helpful to us. (193-4)

This latter comment is a response to the interviewer's question and can be heard as a forthright rebuttal to any suggestion that the welfare agencies might be unfair with this mother—even her own parents are "disgusted" (line 185).

The depraved character of the mother is made available through a very large number of contrasts with normal reasonable people and entities. There are few points where her behaviour is anything other than unreasonable. Even the successful assessment which resulted in the supervision order, is heard as the success of the social worker rather than the co-operation of the mother—"I managed to develop a relationship with..." (line 69).

In contrast, the social worker appears throughout as reasonable and committed. This can be demonstrated in four ways—he is reasonable with the mother, is supported by other professionals, is concerned with the welfare of the child and acts professionally.

First, as mentioned above, he is initially successful with the mother (line 68) and is able to recommend a 'low tariff disposal' at court. He offers a wide range of services—counselling (line 93), parenting skills (line 94), a two weekly family aide (line 96). When co-operation breaks down, he wants to know 'why' (line 115) and even when the ultimate sanction is being prepared, he twice tries to negotiate (lines 154 and 158). Second, other professionals and the grandparents are enrolled at many points, in contrast to the mother who only has the 'delinquent' father as an ally. Third, although the 'welfare of the child' principle is not explicitly invoked, as in the 'broken nose' case, at several points the children's health and welfare is portrayed as the immutable referent. At line 102, the 'statutory supervision order' is heard as the state's instruction to safeguard the child, as is placing the baby on the register (line 114). The further hospital treatment of the baby at line 149 is another prerequisite. These are 'non negotiables', standards which cannot be breached. Finally, the competent social work reader can recognise a full range of possible interventions and professional rhetoric—a clear objective (line 51), assessment (line 52), use of and liaison with voluntary and statutory organisations, case conferences. At no point could a charge be made that an appropriate intervention was not on offer. Can any hearer accuse this worker of being anything other than competent and reasonable and the mother anything other than culpable? Our social worker/hero contrasts with the ultimate depravity of the villain—there are no excuses, no mitigating circumstances. At the same time, our hero is long suffering and professionally competent.

But wait a minute! How come the child was "developing acceptably" when the police removed the child (line 163)—a misjudgement? an unnecessary use of coercive action? The interviewer was surprised 'oh' (line 164). And later in this interview, the judge considered that social services had "overwhelmed the family with support" and "suggested social services should take a back seat". And in the file, there is record of a phone call from the health visitor which does not suggest good inter-professional co-operation:

> 5/11 Telephone Call from (health visitor) used a very rude and abusive tone of voice. 1) Neither she nor (her colleague) were attending the informal meeting. 2) Procedure dictated that a case conference should already have been called. 3) She had written to (the Principal Officer: Child Protection) and received no reply. 4) She and her colleague had made "all the running so far". She had visited the baby in hospital and liaised with the midwife. 5) Social services had clearly not planned or prepared. At her request, I gave her the name of my team manager and area manager. She also said that everything had come to her through "rumour".

And besides, can anyone be as depraved as this mother. Surely she must have done something reasonable. And so the 'unheard story' of the mother threatens the strength of the social work story, but we can explore this further in chapter 8.

In summary, the three stage pattern and moral contrasts are available throughout this account and can be heard as a progressive and cumulative series of clashes between the social worker, supported by his allies of doctors, scales etc, and the parents with their predispositions and patterns of deviant behaviour and depraved moral character. Compared with the 'broken nose' case in chapter 3, this account moves through more and complex encounters to arrive at the same intervention, removing the child with police help (line 160). The repeated use of the three stage feature can be heard to offer an ongoing pattern of communication with the hearer/reader, within which a series of morally charged encounters makes available a competent social work story. The various entities are invested with moral attributes and the characters provided with roles of heroes, allies and villains. As with the 'monsters' described in the journal reports, the parents here are given no voice, point of view nor any legitimation for their actions. Unlike the journal reports, blame is not directly aimed at the social worker, but considerable contrast work can be heard to (over)kill off any potential criticism.

This chapter has investigated the construction of moral character and the allocation of blame in the performance of social work accounts. It has suggested that morality is not inherent in actions and entities but actively made available in performances and reading relations. A range of textual accomplishments draws on contrasts and rhetorical features, littered with appeals for the reader to side with the forces of propriety. In none of the data have there been explicit moral categorisations, no one is described as a monster nor undeserving. There is no direct description of the mother in the interview, but the subtlety and power of the storytelling enables a complex characterisation to be discovered in the reading of events. Morality can be heard through everyday storytelling. Similarly, blaming is made available in the depiction of characters and events, without direct rebuttals or excuses.

We thus see that social work accounts use deeply moral storytelling strategies. The power and excess of the moral formulations can be heard to attempt to bind the reader to the appropriate reception of the moral tale. Significantly, disagreement would involve taking a morally abhorrent stance. In the journal reports, critics are directly embarrassed–Mr Mellor (report 4), the press (report 1) and national press reporting generally. In the interview, how could a critic side with such a mother against so many reasonable professionals and such flexible invitations to co-operate.[11] The interviewer's surprise at line 164 can be heard as a marker that he had been convinced.

In terms of the overall aim of this study, this chapter has demonstrated the importance of moral construction and blame allocation in social work accounting. Whereas the last chapter showed that a ratified and competent reader is constructed in order to read social work accounts, this chapter has been concerned not only with the identity of the reader, but the dynamics of moral persuasion. Here the reader has been addressed as a ratified reader who can distinguish between right and wrong. The journal reports speak to a social work reader by definition and can be heard to champion the social work cause. The social worker in the interview, as in the chapter 3 'broken nose' case, binds the reader through mutually accepted views of appropriate client behaviour, but here plays on the sheer moral depravity of the mother–this is someone for whom it is impossible to have sympathy. In the next chapter, the investigation of the persuasion of the reader explores use of facts rather than morals; the reader as an empiricist.

> How does a discussion of morals inform this investigation? Have I deployed morality and enlisted you into my interpretive community? If the aim of this project is to discover the methods of the social work storyteller then this text must make available a storytelling performance, with a moral dimension.
>
> So, how have I been moral? Well, I have included a range of persuasive features similar to the social workers and journalists. I have not claimed to be more righteous, just or plausible, but then neither did the social workers: we are all more subtle than that. Inevitably, the 'documentary method' has been a feature of my analysis, as patterns of textual organisation are uncovered and considered to stand for an underlying reality–the normal activities of accomplishing social work accounts. Like the social workers, I have looked for and found a pattern. I have used irony to suggest that social work is not a set of working practices, skills and principles, but instead it is a set of storytelling features and rhetorical strategies, in the same way as the social worker depicted the mother as not a proper parent, but deficit. Things are not what they seem, but are they something else?
>
> You might ask what right have I to ironicise? Irony, according to Collins New English dictionary, 1964:534 is " accompanied by an implied conscious superiority, of what is the true state of affairs." And yet given the deep scepticism in this study, I am clearly reluctant to offer a 'true state of affairs' (see Woolgar's key principle of 'uncertainty', 1988:29). Edwards et al. (1992) asserts 'the moral strength' of sceptical inquiry, claiming its radical credentials against the orthodoxy of scientific realism and its liberating potential. My search for morality is partly my scepticism but also claims that my methods are more revealing. Narrative analysis is offered as a better approach to understanding social work texts with extensive and meticulous textual fingerpointing–look here! and there! As the social worker

brought in lots of allies, so I have 'name dropped'. Have I persuaded the reader by my thorough analysis?

I have also made much of the inevitable moral dimension of child abuse. Constructing child abuse involves constructing versions of moral worlds. We cannot identify child abuse, at least not a version that is objectively available. We have instead heavily loaded representations of events, not the events themselves. Is saying something is socially constructed the same as saying it does not exist? Surely not. Relativism is committed to impartiality towards competing claims, so does it undermine the claims of the claims maker? This is a big topic to which we'll surely return. Others have discussed the Nazis, poverty or domestic violence with similar concerns (Herrnstein Smith 1987, Code 1994, Loseke 1989). They have investigated the socially constructed nature of such entities whilst resisting accusations of moral paralysis or 'quietism'. This investigation can side-step this issue to some extent, since we can say we are only concerned with social workers' 'accounts' of child abuse, not the 'real' thing. We can go along with Hacking (1991:285) when he makes a distinction between abusive actions and child abuse:

> There is only one viable attitude: child abuse is bad and we'd be glad if there were a lot less of it. But when we turn from abusive actions to the idea of child abuse there is and should be no unanimity in attitudes.

Schneider (1985:223) considers "the contained can only be seen through the containers". We can all acknowledge the reality of abusing actions, although we have no direct access to it (except as victims or abusers). But the attempts of social workers, doctors, journalists, police, sociologists to construct, explain, manage child abuse is available to be deconstructed. As we have shown child abuse, as opposed to abusive actions, is malleable, negotiable and uncertain. That's a relief.

And besides, the social worker in both the 'failure to thrive' and 'broken nose' cases appears to leave the facts, the reality, to the Doctors. The child **was** failing to thrive, the scales proved it. The injury was/wasn't deliberate, according to the Doctors. Yet Atkinson (1995) has shown how medicine is socially produced, doctors tell stories, novices have to learn to see disease. Medicine is replete with images and inscriptions–blood tests, x-rays, smears etc.,–which require a particular reading, a 'clinical gaze', in order for the body to be constructed as healthy or diseased. As Atkinson notes "Seeing is not straightforward" (1995:28), a professionally constructed competence is required. Still, we are not here to discuss the social construction of medicine, only to note that the 'facts' that social workers receive have already been through other processes of reading, persuading and performance.

However, Atkinson does raise a more general point about the link between social construction and the material world. He argues that social construction involves 'real' collective processes, not something inside the heads of actors.

> ... the collective acts of reality construction are themselves real. The everyday social actor and the expert (such as the natural or medical scientist) engage with a material universe in acts of exploration ...

> 'Reality' is not to be viewed as a construct in the sense that 'there is nothing there' independently of social actors. (Atkinson, 1995:43)

The social constructivist, however, is involved in a process of 'bracketing' the material world in order to explore social processes, a necessary methodological procedure:

> A methodologically inspired scepticism about what we know and how we claim to know it does not necessarily lead to a nihilistic perspective. It is quite wrong to confuse a methodological precept with an ontological position. (Atkinson, 1995:44)

I'm not sure about this accommodation with the real world. Surely by suggesting that social work or medicine is replete with social processes and that a reality outside the phenomenological brackets is not independently verifiable, then we are involved in a sort of nihilism. It is certainly a scepticism about the reality of the professional gaze, if holding back on a scepticism about child beating, pain and death. Reality is real enough even though it is only made accessible through complex social processes. Still, we are getting into a different issue here; the fact construction of social work is the subject of the next chapter.

But I still have a (moral) obligation to the social workers, after all I used to be one and that in itself must alter your expectations of me. Besides, even theoretical research should consider policy implications, if not necessarily provide easy answers. I'm rather hoping some of my readers are social workers. Look, social workers are required to describe, report on, identify and prevent child abuse; if they don't, we have seen how they are criticised and how they respond. We have also seen how the criticisms and the responses depend on moral construction for authority and self justification. Much more than the rest of us, social workers' claims about what constitutes child abuse matter.

I've avoided saying this so far, but social work is inevitably tied up with social control...

Families are split up on the basis of your claims...

Look how the social workers in the 'broken nose' and 'failure to thrive' stories took very serious action based on strong claims, only for it to be reversed by the judge...

Were you too hasty? Did we reveal your deception?

Is performing social work and research inevitably a display, a con trick, somehow deceptive?

Am I reflecting uncertainties which many social workers (and researchers) confront but prefer to cloak in good performances?

Note how a 'superaddressee' of Social Worker reappears even when s/he does not speak...

And I still worry about children; well, don't we all?

But I do want to help and perhaps I'm not...

See my heart is in the right place, isn't it?

NOTES

[1] Ken Livingstone MP on a BBC TV 'Question Time' debate, discussing a prominent official accused of having collaborated with the Nazis, said "next to child abuse..." this was the most serious accusation that could be aimed at anyone. Hacking (1991:259) comments that "child abuse is an intrinsically moral topic... the most heinous of crime." Dingwall et al (1983:87) consider:

> If it is assumed that all parents love their children as a fact of nature, then it becomes difficult to read evidence in a way which is inconsistent with this assumption. The challenge amounts to an allegation that deviant parents do share a common humanity with the rest of us.

[2] The breaching experiments were a range of studies where Garfinkel' students were given various tasks to break normal conventions of everyday interaction–to barter in shops, to ask continually for clarification, to break the rules of simple games. As Heritage notes (1984:83):

> In each case the subject treated the intelligible character of his own talk as something to which he was morally entitled and correspondingly treated the breaching move as illegitimate, deserving sanction and requiring explanation ...such compliance already appears to be the object of spectacular moral constraints.

[3] Much of the constructionist tradition has looked at the wider societal construction of child abuse by important claims makers, like the media (Best, 1989).

[4] The journal from which the reports are taken, Community Care, is widely available in social work offices. Whilst a professional journal does not speak for social workers, given its readership it might be expected to attempt to represent their world. As its editor noted (Philpot, 1991:59):

> The primary aim of a professional magazine (indeed of the media as a whole) is to reflect the facts and changes of the world which its readers inhabit, to try to be, as the playwright Arthur Miller said of a good newspaper, 'a nation talking to itself' ...it must angle its news to suit its readers' interests.

[5] I have, with colleagues, noted the difference between crime stories and child abuse stories, the former unable to perform adequate closure, seeking explanation and blaming (Hall, Sarangi and Slembrouck, 1995). We thus see it as a rhetorical feature, in contrast to Hartley (1985) who sees it as de-criminalisation and an underlying pattern of press criticism of social workers.

[6] These data and part of the analysis were used in a paper to the 'Discourse and the Professions' conference, Uppsala, 1992 (Hall, Sarangi and Slembrouck 1997a). This section develops further the themes of that initial paper.

[7] Maclean (1988:25) describes this as the two way contract implicit in every narrative performance '*Listen* and I will tell a story'.

[8] Some medical writers dissociate 'failure to thrive' from child abuse (see Batchelor and Kerslake, 1991). But in some highly publicised cases children were underweight (Beckford Report, 1985:72) and other writers make strong connections. Gilmore (1988:52) considers:

There can of course be an almost endless range of mixed causes whereby a medical condition may indeed be responsible for a child's failure to thrive, but that such a condition occurred or was not dealt with sooner, or did not have a persistence in treatment, may be poorly or wholly due to neglect on the part of the parent.

[9] The three stage feature was suggested by Srikant Sarangi (see footnote 6).

[10] An example of a last resort is available in a newspaper article with the figurative title "I've crossed the Rubicon on conflict Bush reveals" (Daily Telegraph, 21/12/1990 p.10):

A senior White House official said that Mr. Bush had been under considerable pressure wondering if all alternatives that might provide a solution to the crisis had been examined. That is why he had decided to offer direct talks between Saddam and James Baker, US Secretary of State, to exhaust all possible options. Saddam has not offered a date acceptable to the US. "That makes it a lot easier," the official said. "When you're satisfied that everything has been done, it removes a lot of the pressure."

This suggests relief in achieving the last resort; is it then really dispreferred?

[11] There are of course unheard stories and non-ratified readers. For example, one might ask how reasonable parents might act to protect their families from unwarranted intrusion, see chapter 8.

APPENDIX 4.1

1. *Community Care* 21/28 December 1989

Judgements flawed says child death review

BY DAVID MITCHELL

Child protection workers made "flawed judgements" and "faulty decisions" in their handling of the Sukina Hammond case, a report from Avon's Joint Child Abuse Committee has concluded.

The report claims that despite the best of intentions, the standards of practice expected and required of all agencies in child protection work were not fulfilled.

In particular, there was a lack of objective assessment and evaluation of the information available.

"The indicators of predisposition to abuse and neglect in this family were not recognised and there was an unwarranted optimism... which led to a serious underestimation of the potential risks to the children," says the report.

But despite the criticisms, the committee concurs with the SSD's own internal review that Sukina's death could not reasonably have been anticipated and therefore prevented.

"What we know is that no evidence of the children being beaten was ever observed — although more frequent and more thorough medical examinations would have been advisable in checking on their welfare," says the report.

Five-year-old Sukina of St Paul's, Bristol, was beaten to death by her father after she was unable to spell her name. David Hammond was jailed for life at Bristol Crown Court last month.

Avon director Wally Harbert welcomed the report as "fairly balanced" in its criticisms.

"You can't do our job without taking a risk, but in this case the risks were unacceptable and the staff involved should have realised that," he said.

But he added: "It is unfortunate that the press has tended to pick this up as a criticism of social workers, whereas mistakes were made by pretty well every organisation which had any involvement in the case."

Harbert said the Social Services Inspectorate had been invited to review the department's child protection procedures and could well begin work early next year.

As for a possible public inquiry, he said: "That is a matter of judgement for the minister but I do not think it will come to that. She may well weigh it against the possibility of the SSI doing some work with us."

2. *Community Care* 14 December 1989

Legal expert to head child death review

BY DAVID MITCHELL

Child care law expert Richard White has been called in to head an independent review of the death of Christopher Palmer, who died three weeks after being placed on Ealing's at risk register.

White, who earlier this year produced the Doreen Aston report for Southwark, has already begun work and hopes to produce his findings early in the New Year.

Assistant director Stephen Barber said the review would be carried out along similar lines to those recommended in the Doreen Aston report.

But he added it seemed unlikely that an inquiry of that scale would be needed.

Seventeen-year-old Danny Palmer was convicted of murdering the seven-month-old baby at the Old Bailey last week.

Palmer, who was also found guilty of causing grievous bodily harm, actual bodily harm and cruelty, was jailed for an indefinite period.

After the child's death in December last year, Ealing ordered an internal inquiry to be carried out by Terry Cooper, a senior manager in the SSD, and Abigail Sargent, a GP and a member of the area child protection committee.

The investigation concluded that social workers were not to blame for the child's death.

"Within the limitations set by the law we felt all the workers carried out their duties conscientiously and satisfactorily and that no blame can be attributed to those involved," they said.

"We are satisfied that at no time was there evidence which would have allowed the department to have instituted legal proceedings."

The court heard that Palmer was 16 and in council care when he was initially allowed to set up home as father to his girlfriend's baby.

Palmer, who had been in children's homes since he was three, was subject to a court order which gave the London Borough of Hounslow full parental rights.

But a spokesman for Hounslow said: "Danny made his intention to move very clear. Even though this was against our advice, we could have done little to prevent him going.

"In this situation, it is preferable for a local authority to try to work with the adolescent, rather than risk losing contact with him altogether," he added.

3. *Community Care* 21/28 December 1989

SSD was mistaken

South Glamorgan SSD last week accepted it had made a mistake in allowing a two-year-old girl to return to her home where she was physically and sexually abused.

The department was strongly criticised in a damning report into the child abuse case — the first to be called into a case which did not result in a child death.

NEGLECT

The inquiry, which was undertaken by barrister Mark Evans and a panel of three child care and health experts, was established after the child's mother and her boyfriend were jailed in December last year after admitting charges of neglect, assault and indecent assault.

The report finds that a decision made at a case conference to return the child to its home was based on "inadequate information and a superficial assessment of the case".

"The fateful decision to return the child was ultimately a collective decision, reached in a properly constituted case conference. Our view is that such a decision was the wrong one," it concludes.

The report does not criticise any of the individuals involved, but states it was the system which broke down, "letting down those who worked within it".

"While the most perfect and best resourced system will never prevent individual misjudgment, inadequate procedures and overstretched resources will guarantee the occurrence of frequent mistakes and misjudgements," it warns.

"In this case the resources of that part of the department charged with the conduct of this case were overstretched and patently inadequate to the task."

South Glamorgan director Chris Perry told *Community Care* procedures in the department had changed considerably since the child's case.

REORGANISATION

In addition to new national guidance, as a result of the Cleveland report, the SSD had reorganised into eight child care teams and had appointed eight senior social work practitioners.

"Everyone recognises that the decision to return the child to its home was wrong, but it should be remembered that at the time it was made with the best interests of the child in mind," he said.

5. As for 3.

Deaths could not have been prevented

Central SWD could not have predicted nor prevented the tragedy when a Clackmannan mother killed her children in April this year. The woman was receiving considerable social work support at the time.

These are understood to be the main conclusions of the independent and departmental inquiries into the children's deaths in a house fire, which director Ian Ross will report to his social work committee today. Linda Thomas, who was acutely depressed and also trying to kill herself, was subsequently jailed for ten years.

The report will also make recommendations in the light of lessons learned from the case, and details will be passed to the Secretary of State. Thomas's appeal against sentence is expected early in the New Year.

4. *Community Care* 30 November 1989

Mellor's attack on staff ill-judged says inquiry

BY LINDA CHAMBERLAIN

Former Health Minister David Mellor has been strongly criticised by a child abuse inquiry for his hasty condemnation of professionals following the death of three-year-old Liam Johnson.

Liam died from 16 spinal fractures at the hands of his father. He had never been in care, was not on an at risk register and was not regarded by welfare agencies as neglected or ill cared for.

Following Robert Johnson's conviction in June for manslaughter Mellor called for an inquiry demanding to know what went wrong. He said Liam had been entitled to "more protection from the authorities than he received".

Yet the inquiry commissioned by Islington area child protection committee found that the professionals, particularly social workers, had not failed and had not made any serious errors of judgement.

The team, led by lawyer Elizabeth Lawson, challenged Mellor's "dangerous assumption" that all violence to children was predictable and preventable.

The report concluded: "Children do die, sometimes tragically, and sometimes at the hands of those who should care for them.

"Responsibility for these deaths lies overwhelmingly with those who kill them, not with those whose role has been to try to help the family."

The team, which included former Wandsworth director, Leo Goodman, questioned the seemingly inevitable need for an inquiry following the death of a child particularly when there was only limited contact with social services.

This one was held in private and therefore considerably cheaper than most at £100,000. But the report notes that it still diverted scarce resources away from the solution of problems "which are already known and identified".

There had been contact between Liam's family and social services in both Sheffield and Islington. Prior to Liam's birth his mother alleged that Johnson had assaulted her and injured Liam's brother.

The boys were in voluntary care for a while but later lived with their father in London and appeared to be well.

Liam had been taken to hospital a month before his death with a badly swollen thigh but the injury was considered to be accidental.

The inquiry makes a number of recommendations including the provision of specialist child abuse practitioners.

It raises concerns about Islington's decentralised neighbourhoods which mean the only centralised social services record is the child protection register. Had doctors wanted to check whether Liam's family was known to social services they would have needed to contact 24 neighbourhood offices.

Islington social services director John Rea Price said staff were distressed that a child had died but pleased that the quality of their work had been upheld.

6. *Community Care* 24 May 1990

Boy's death no fault of social workers

Social workers in Bury, Greater Manchester, have been cleared of responsibility for the death of a three-year-old boy in 1988. The area's child protection committee has concluded that no blame should be attached to staff.

The boy was suffocated with a pillow by his mother following a row between the woman and her ex-boyfriend. The woman then tried to commit suicide by setting fire to the hotel which she had booked into.

NO INVOLVEMENT

The committee's report on the case said there had been no SSD involvement with the mother.

There was no evidence that her care of the child had been anything other than satisfactory and no sign that she rep-

Hewitt: Unforeseeable death

resented a physical threat to her child.

Bury director Peter Hewitt, who chairs the area child protection committee, said: "This tragic death was unforesee-

able. Nothing we could have done would have saved the child."

● Manchester director Mike Bishop reacted angrily this week to newspaper reports of a "sex scandal" in one of the SSD's children's homes.

HORRIFIED

He said staff at the Westdene children's home in Cheetham Hill were horrified at the sensational reports concerning a 12-year-old girl. She allegedly became a prostitute while living at the home.

"The scandal is not that a very disturbed young girl became a prostitute, but that there are men on the streets who will abuse children in this way and who are prepared to pay for it," he said.

The girl has now been placed in a more secure, specialist setting elsewhere.

7. *Community Care* 23 November 1989

Social workers failed to spot and stop abuse

BY IAN McMILLAN

Basic and "potentially dangerous" flaws in the way the Cumbria-based social workers respond to cases of suspected child abuse have been uncovered by SSI inspectors.

The inspectors, who investigated a number of SSD cases during last autumn and this spring, found that management roles are inadequately defined and social workers are failing to make accurate assessments.

The three-member SSI team conducted its investigation in the wake of widespread public concern over the death in 1986 of two-year-old Karl McGoldrick.

The results of the SSI investigation were released last week to coincide with the publication of a hard-hitting health authority report, which criticises senior social work and medical figures for failing to protect the boy.

Karl suffered a series of injuries which culminated in his death at the hands of Mark Knowles, his mother's boyfriend. Medical and SSD staff saw his earlier injuries as the result of "poor parenting" and no one was willing to confirm abuse, the health authority report claims.

"The SSD, like some others concerned, seemed to fail to appreciate the gravity of a situation that progressively and insidiously unfolded," it notes.

Following Karl's death, the SSD made a "serious effort" to respond to a number of recommendations from the area review committee and a team of independent consultants, the SSI report comments.

The inspectors found evidence that some social workers were acting professionally, though much of their contribution went "unrecognised and unacknowledged" by colleagues and managers alike.

There were "potentially dangerous practices" in the identification of abuse, with "shortcomings in both individual practice and management control".

Staff should plan casework carefully, look at all sources of potential harm to children and have easier access to SSD records, the SSI report adds.

Cumbria's assistant director Deryk Mead stressed that the SSI inspection, carried out jointly with three SSD representatives, took place before vital parts of a five-year overhaul were implemented.

Earlier this year, completely revised procedures on child protection were introduced and staff offered specialised training.

A child protection consultant, David Pithers, was appointed to support a new monitoring unit, which now oversees child abuse work across the county, scrutinises case conference minutes and gives independent advice.

8. *Community Care* 30 November 1989

Avon director admits mistakes were made

Avon's social services director Wally Harbert has admitted that mistakes were made by social workers and other professionals working with five-year-old Sukina Hammond who was battered to death by her father.

But he has denied they could have foreseen the tragedy or prevented it and warned that this would not be the last child death.

David Hammond, 26, was given a life sentence last week for Sukina's murder. He had subjected her to a 20 minute beating with a ruler, plastic piping, fists and a kettle flex because she had failed to spell her name. She died from pain, shock and exhaustion.

Sukina and her family had been known to social services for three years but four months before she died her name was removed from the at-risk register.

Harbert said this week that the decision — taken by a multidisciplinary team of the department's staff, health professionals, the police and NSPCC — was a mistake.

He told *Community Care* that it was normal procedure for such decisions by a case conference to be ratified by another panel.

Sukina had suffered a broken limb after the case conference but the incident was never reported to the panel prior to its meeting.

"Had they known, it is pretty unlikely she would have come off the register," he said.

Harbert doubted social workers could have foreseen what was going to happen and therefore, could not have prevented it.

"Staff rely heavily on medical opinion to identify whether physical injury is non-accidental. In this family, medical opinion was that abuse had not occurred," he said.

Three weeks before her death social workers had received an anonymous allegation that she had been beaten. Staff could see no injuries to her but arranged for her to be examined by a doctor who advised there were no marks. Contingency plans to remove her from the home were not implemented as a result.

Harbert said there had been evidence over a long period of poor parenting, domestic violence and involvement with drugs. This was not sufficient to take Sukina into care.

He said staff had faced angry and aggressive outbursts, personal abuse and complaints of harassment in working with the family.

"It is becoming increasingly difficult to tread the careful balance that is required between over-reacting and under-reacting to events.

"As the death of Sukina shows, we are not always able to avert a tragedy but there are good reasons for staff to be vigilant," he added.

The department's review of the case is due to be considered by the social services committee in December and may be made public. Harbert hoped an independent inquiry would not be needed.

9. *Community Care* 14 December 1989

Inquiry after foster mother jailed for manslaughter

An independent inquiry has been launched by Derbyshire County Council after a registered foster mother admitted killing a nine-month-old baby in her care.

Former Wandsworth director Leo Goodman is to head the inquiry, which is expected to open in January and last for several months.

Forty-seven-year-old Janet Jones was jailed for life admitting the manslaughter and several other charges concerning the child at Nottingham Crown Court last week.

The court heard that no criticism could be levelled at Derbyshire social workers, who had kept in regular touch with Jones while she fostered ten other children.

Derbyshire said the inquiry would be held in private but its findings would be made public.

Goodman is to announce the terms of reference at a later date.

10. *Community Care* 7 Spetember 1989

Central inquiry into child killings

Central SWD has launched an independent inquiry after a single mother was jailed for 10 years last week for killing her two children while they were under social work supervision.

Linda Thomas, 35, also tried to kill herself when she set fire to her home in May. She was severely depressed and wrongly believed social workers were about to remove her two sons, aged 10 and three.

At the High Court in Edinburgh the judge, Lord Milligan, blamed Thomas' heavy drinking for her "horrendous" crime, and said her problems were "substantially of her own making".

Central SWD hopes to complete its inquiry by the end of this month. It is to be led by Dick Poor, retired depute director of social work in Strathclyde.

For legal reasons, Central's depute director Iain Crawford, was unable to comment on the Judge's remarks or the length of the sentence, nor to confirm reports that social workers involved in the case have been shocked and upset by the outcome.

But he confirmed Thomas had no history of violence or abuse towards the children: "It was felt the family needed help and support. Neither prosecution nor defence had criticised the SWD," he said.

Thomas's children had been returned to her care, under supervision, in November 1988 by a children's home. They had earlier been placed with relatives when she attempted suicide after her relationship with the children's father broke up.

The three-strong inquiry team will examine the effectiveness of support and supervision, evaluate Central's guidance on children at risk; and study the case conference involved.

11. *The Guardian* 19 August 1989

Death of child in care sparks inquiry call

David Brindle, Social Services Correspondent

A MAGISTRATE called yesterday for a full inquiry into how a child in the protection of social services was allegedly battered to death by her father after she and her two sisters had suffered a series of suspicious injuries.

The 22-year-old father, who has been charged with murder but cannot be named for legal reasons, was also involved in the accidental death of his first child.

Mr Rex Cowan, chairing the bench at Inner London Juvenile Court, said: "This is a disturbing, horrifying case involving the death of a child in care and I assume that at the end of it there is going to be a very penetrating inquiry into how it all came about."

The court rejected an application by the man's partner that their two younger daughters be returned to her or her parents rather than kept in the care of Wandsworth social services, south London, where they have been since the death of their sister two weeks ago.

Mrs Janet Digby-Baker, acting as the children's guardian at litem, opposed the application on grounds including the chance that the father, who is remanded in custody, might get bail.

The court heard that police were called to the family's council flat in the early hours of August 6 and found the elder child, aged almost three, with serious head injuries.

Police Inspector Peter Stenning said the father was threatening. Blood stains and human tissue were found in the toilet.

"The whole flat absolutely stank with excrement and urine," said the inspector. The younger children's nappies did not appear to have been changed for 24 hours, he said.

They had been found in a small and dirty bedroom which they were apparently sharing with their sister.

"The children were lifeless, there was nothing in them. They didn't respond to kindness, to cuddles or laughing. Obviously they were in a state of shock."

The 20-year-old mother said that the flat had been clean and the children freshly changed when she had left the previous afternoon for an anniversary party at her parents' house. She returned at 5 am.

The court was told that the father's first child, a boy, had been the subject of a supervision order. He had choked on his vomit when apparently being fed and then thrown in the air by the father. A verdict of accidental death had been recorded. There had been no known police inquiry.

Injuries to the second child had been first reported in 1986, when she was two months old. She had been made subject of a care order as well as being placed, with the other children, on the at-risk register.

Mr Michael Watson, the family's social worker since May, said he had recorded four incidents of bruising to the elder girl and one to each of the others. The mother said they were due to accidents, he said, and a doctor on one occasion had substantiated this.

Mr Watson said he had not had much experience of such cases but that he had said this to his superiors.

In this section

Arts, Reviews	18, 19
Crosswords	22
Financial News	8–10
Guardian Money	11, 12
Home News	2–4
International News	5, 6
Listings	17
Sports News	13–16
Weather	22

Weekend tabloid

Cartoons	18, 19
Crossword	48
TV and Radio	44–47

12. *Community Care* 10 August 1989

Inquiry follows death

Wandsworth social services has launched an inquiry following the death this week of a three-year-old girl who was in its care but living with her mother.

Stephanie Fox died in the early hours of Sunday morning and her twin sisters are recovering in hospital suffering from bruising.

Her father, 23-year-old Stephen Fox, has appeared in court charged with murder and was remanded in custody.

Sheila Poupard, acting director of Wandsworth social services, has launched an "urgent and thorough" review of the case.

A spokesman said the aim was to establish the facts, check whether proper procedures were followed and recommend appropriate action.

The inquiry is being conducted according to DoH guidelines and will work to a tight three to four week time scale. Its findings will be considered by a special meeting of the social services committee in September.

That meeting will decide whether further action or inquiries are necessary.

The spokesman said: "We are greatly concerned at the tragedy and deeply sympathise with the grief the child's mother is experiencing."

APPENDIX 4.2
The failure to thrive case

Int: = Interviewer
SW = Social Worker

Int: start when you took it on and (-) I gather from what I could see you took it on in about er September [year]

SW: yes yes...

Int: and the kids were already in care is that right...

SW : well look I'll speak because I can I can ...

Int: I'll leave to you [laughs]

SW: I was allocated to this case in September [year] the case er had originally been allocated in west area er for a period of about six weeks prior to me taking it on the circumstances were (-) that er a child by the name of Catherine er (-) had been taken to [hospital] by the child's mother in July [year] the circumstances were that Catherine had been born in December [year] she had lived with her mother who was then aged seventeen just turning eighteen er at the grandmother's the maternal grandmother's home and er the mother had subsequently moved to her own [council] provided accommodation in west area and had moved in with er a cohab so there was a young cohab of aged eighteen there was the mother who was eighteen and the baby (-)

now the baby was at some stage I think when she was about five months old er taken to the GP who was **very** concerned about the child feeling that the child was under weight er was not developing as it should and a referral was made to [hospital] it would appear retrospectively that there was a a breakdown in communication between the GP and the hospital the hospital perhaps not quite realising the er the priority that this er situation should have so it turned out that it was a further four weeks before the child was taken to the hospital for an appointment on being taken there er the hospital felt that this was a clear picture of a failure to thrive the child was as I recall off the top of my head I think it was two and a half kilos under weight was very dehydrated and in fact had the situation been left further longer the child could have died (-)

the child was admitted and what then happened was the mother er the the staff found the mother very very difficult very hostile unco-operative er and the the situation er caused so much anxiety that [an emergency court order] was taken and child was kept in hospital

there followed a number of case conferences the number of which I

10

20

30

cannot recall but something in a region of three or four er and at
one of those conferences the mother actually physically assaulted the
chair (-) er now a social worker from the hospital was appointed at
that time the family is a a black family and the social worker at the
hospital was a a black worker but that didn't seem to help at all in
that the parents found it **very** difficult to co-operate with this man
(-) the case was allocated in west area and I think it was in August
[year] because of course the family actually lived in west area and
again er a black social worker was allocated (-) there was an incident
however involving this worker when he was assaulted he was kicked
and punched and it was really a very serious matter on the basis that
this worker would find it extremely difficult to proceed I was
allocated (-) which was in September now at that point various
interim care orders had been granted but when I took on the case I
took it on with a very clear objective in mind and that was one of
assessment (-)

now unfortunately the child had been placed with a foster parent
but again because the mother was so hostile the foster parent found
it impossible to work with her and was actually in fear of having this
mother come to her home and she in fact was so frightened that she
asked for the child to be transferred (2)

when the child was transferred **again** we were in some difficulty
because we felt that we couldn't arrange access in in the foster home
as we normally would so what happened was that access had to be
arranged in the office which was a horrendous task (-) to overcome
this and to enable me to assess this family's ability to care for this
child we involved the family welfare association in [area] and we
involved them with two er objectives one was that they would assist
in the assessment of the parenting skills of these parents and secondly that they would provide a venue where access to the child
could could happen (3)

er cutting a long story short the assessment went very well and I
managed to develop a relationship with the mother in particular the
father unfortunately was in detention centre at that time and this
caused some difficulties (-) but the the assessment did go well and
by the November when the full care proceeding date was set I had
called a further case conference and the case conference accepted
my recommendation that we should go forward with care proceedings but that we should seek a supervision order rather than a full
care order (-) we took it to court in November and this recommendation was accepted by the court albeit that we had reservations and
the reservations were put very clear to the magistrates we were
recommending supervision but we wanted the court to know as
indeed did the guardian ad litem (-) er that the supervision order
gave us no er statutory powers to remove the child or to do **anything**

should the situation break down and that is the significant point for the future (-) anyway er we came to a voluntary agreement which was agreed in court although again it couldn't be part of the order that mother was to continue er her work with the family welfare association and that there was agreements made about her visits there about my work with the family

what then happened was that as soon as the baby went home **very** sadly the parents refused to co-operate and things became extremely difficult the situation was exacerbated by the birth of a second baby in the December of [year] (-) we then had a a double problem (-) that work-wise we were putting in the family welfare association who were meant to be there to counsel the family and to offer them er primary care which would involve them developing their parenting skills so they were heavily involved secondly there was myself who was the key worker thirdly there was a family aide from west area who was visiting twice a week

and it got to the point that by sort of January February [year] that none of us were actually able to work with this family at all and because they weren't allowing us in too and as I said they just stopped co-operating er (-) our concern was that here we have a statutory supervision order er and we were not able to work on it at all we were not able to supervise (3)

we attempted to hold case conferences where we could review this situation and we did this unfortunately parents failed to attend and there was a rather climax and I can't remember the month but I think it was in March [year] er when I did a home visit to the family a joint visit with the family welfare association and it was found that er [interruption]

at the home visit in March we went to to cover three things one was that we wanted to to let the family know that there was another case conference coming up and we wanted to tell them how important is was because clearly we were going to have to consider putting the new baby's name on the register (-) secondly we wanted to to see if we could investigate with the family why they were unwilling to co-operate er and thirdly really to let them know that we were viewing the situation very seriously (-)

basically I was threatened at that interview it was a very frightening experience and and both of us felt very lucky to get out without being physically assaulted er (-) the situation got to the point where ah because no one was seeing the family we were getting second hand information that the new baby was also failing to thrive and we tried very hard to liaise with other agencies like the GP and the health visitor we did this successfully but the family were not co-operating with them either (-)

the baby was actually admitted to hospital in April for a short period and was diagnosed as having reflax which is a condition whereby er the the the food er is is is not or that the milk as it was the liquid is not retained it it's just goes down so far and a valve then forces it out again and it's vomited up and so of course the baby doesn't get nourishment (-) that was diagnosed and mother was shown how to er how to act y'know how to actually deal with this but after I think it was a further three weeks er three or four weeks having failed I may say to keep follow up appointments at the hospital the baby was again seen by the GP who felt further concerned and the baby was taken to [hospital] where it was admitted and a diagnosis was made of a very er clear failure to thrive in that from the time that it was admitted to the time ah sorry from the time of discharge to the time of readmitting again had failed to put on much weight at all and indeed by the time we had the next case conference which was at the end of April er stroke beginning of May [year] the baby while it had been kept in hospital had actually put on weight having been fed under a normal regime indicating so the medics felt that clearly it was a question of the way the baby was being handled and fed (-)

what (-) the the mother came to that case conference but went off in a temper before we could explain the recommendations or the decisions and the decisions were that we should take [emergency orders] on both children one because we wanted to ensure that the baby was kept in hospital er for further treatment and secondly that the second the first child Catherine who we were meant to be supervising because we had not managed to just see her we've been prevented in effect from seeing her er we'd no way we we felt that the child was probably progressing quite well but we couldn't prove it and we felt we needed to see her to prove it (-) this was we tried to discuss this with mother but she wouldn't hear of it and regrettably I was forced into a situation where not only had I to take [emergency orders] that I had to apply for a section forty one allowing me to to go with the police to gain access (-) we further tried to negotiate this with the parents but again getting no cooperation I had no er alternative but to go with the police (-) both the the baby was already in hospital but the other child we removed of course not to my surprise when she was removed and examined was found to be developing perfectly acceptably ..

Int: oh

SW: which is what we anticipated

Int: yeah

SW: but we had to prove it (-)what then transpired was that we went of course for interim care proceedings and we got the interim care on the baby but not on Catherine the first child

Int:: ...oh, I see yes

SW: however the parents took a decision er to (-) er leave or to place Catherine with the maternal grandmother and grandfather who had always kept in touch with the situation that was their choice it wasn't by any order

[A few minutes later]

we now understand from the guardian that the natural parents or the mother has decided that she does not want either of the two children returned to her that she is making things difficult because she insists that she wants the two children to be together and she full well knows that the grandmother is only prepared to keep Catherine er because she feels that it would be too much for her to have to cope with two young children so that's the position at the moment and that in summary is the case

Int: how in terms of the grandparents have you found them much easier to work with

SW: oh they are very co-operative and no problem they are disgusted of the behaviour of the natural parents and they are very resentful because their position is they say why why that they bring these children into the world er if they cannot care for them and they are not interested in them that's their sort of er sort of blinkered view they are not looking at the wider perspective that they can hardly expect to there is a lot of anger

Int: and they were much easier

SW: oof no problem they're happy and they've always been very helpful to us

5 Explaining the 'facts' and claiming entitlement

> I'm called a philosopher, a theologian, a historian, a psychologist, sometimes a psychiatrist. But basically I'm a storyteller and I'm interested in what makes stories powerful.
> William Golding ('The Late Show', BBC 2, 23/6/93)

The last chapter demonstrated how moral concerns and blame allocation are made available through a range of rhetorical and narrative features, persuading the reader that the storyteller is virtuous and believable. Such formulations enable the reader to (re)construct a social work account as a moral enterprise and to read social work as a moral tale. This chapter and chapter 6 investigate the textuality of social work accounts by looking at how entities are constructed as factual and endowed with attributes. How can social work accounts be heard as powerful and authoritative as well as ethical and virtuous?

Moral and factual formulations overlap and interact. To attend to an account on the basis of its factual status is to appeal less to the virtues of the storyteller and more to his/her accuracy; to be right rather than righteous. A 'fact' is outside personal interpretation, anyone would read an entity in this way. It is "independent of the wishes of the observances" (Smith, 1993:25). The task of fact construction is to persuade readers that they too can recognise the 'out-there-ness' of entities. A social worker provides evidence that parents are not caring adequately for their children, a researcher that their data supports their conclusion, whether the writers like it or not. Smith (1993) analyses how a speaker, Angela, organises an account of her friend, K, becoming mentally ill, by placing events and their interpretations outside her control. The listener is taken through a series of incidents in which K's behaviour is depicted as anomalous and which others recognise as mental illness. Angela was constrained by the facts to recognise K as mentally ill, indeed the account begins: "I was actually the last of her close friends who was openly willing to admit that she was becoming mentally ill" (Smith, 1993:18).

Social workers create explanations around facts constructed by others. In the last chapter, we saw how 'failure to thrive' was established by doctors and their scales. In the 'broken nose' case (chapter 3), doctors and police were heard to negotiate the factual status of the injury. For social workers, child abuse or delinquency are 'givens', undisputed entities but medical/criminal entities. Social work accounts make available explanations and descriptions about the 'how' and 'why' of child abuse, not the 'what'.[1]

This chapter investigates how social workers organise accounts which explain and weigh up the significance of 'facts' and at the same time produce a story which displays the authority and entitlement of the storyteller. There is a discussion of some theoretical themes associated with fact construction, followed by an analysis of events and character depictions in, first, different types of social work stories, low risk and serious situations and, second, in the case of a teenager, Donna.

Theoretical approaches to fact construction

There are a number of interrelated themes in the study of facts. Fact construction, displays of authority and entitlement cover similar concerns about how the writer/speaker is able to convince the reader/listener of the independent status of entities and their attributes. These concepts are discussed here and illustrated with examples from various social work accounts.

We have already defined a 'fact' by its 'out-there-ness', devoid of ownership (Latour, 1987:23). Such independence can be displayed by various methods. Entitlement and authority involve establishing the storyteller's personal capacity to relate events or make descriptions. Shuman (1986) offers an approach to displays of entitlement by analysing teenagers' storytelling. Smith (1993) explores the methods of a storyteller in authorising her version of events and entities. How are they displayed as the trusted teller of the tale? Taking fact construction and entitlement together, how does the storyteller balance the 'out-there-ness' of his/her account with displays of personal authority?[2]

Fact construction

One of the problems of investigating fact construction is that something becomes a fact when its construction is no longer debated. Its status is obvious and the "processes of literary inscription are forgotten" (Latour and Woolgar, 1986:76). As Latour (1987:23) notes:

> [positive modalities are] those sentences that lead a statement away from its conditions of production, making it solid enough to render some other consequences necessary. We will call 'negative modalities' those sentences that lead a statement in the other direction towards its conditions of production and that explain in detail why it is solid or weak instead of using it to render some other consequences more necessary.

A 'fact' has no trace of ownership or self reflection. In contrast, an artefact is a metastatement concerned with it own construction. They lead the reader in different directions. An artefact leads further into the statement and the controversy of its disputed construction, a fact leads on to other questions on the basis of its affirmation. For example, at the beginning of a case conference report in the case of Donna (Appendix 6.1, discussed in chapter 6), the mother's version of events is treated as uncertain and open to dispute:

> [Mother] has indicated that she thinks she can manage with one daughter [i.e. sister] at home. She wishes to keep her daughters apart. Donna is seen as immoral and badly behaved and if [sister] misbehaves it is invariably seen as Donna's fault.

The mother's views are reported using ironic terms like 'she thinks', 'Donna is seen' and 'invariably seen', displaying her version as untrustworthy. The reader is encouraged to explore the mother's viewpoint as biased. Her view of family relations is further relativised when in the next sentence, the report writer displays the mother's version as masking her own inadequacy:

> [Social Worker] did not think that Jane would be at home for long as [mother] does not have the emotional capacity to cope with adolescents.

The latter statement is a fact with no qualification, the mother's care is the problem. The report can now proceed on the basis of an authorised fact that mother is the problem, and an ironicised artefact that Donna is the problem.

Latour and Woolgar (1986:75-81) delineate five levels of statement from fact to conjecture. Type 5 statements need no comment, they are self evident. They are taken for granted by ratified readers, so much so that they are rarely heard within the community of competent hearers. In Type 4 statements, attributes are described but treated as uncontroversial, for example "M is a likeable pleasant girl". Type 3 statements indicate attributes but the use of modalities relativise the statement "She likes to be her own mistress I suppose and take charge of things." Type 2 statements are claims rather than facts, as the modalities draw attention to the circumstance of the relationship. For example, having established M's maturity, it is relativised: "... but I think she still needs guidance although she does seem quite mature and able to cope with most things". Type 1 statements are conjecture or speculation: "I'm struck by her unhappiness."

All these statements are from the same description of a young person by a social worker and indicate the wide range of fact, claim and conjecture used in accounts. Latour and Woolgar (1986:80) note that the change from one statement type to another does not necessarily indicate a change in the degree of facticity. For example, by deleting the modalities from a type 3, we would have a type 4 statement. However, without the support of the reference, "I suppose", would it be more authoritative? This suggests that 'facts' can be strengthened or weakened by denoting personal agency.

Facts and personal agency

Whilst fact construction might aim at 'out-there-ness', the methods used to achieve this may trade on personal agency. Shuman (1986:195) notes that personal narratives are concerned with the occasion of the telling rather than the content of the story:

> In stories about actual occurrences, the assessment of tellability requires an assessment of the teller's accountability.

Shuman (1986:195) quotes Sacks's lecture:

> the point of the witness's story about the car accident was the ways in which, in this case, she's making the automobile wreck something in her life ... Stories are plainly ways of packaging experiences. And most characteristically stories report the experience in which the teller figures. And furthermore, in which the teller figures—for the story anyway—as a hero. Which doesn't mean that he does something heroic, but that the story is organised around the teller's circumstances.

Personal agency can foster fact construction by attending to 'pathing devices' (Woolgar, 1980:256) or 'interpretative frames' (Smith, 1993:29) as readers are encouraged to follow the path of the storyteller. Through observations, directions and events, the journey of the storyteller displays the discovery of the independent 'fact', as Smith (1993:27) notes "whether I wish it or not, whether I admit it or not, it is a fact". Such routes enable the use of personally orientated storytelling, the opportunity to introduce entities and characters to the reader through, for example, chronological markers, institutionally recognised events and processes; what we all know about social work and clients. For example, in a number of the interviews, the social worker began to tell the story from being allocated the case:

> I got allocated it not long after I started the job I'd discussed it with the senior and probably spoke to the previous worker ...
>
> It was one of those cases I was given when I arrived ...

These accounts lead the reader through the social worker's attendance in court proceedings and case conferences, home visits and office interviews, the personal testimony of the storyteller. Indeed, the construction of a social work case is isomorphic with being guided through specific social work relations and institutional processes. Such processes provide the competent listener with a demonstration of the 'proper procedures' for recognising and justifying a social work case. Shuman (1986:181) refers to 'contextualisation' as a way that the listener is instructed as to what occasion of storytelling is being performed and how it should be interpreted. Atkinson (1990:55) notes how accounts rely on an internal coherence, being 'true to itself', both factual and realistic. Social work entities are established as 'facts' through the ratified reader's familiarity with institutional processes, as experienced by the storyteller.

Wooffitt (1992:103) investigates paranormal stories, noting the absence of personal agency. He distinguishes between events that happen to people and those which are a product of intention, planning or decision making.

> By formulating their paranormal experiences as an 'it' that 'happened', speakers in the anomaly accounts are thus trading on conventions which inform the way that we refer to events the occurrence of which were not contingent upon human agency and involvement.

Paranormal stories are brought off by describing events which are entirely non-human in origin, not traceable to any human action or perception, but imposed on the individual. I am suggesting that social work accounts establish 'out-there-ness' by hearing personal experiences, duly assessed and authorised by competent, trusted storytellers.

The organisation of accounts

We have seen how 'pathing devices' are an example of how readers can be guided through an account. Approaching accounts as narrative suggests viewing the organisation of the whole account as concerned with constructing and linking entities and characters. Rather than merely deploying categories, narratives construct and configure them into a plot. Entities like mental illness or child abuse are only available through the organisation of accounts. Woolgar (1980:246) notes that Smith's assumption of isomorphism between notions of mental illness and the way a text is organised seems to suggest that:

> ... there is no sense in which we can claim that the phenomena mental illness has an existence independent of the means of its expression

> ... the only way to recover the character of a phenomenon is to examine the work which is carried out by participants in effecting or bringing off its existence

Facts are dependent on how they are represented in telling stories, writing reports, weighing babies. As Smith (1993:27) notes:

> The actual events are not facts. It is the use of proper procedure for categorising events which transforms them into facts. A fact is something that is already categorised, already worked up to conform to the model of what that fact should be like.

Embedded in descriptions of instances of mental illness or child abuse are instructions for how to read events and characters in terms of the appropriate category and how to construct categories in terms of events and characters. Smith (1993:30) argues that in the account which depicted K as mentally ill:

> The problem presented by the account is not to find an answer to the question 'what is wrong with K?', but to find that this collection of items is a proper puzzle to the solution 'becoming mentally ill.'

There is not merely a list of K's symptoms. A story is offered which is organised around the 'proper procedures' for both displaying the attributes of the category mental illness and identifying them as present in this case. By sharing interpretative resources about what constitutes mental illness, the reader is able to recognise and re-establish mental illness as a category and K as an example of it. Bringing in witnesses is another way that establishing facts can be located in the progressive and cumulative nature of social work storytelling. Smith (1993:28) notes the gradual addition of trusted witnesses to the account, each witness is heard as independent of the others. This solidarity of allies was observed in the 'failure to thrive' case (chapter 4). The social worker introduces allies and supporting witnesses gradually and cumulatively: GP (line 20), first hospital (line 28), hospital social worker (line 41), other Area social worker (line 46), first foster parent (line 53), second foster parent (line 59), family welfare association (line 63), case conference (line 73), court (line 78), family aide (line 96), GP and health visitor (line 123), second hospital (line 126), police (line 160), grandparents (line 185). Crowding the text with allies and supporters can be heard to make available independent and trusted witnesses who agreed to follow the social worker on his project. They too experienced the mother in the same hostile way; there is no conspiracy, all these people (and the institutions they represent) had the same experience.

Entitlement and authority

Displaying the attributes and status of the storyteller and their right to tell stories are important issues in substantiating 'facts' and creating strong texts. In Shuman's study (1986) of adolescent fight stories, entitlement to tell a story was as important to negotiate and defend as the content of the story. She sees authority and entitlement as closely linked:

> Authority and entitlement are related concepts, the first referring to the right of the storyteller to tell a story in a certain way and the second referring to the negotiable right of any person to tell a certain story. In the first case, it is the mode of telling that is in question; in the second case, it is the relationship between the teller and the events described. The two concepts invoke each other, and when one is called into question, so is the other by implication. (p.61)

Shuman's adolescent girls had to negotiate the right to tell stories about their classmates. In contrast, social workers are required to report on the private lives of their clients. They do not need to negotiate the authority to tell the tale but still must display entitlement. A poor performance or inadequate information can be dismissed as incorrect, inaccurate or just not convincing enough. For example, in a case conference observed, a care worker was in attendance to represent her absent colleague. The family contested this contribution on the grounds that they had never seen this person; she had authority but no entitlement.

Authority is invested in the position of the allocated social worker. This status can be heard to carry with it privileged access to encounters and a history of contact which entitles such a social worker to talk with personal authority. An entitlement to talk for the client may be extended to claim professional expertise to represent the clients' history, attitude and behaviour. Such a performance must still be brought off as competent and appropriate; the danger is that it is heard as biased.[3] The social worker may automatically be given the floor at the case conference or at court, but what is said and how it is delivered and received constitute the performance of professional efficacy.

Shuman (1986) offers three concepts which enable an analysis of authority and entitlement—contextualisation, the use of reported and described speech and mediate and immediate storytelling. All these features control the distance between the storyteller and hearer/reader. The first has already been discussed: how an account produces 'context' and instructs the listener as to what this occasion of storytelling constitutes. The second concept, reported speech, has been noted by Bakhtin as a key feature in providing a text with speech of other places and speakers (discussed further in chapter 7).

The third concept of mediate and immediate storytelling is particularly important as social workers take stories from other periods and make them relevant for telling in a case conference, court, supervision session or research interview. At the same time, the relationship with the audience is negotiated and mediated.

> ... a mediate relationship presents stories as stored over a long period of time, as part of the storyteller's repertoire. The stories and the occasions on which they are told may have several possible mediated relationships ... In contrast in an immediate relationship, a story and the occasion on which it is told are explicitly connected such that the story is about the current occasion. (Shuman, 1986:55)

Mediate storytelling relates the past in a way which explains current events, requiring an authorised connection between present and past stories: how the past is relevant to and determines the present. For example:

> ... I think some of S's behaviour patterns which sets him into a circle of needing special placements has a lot to do with his background how he was brought up ... (interview 7.1.1)

> ... then two or three sessions about the family when he almost was crying (-) he talked about how his dad always favoured his sisters about the pain non-specifically at first (-) talked about pain outside the family a girlfriend he went off the rails he said and he was linking up his behaviour with this pain ... (interview 2.2.1)

These examples of mediate storytelling can be heard to locate social work accounting in key stories which sum up how the client is as s/he is—because of early childhood relations, events, actions, contingencies. That they are distant and incontestable allows them to present the metastory of the case. If you understand this story, you will understand why the client acts as s/he does now.

In summary, theoretical approaches to fact construction, entitlement and authority offer important concepts in investigating social work accounts. The facts of social work are human entities, but the 'out-there-ness' of fact construction relies on displaying objective formulations of categories and attributes of people. The discussion of the overall organisation of the account reinforces our earlier concern to explore the whole utterance, since the 'proper procedures' of social work require complex rhetorical displays and unfolding narrative forms. In the next section, we analyse social work accounts, concentrating on how character depictions are deployed to establish definitive categorisations of clients, their behaviour and circumstances.

FACTS AND CLAIMING ENTITLEMENT 125

Ideal Reader: I feel a bit let down by this chapter so far. I mean at the end of the last chapter, some very interesting questions were raised about the 'reality' of child abuse, morals and the consequences of the debate so far. This discussion of fact construction is fairly interesting but the implication was that the reality questions would be raised again here.

Allies: Grint and Woolgar (1992: 379):

> Spector and Kituse (1977) show how it is more useful to develop a theoretical (social constructivist) framework for the analysis of social problems than to engage in a piecemeal argument about the "objective conditions and causes" that apply in any particular instance.

Ideal Reader: Yes, I can see that social construction is very important but it was you who raised the reality question. You were worried about the strong moral position of asking whether social constructionism in some way underined the true status of the child abuse.

Allies: Grint and Woolgar (1992:371):

> Our knowledge of what bombs can do is not based simply on our looking at them or watching them go off. It depends, instead, on a complicated variety of factors including our reading or listening to accounts of others, our susceptibility to persuasion by authoritative sources, our willingness to credit claims to expertise, and so on ... Some accounts will turn out to be more persuasive than others, but they are still accounts—not definitive nor undeniable truths.

Ideal Reader: So this means that child abuse, like the bomb, is only available through accounts which may or may not be persuasive. But surely there must be a reality about the bomb or child abuse underlying these accounts and some accounts must be nearer the essence than others.

Allies: Grint and Woolgar (1992:371):

> Our knowledge of the "effect" of the bomb [on Hiroshima] would be the contingent outcome of reading other people's reconstructions in a contextually specific way. This does not mean we have to deny that the nuclear bomb of Japan was influential in its surrender. But our acceptance of this "fact" does not entail, nor is it entailed by, our acceptance of some categorical truth about what the bomb (actually) did.

Ideal Reader: So the reality of child abuse or a nuclear bomb is always dependent on social construction. There is no point at which we reach a reality uncontaminated by storytelling and persuasion.

Allies: Grint and Woolgar (1992: 376-7)

> John F. Kennedy's assassination is a classic example of the difficulty of providing an irrefutable, "objective" account of the damage caused by the bullet ... We do not argue that the bullet is irrelevant but that the process by which it achieves relevance is irredeemably social.

Ideal Reader: Yes, of course there might be controversy about who shot Kennedy and from where, but in the end he was shot, wasn't he?

Allies: Grint and Woolgar (1992:376)

> It is not necessary to deny that bullets may tear flesh or splinter bone to argue that it is nevertheless a social construction. If a gun goes off and the victim falls over with a hole in his or her head, you would have to be insufferably stubborn to deny that the bullet made the hole. The point is that our knowledge that the bullet made the hole depends on a series of social (re)constructions. It is only the end result of these constructions that makes the constructions themselves seem irrelevant and makes a distinction between the fact of the hole and knowledge of the hole seem arcane.

Ideal Reader: So you mean that the 'fact' of the injury is only one of many social constructions and re-constructions which storytellers might use to link events and people. Children are injured but how, when, why, by whom, with what consequences are questions which constitute child abuse as much as the 'actual' pain and death. So the analysis of fact construction is confronting the reality of social processes, as have many others about Kennedy's death.

Depicting clients and their attributes

Social work accounts are concerned with categorising people, their attributes and behaviour. This section compares social work accounts which differ in the investment in and distance from characters and events. Shuman (1986:48) notes the lower level of investment in stories about fights told after the event compared to those at the time. Similarly, social workers talk about cases with varying degrees of concern. How does the account change when the crisis is over and intervention is no longer considered appropriate? A distinction is offered between 'low risk stories' and 'serious situations'.

Low risk stories

Some accounts depict situations as 'low risk': the social worker no longer envisages ongoing contact with the family and can be heard to downgrade any sense of alarm. In these examples, it is accepted that not all the problems have been solved but the social worker persuades the interviewer that characters and events can no longer be constructed in social work terms. The link between events and character depictions can be heard as significantly different from 'serious situations'.

Interview X.4.1. concerns a case of a single mother and young child. The social worker has just closed the case, believing the client does not benefit from her contact. The case had previously been known to social services with reports from the health visitor of mother's attempted suicide. The interview has concentrated on the events of a one night admission to care. The child had been found wandering with no knowledge of mother's whereabouts. The account offers no discussion of why the admission had occurred, only a chronology of the times and action. The child returns to the mother the next day after an interview with the duty officer but, given the previous concern, the case is considered to warrant a social worker being allocated. Contact does not develop and the case is closed. As the interview ends, a summary of the present state of affairs is heard:

> Social Worker: it was just a long sort of (-) catalogue of her not being at the [bed and breakfast] hotel and things it's not (-) the whole thing's not satisfactory but (-) I don't think there is anything else we can actually do at the moment.
>
> Interviewer: no I mean it's not the sort of case in which you would imagine er reception into care's going to happen in anything but the odd situation.
>
> Social Worker: I wouldn't be surprised if this came up as an emergency again yeah but in terms of mother and what she says about the child and her situation (-) er there is nothing we can do I mean she is saying basically she's got things sorted out ok moved out of the B and B to live with er someone that she knows she's saying that she doesn't need help I mean our only concern is that the child is developmentally behind but that's being dealt with by the health centre really and I mean they know the situation so they'll contact whoever if they're concerned (-) so I think it's one of those that you have to live with really

The social worker and interviewer can be heard to co-operate in reducing the evaluation of future risk and what social services can do. A 'low risk' category is negotiated around "not the sort of case which will happen again" and "it might happen again [but] it's one of those that you have to live with". For the first time in the interview, the mother's present circumstances are now made available—she has got things sorted out and is no longer in B & B. The interviewer now suggests an alternative intervention which the social worker can be heard to reject:

> Social worker: No I don't know I mean I think she's er (-) she came over from Ireland er I think about a year ago and I think she's not been able to settle at all since she came over from Ireland but certainly she er (-) she's dependent very much on er (-) well her kind of network seems to be well there's a lot of these there's a lot of single Irish blokes who sit over in the park and they seem to be her reference point really although having said that she actually presents as a sort of respectable person I mean not that they are not respectable but er I mean she is involved in [family centre] which

> she goes to sometimes but I I actually feel that she needs some work done with her around how to deal with children and stuff and er [family centre] would be quite good in helping her with that but she uses the toy library down there she is not saying that she doesn't want to look after [child] or that she finds that a strain and I feel very apprehensive about removing children from parents
>
> Interviewer: oh sure (-) so some sort of help with parenting skills ...

The interview moves to an ending with no further discussion of this case, except to compare it with 'other priorities'. This utterance is of interest because, after a pause, a detailed depiction of the mother is offered. Her character, history and relationships are made available in a definitive form that has not previously been heard. Such details could form the basis of a formulation of high risk—unsettled, her associates, the need for some work on parenting. However, this display of detailed information and assessment can be heard to reassure the interviewer that the social worker understands this woman's situation. Appropriate resources are available elsewhere. Finally, an extreme case formulation can be heard to mock the interviewer by exaggerating his suggestion—surely, you are not suggesting this kind of mother should have her child taken away. The hesitant beginning suggests a reluctance to go into this detail, but precise contrasts through complex modalities, depict the mother as someone who is now coping pretty well. A careful character depiction, grading her respectability and coping, is eventually made available in order to categorise this as not a social work case.

A similar feature appears in interview Z.6.3. which also ends with a character depiction. More detailed previous contact is described but only at the end is this summarised into a categorisation:

> Interviewer: as far as future contact with the department is concerned
>
> Social Worker: er I think the only contact that G will need (-) from the department whether it be from whatever social service office will be for nursery I don't think she needs anything else G is a survivor she is able to survive on her own and I think as [child] is getting older she is actually going to do more and I actually think the relationship with her and her own mother will actually right itself
>
> Interviewer: you don't think she needs help looking after after the baby
>
> Social worker: I don't think so
>
> Interviewer: ok thanks

Despite having reported concerns by the day nursery about the mother's ability to look after her child, the categorisation of a "survivor" underines any reason for further intervention. The future only offers improvements. Three uses of "actually" can be heard to pinpoint the definitive facts of the case—the restrictions of a young child, her relationship with her mother and the social worker's own definition of the state of affairs, "I actually think". None of these concerns require further social services contact.

In summary, these accounts of 'low risk' cases can be heard as presenting only chronological events. When the social worker is challenged to justify no further contact, a character depiction is made available. The definitive portrayal of the mother does not bring in witnesses nor reported speech to create 'out-there-ness'. However, 'pathing devices', complex categorisations and contextualisations of weighing up priorities enable the competent hearer to locate these cases. Character depictions are a stock in trade of social work accounts but in these examples they are deployed sparingly in response to local interactional requirements.

Serious situations

In contrast to low risk cases, there is no reluctance to offer background circumstances and character depictions where the case is allocated to a social worker, formulated as serious and long term contact is envisaged. At the beginning of an account, attributes are allocated to characters, as Smith (1993:24) suggests, to instruct the reader that the account s/he is about to hear should be read through this categorisation:

> J is a very complex young woman very inward and holds things in very unwilling to share much with anybody... (Interview 8.1.1)

> I think she is quite independent now and seems to know what she wants there are a lot of things I could say but that's where she is at the moment... (Interview 1.1.1)

Each opening can be heard to include a strong instruction that this is the definitive portrayal—the first has a three part list using 'very' and the second tells the listener that 'a lot' of information is available to back up the assertion.

Interview Y.8.5. does not start with a categorisation. It is concerned with the possible adoption of a new-born baby. The social worker explains the racial background of the family has influenced decisions: grandfather's 'undue' pressure and the uncertainty of the mother's reaction to her new baby. After eight minutes a character depiction is made available, which can be heard as instructing the interviewer as to the definitive state of affairs:

> Interviewer: that [placement] would have been for mother and ...
>
> Social worker: no (-) just the baby because mum at that time was not prepared to leave home

Interviewer: (-) oh I see

Social worker: no

Interviewer: I see

Social worker: she's a girl that (-) she's a girl that to some extent is quite weak willed on the personality basis but also caught into her culture and she didn't in fact feel able to leave home until very recently

Interviewer: right (-) right

Social worker: so whatever happened with the baby had to happen separate from her because she wasn't prepared to leave home at that time it took her a long time to actually (-) develop the the courage and the skill and the confidence to actually leave home she wasn't ready at that time

The use of 'actually' and 'in fact', three repeats of 'not prepared to leave home' and a three line list 'courage, skill and confidence' can be heard to establish this formulation as the definitive portrayal which determines the overall state of affairs. The interviewer has at last been made to understand the uniqueness of this case and agrees with the social worker that the mother and baby facilities are not appropriate here.

To summarise, these social work accounts can be heard to manipulate and configure the entities of social work–character, events, states of affairs–in various strategic and local forms. It is in making available the depiction of character, background and circumstances that the hearer is enabled to locate the 'facts' of the case. Offered at the beginning of an account, such character depictions can be heard as instructing the reader that what follows is a story based around the client as a particular type of person. Heard later, it can signal an 'evaluation' of the narrative (Labov and Waletsky, 1967) or 'warrant' for a 'claim' (Toulmin, 1958), the point where the hearer is put straight. To describe these accounts as 'low risk' or 'serious situation' does not denote an objective measure of the case. Rather it shows that events, characters and states of affairs are available flexibly and interactionally. Deploying definitive character portrayals at strategic points in the account can be heard to persuade the hearer of the factual status of the case.

Telling a strong story: Donna

So far features of social work accounts have been displayed as facts by indicating specific moves or formulations. In this section, a single account is investigated for its overall organisation and as a site for reading a text as persuasive and intriguing. Facts, claims and conjecture are not only constructed but used to manipulate and fascinate the reader. In social work accounts, it is the overall display to which the reader reacts and the overall trajectory of the argument along which the reader is carried. The reader may be unhappy with parts but such dissent is minor when faced with a decision to accept or reject the overall efficacy of the account. The document (appendix 5.1) is the first report produced at the beginning of the case of Donna and, hence, does not offer features which have been developed as a result of repeated storytelling. In the next chapter, the story of the case of Donna is followed through later reading performances.

In August 198_ Donna's mother contacted the social services department to ask for her daughter aged 14 to be received into the care of the Local Authority. The social workers made inquiries of other welfare organisations and, whilst refusing the reception into care, agreed to help the family. There was some contact over the next few weeks but at the end of August, Donna ran away from home. When the police took her home a few days later, her mother refused to have her back. Donna was taken to a children's home and it was decided to request a full social and psychological assessment in order to decide what to do next.

Creating the ratified reader

The document in appendix 5.1 is a report from the social worker to the Principal Social Worker asking for his agreement to proceed with a 'Full Assessment'. The ratified reader is specifically addressed, being the recognised access to the resource. The purpose of the account is to convince the Principal Social Worker that the situation is serious enough to warrant a Full Assessment. As already discussed a categorisation of events is isomorphic with the textual organisation of that category (Smith, 1993:16). The categorisation 'a serious breakdown in mother-daughter relations' is not separate from the performance of that assertion in a social work text. This is achieved, however, not by laying out 'facts' leading to a conclusion of 'serious breakdown requiring a Full Assessment'. Rather the categorisation of a 'serious breakdown/ full assessment' is rendered observable by the events and depictions made available. As Smith (1993:30) observes, a 'proper puzzle' is required to display the category 'serious mother-daughter breakdown'.

The lay out of the report produces the context for reading the account as a request for action. The heading 'Case-History (Summary) Sheet' might be expected to summarise the history of the case. However, lines 3 and 4 signify a memo with 'From' and 'To' indicating a particular channel of communication from one specific actor to another. In the space after 'Recommendations' (line 48), the recipient writes 'agreed', also treating the document as a request. This document is thus not attended to as a summary nor a case history for the purposes of any reader of the case file who is looking for a definitive version of the case of Donna. Instead, it is to be read as a request for agreeing an action and the proper site for reading is the Principal Social Worker's office.

Whilst a request for full assessment is not an unusual response to a mother-teenager dispute, a more favoured strategy would be to work with the family and young person at home. Full Assessment commits expensive and hard pressed resources, to which the ratified reader (the Principal Social Worker) controls access. An alternative reading of the case of Donna might be that the mother and daughter are having a few problems, which is normal in some families with teenagers. The request could be refused with a recommendation that the young person be returned home and social work intervention be located there. It would also be cheaper.

This account can be heard to negotiate these alternative formulations of the situation as a justification for social services involvement is produced to configure characters and events, thereby constituting a legitimate social services case. A reading occasion is constructed as the location for justifying professional action by the manipulation of the categories—'serious breakdown of mother-daughter relationship' and 'Full Assessment', which are set against dispreferred versions of 'normal teenager upset' and 'work in the home'.

Fact construction and entitlement in character development

The construction of facts has been considered above to be an important feature of persuasive accounts. We have seen, in particular, how social work accounts trade on entitlement through the social workers' experience and privileged status. Unlike accounts where professional affirmation is based on long term contact, in this case there has been little previous work. The report writer can be heard to manipulate externally-established facts with initial impressions to display the 'proper puzzle'.

Reporting events and introducing trusted witnesses are presented at the beginning to set the scene. Both pages begin with facts—"Donna was received into care on 2nd September" on page 1 and "Donna has never been received into care before" on page 2. The introduction of the police provides not only external witnesses but also an external measure denoting the seriousness of the problem: "Police failed to get mother to take her back" (lines 8-9). The main witness of Donna's character and her "maladjusted behaviour" is her mother, with some confirmation by the EWO (education welfare officer) (line 15).[4] The mother's assertions (lines 13-15) about Donna's behaviour appear to offer extra support for the proposition of 'maladjustment' with a strong list "steals, lies, rude and abusive" (line 14). This is more than a three line list (Heritage and Greatbatch, 1986), as the third item consists of two linked elements "rude and abusive" denoting a more general anti-social attitude. There is in this phrase a strong rhythmic pattern. The state of Donna's unhappiness (line 23) trades on the entitlement of social worker assessment. Despite only having two meetings, the social worker offers an initial assessment of the child's state of mind. A three line list is again heard: "very unhappy, withdrawn, totally shut off emotionally", which again denotes an escalation of problems. A provisional categorisation of Donna as unhappy and disturbed is made available.

The character of the mother involves a more complex reading. On the one hand, she is offered as the 'trusted teller of the tale' (Smith, 1993), but, on the other hand, she is presented as a rejecting mother (line 32); hardly a reliable witness. The words of the mother can be heard as accomplishing both tasks, providing an external witness of the events while indicating the seriousness of the mother's rejection. This is a serious situation because of what mother reports and the fact that she reports it. The ongoing poor relationship is presented through mother's 'described speech': "Mother saying [Donna's] maladjusted ..." (line 13) and "Mother saying Donna completely bad and she never wants to see her back" (lines 44 -46). However, irony can be heard in the trust given to the mother. First, she is seen as manipulative: "agreed to discuss problems but when it did not get results ... she refused to have her back" (lines 42-44). Second, the extreme case formulations attributed to her description of Donna (lines 13-14 and 45-46) could be read as someone who might be overreacting.

It is mother's description and reaction to the sexual activity of Donna, which moves the case from a mother-daughter dispute to a young person in moral danger and hence appropriate for social services action. Donna is portrayed as a possible teenage prostitute:

> Mother requested RIC after she discovered that Donna had had some sexual contact with a 37 yr. old pimp. (lines 39-41)

This can be heard as the most serious but unsubstantiated 'fact' in this account and raises the stakes over appropriate categorisation. The only witness is the mother and the lack of police involvement (the appropriate external informant) is accounted for: "Mother reluctant to inform Police" (line 41). There are other comments on her possible sexual activity but all are mother's assertions: "she might have had sex" (line 32) and "discovered had had some sexual contact" (line 39) which are reported as the basis for the mother's present rejection. Perhaps the 'maladjustment' might have been tolerated. The possible sexual behaviour can be heard as such a serious claim that, even if not eventually proven, to ignore it would be negligent. Hence, mother must be taken notice off since her 'facts' are a plausible cause for concern. Even though mother is an unreliable witness and is morally suspect by rejecting her daughter, the situation being suggested–'teenage prostitution'–cannot be ignored. Whilst not a 'fact', rumour and conjecture are heard as requiring serious attention.

The mere suggestion of such a serious categorisation can be heard to invite a reader response which demands a reaction; it needs no further factual substantiation to require grave concern. Pithouse and Atkinson (1988:193) note a similar reaction to the term 'incest' in a case presentation by a social worker to her supervisor:

> It is significant how the term 'incest' is introduced early in the social worker's account. It hangs in the conversation without qualification, elaboration or clear attribution ('some sort of incest'). The term is not attached to any members of the family nor to any behaviours. Here, as in other accounts of the sort recorded in the same setting, there are hints, clues, innuendoes and unverifiable guesses.

Pithouse and Atkinson suggest that such talk demonstrates shared occupational assumptions. Here, however, it appears less an example of the '*et cetera* principle' (Cicourel, 1973:86), where the competent hearer fills in the gaps, than the use of morally laden words to posit an unheard proposition that cannot be substantiated, but cannot be ignored. The least 'factual' part of the report is the strongest statement. The consequences of substantiation would be so serious that the reader is required to invest in its possible truthfulness. Child abuse, teenage prostitution and incest are moral entities, which by their force enable everyday events, concerns and witnesses to be sorted into moral categories and characterisations which demand action.

Unlike the construction of K's mental illness by Angela (Smith, 1993), there is available here a less explicit relation between the category and the 'facts' which constitute it. The account is heard as positing a categorisation of 'mother-teenager breakdown', but with the categorisation 'teenage prostitution' not proven but possible. To have ignored it would lower the moral force of the story and the legitimacy for the Full Assessment. It is also early in the development of Donna as narrative.[5] Social workers telling accountable stories means covering all possibilities, especially the worst case. Facts, claims and conjecture all require attention, with perhaps the 'facts' the least interesting.

Strengthening claims through reading a narrative

In chapter 2, it was suggested that narrative requires less a set of necessary features indicating a story outside the context of its performance and more a way of performing reading relations. This report offers an opportunity to study aspects of an account which has both a narrative and non-narrative structure. Page 1 is a series of answers to questions whereas page 2 offers the opportunity for an extended report, available as a narrative. How do the narrative and non-narrative sections contribute to a strong story? Goodman (1980:115) considers that a psychological report can be presented in a narrative or non-narrative form.

> A psychological report recounts a patient's behaviour chronologically. It is a story, a history. But rearrange to group the incidents according to their significance as symptoms—of first suicidal tendencies, then claustrophobia, then psychopathic disregard of consequences—it is no longer a story but an analysis, a case study. Reordering of the telling here turns a narrative into something else.

Page 2 is hearable as a story in a number of ways. It can be heard as a chronology of events and divided into the elements of story structure, similar to Labov and Waletsky's model (1967), discussed in chapter 2:

Setting: Donna has never been received into care before (line 37).
Orientation: There have been many problems with Donna's behaviour (line 38).
Complication: She agreed to discuss problems but when it did not get results i.e. Donna received into care and Donna ran away, she refused to have her back (lines 42-4).
Evaluation: Mother saying Donna's completely bad and she never wants her back (lines 45-7).
Resolution: Recommendations (if any) Full Assessment (line 48).

The 'Resolution' as the request for Assessment can be heard as an important aspect for reading a narrative, since it would be an incomplete story if the Assessment is not agreed. Prince's (1973) story structure as moving from one state of affairs to another can also be read as a contrast between a period where the family problems could be discussed at home, to a situation of complete rejection. A third approach to narrative is the 'point' or claim that the story warrants, the answer to the 'so what?' question. The account starts with "Donna has never been in care"(line 36) and ends with the claim that mother "never wants her back" (lines 45- 46). The reader seeks narrativity in the move between these two statements in order to substantiate the recommendation at line 48. This account, then, can be read as a narrative in the process of constructing the context of a request for full assessment.

Narrativity can also be seen as accomplished through the use of tenses. The work of 'mediate storytelling', discussed earlier, links various past events with the present situation. The first sentence "Donna has never been received into care before" (line 36) can be heard to set up a problem for the reader.[6] That this is a request for Full Assessment for a teenager who has not been in care before may be heard as unusual. Most requests for Full Assessment concern children with previous experiences of care. Is this a low risk case? The account has to rebut such a charge.

The main body of the narrative begins with use of the imperfect tense 'have been' (line 38) indicating many problems have been occurring and still are. The continuing nature of these problems can be heard to escalate with mother's request for RIC (reception into care) (line 38) and the next few events are established as recent occurrences. This is achieved through another contrast with the previous sentence—"there have been many problems" (past continuous), now it had reached a request for RIC (recent past). There is no grammatical indication of this stage being the recent past, but the immediate move to mother discussing the problems and then refusing to have her daughter back (line 44) is located in the present. The last sentence brings the situation up to date and lays out the problem which is heard as continuing, escalating and can be heard as a demand for action. The upgraded phrases "completely bad" (line 45) and "never wants her back" link to the "never" at the beginning of the narrative (line 36) and also mark the complete turnaround in the story— never in care, now never to go back. The escalation of the events, moving from "many problems with behaviour" (line 37) to "sexual contact"(line 39) to "completely bad" (line 44) can be heard to move from normal to abnormal teenager/mother problems.

It is thus suggested that the strength of this account is made available by hearing narrative features: the contrast of states of affairs, events and tenses as the sudden escalation of problems is displayed. The 'pathing device' is chronological, unfolding and increasing alarm. The non-narrative on page 1 does not offer the reader an opportunity to read characterisations and events within a narrative structure. However, answers to questions offer data which set up the narrative overleaf. They can be read as contributions to a story which is waiting to be heard. They are facts in search of a categorisation; they can be heard as worrying but not yet tied to a narrative of 'serious breakdown'. Parts of a potential story are available—the 'circumstances' question (line 6) offers an 'orientation', Donna received into care. The 'maladjusted category' (line 12) and her unhappiness (line 21) offer 'complications' but there is no resolution nor evaluation. Some answers make use of extreme case formulations and three part lists—"a very unhappy, withdrawn, totally shut off emotionally" (line 23), "never had a good relationship ... now totally rejected" (line 31).

Thus, the narrative and non-narrative parts of this report combine to offer a strong story which can only be resolved by the Full Assessment. The strong formulations in the non-narrative can be heard as 'over the top' statements, not tied to a framework. In contrast, whilst having fewer upgraded terms, the narrative is heard to use tenses, chronology and a rising sense of alarm to rebut alternative versions.

Narrative puzzle

There is a further narrative feature available to the reader of this report which is followed through other texts and other occasions of reading in the next chapter. This is a 'narrative puzzle'. Recognition of the 'narrative puzzle' can be heard to set up a reading which is unresolved and thus encourages the reader to go further. Such a feature can be heard to add an extra dimension to the narrative work of this text, making it more persuasive, intriguing and stronger.[7] The 'narrative puzzle' creates uncertainty as to the 'true' nature of the problem with two suggestions as to where to seek an answer. It also creates a trajectory to the story as the future resolution of this 'puzzle' in the conclusion of the 'Full Assessment'. The request for the 'Full Assessment' is irresistible.

The narrative puzzle revolves around the status of Donna's sexual activity. It was noted earlier that the category 'teenage prostitution' is dangled before the reader without clarification, setting up a series of possible worries for the reader. Furthermore, its existence is hearable as real and at the same time illusory, as the teller of the tale is not to be trusted. As already mentioned, the mother is the only reporting witness and, having been presented as a rejecting mother, the evidence of Donna's sexual activity can be read in two ways. First, the sexual activity may be heard as an indicator of the depth of Mother's rejection rather than as a 'fact', Mother is making these serious accusations about Donna to justify her own rejection. It is thus unlikely to be true in itself but does signify Mother's deep feelings. This reading can be supported by noting that each mention of the sexual activity is preceded by positioning Mother in the claim. At line 32, Mother's rejection is "on the basis that she might have had sex". The "many problems with Donna's behaviour" (lines 37-8) are introduced as "according to mother" (line 38) and the important conclusion before the recommendation begins "Mother saying ..." (line 44-5). At each point Mother as the sole witness is re-stated.

Second, a distrust of Mother's allegations is never made explicit and an alternative reading is that the claim may be true. The description of "a 37 yr.

old pimp" (line 40) offers some evidence of a tangible evil entity in this scenario. A cumulative sense of alarm of the state of affairs is hearable as the claim moves from "might have had sex" (line 32) through to the appearance of the pimp (line 40). Both possibilities are available and contribute a 'narrative puzzle' which only a Full Assessment will resolve. Having both keeps options open but, more important, the request for Full Assessment is strengthened by the presence of competing versions. Hearing both together, the status of Donna's sexual activity and Mother's reaction offer an unsettled puzzle, with which the reader is intrigued enough to follow further through the Full Assessment. An unresolved story can thus carry incompatible versions and, by tantalising the reader, still can be heard as competent and strong in its claims. Indeed by offering reasonable alternatives, it is harder to undermine and may be heard as fair minded and flexible. Later versions of the story of Donna make much of the 'narrative puzzle', with some emphasising different versions, but ultimately accepting both Blow! I've nearly given the game away. Chapter 6 follows this story further but be reassured that there remain further twists in this tale.

This chapter has investigated some features of social work accounts which can be heard as facts, claims and conjecture. 'Facticity' in terms of Latour and Woolgar's Type 4 and 5 statements has not been seen as central to social work accounts. First, some facts are received by social workers from others—doctors identify 'failure to thrive', the police define Donna as an abandoned child. The social work account is somewhat removed from the process of initially establishing the events as a problem, but an account is required to configure attributes and relations between entities and set out appropriate action. Donna as a rejected child is a fact discovered by the police, the social work account must establish why and what to do. Second, the personal agency/'out-there-ness' balance has been observed as tilted towards the former. The 'facts' of the mother's character and circumstances in low risk stories are known but contrasts and contextualisation through, for example, establishing priorities, enable categorisation. Third, 'facts' and claims have been seen as only a starting point for conjecture and possibilities. Persuasion has been achieved through flexible, provisional, intriguing readings. Donna was found to be rejected by her mother (police-established fact); this is more than a temporary breakdown (claims of progressive and long term problem); the cause may be mother's incapacities or Donna's sexual risk (intriguing conjecture). Despite the shortage of highly protected, robust 'facts', these accounts could be seen to achieve their objective—the low risk cases were discussed no more and Donna had a Full Assessment.

A number of rhetorical and narrative features have been discussed. Some features involve the use of strong rhetorical formulations—three part lists, extreme case formulations, definitive markers. Fact construction has been observed in pathing devices, linking past and present stories, bringing witnesses and displaying entitlement. It has, however, been suggested that the definitive and tantalising portrayals of characters and their attributes have been accomplished through reading narrativity, enabling the reader to follow paths and chronologies, building tensions and offering resolutions. In the last section, enticing the reader through a 'narrative puzzle' suggests a way of intriguing rather than explicitly persuading. Has some of the 'power' of Golding's stories been identified? Are 'puzzles' as strong as 'facts'? This investigation is followed into the next chapter, as the outcome of 'the puzzle' is sought.

A clear separation into moral and factual construction has all but disappeared. The form of some features could equally be made available using moral or factual content, indeed which is which? Are the character depictions in chapter 4 different from the character depictions here? Is the blame for a child failing to thrive based on good/bad contrasts or legitimate/illegitimate information states? And how can you tell the difference? The scales might not lie but the move from readings on scales to court involves a series of transformations, which are depicted as both moral and factual. In the 'broken nose' case in chapter 3, did the police not pressing changes and the judge sending the children home mean the broken nose was less of a 'fact'? The 'fact' of the broken nose clearly changed in its moral and factual significance by such an event. It no longer spoke for the existence of child abuse. Facts do not speak for themselves and morals need entities and characters. Is Donna's mother constructed as a fact: she is really a rejecting mother based on evidence (that she has locked Donna out, said certain things etc), or is she constructed morally as rejecting: a more ephemeral overall 'rejection' which damages Donna's character? Perhaps the answer might be sought in the interaction of the former with the latter, how events relate to the depictions. It also suggests the 'documentary method', how 'documents' stand for 'underlying patterns'.

Given the lack of 'out-there-ness' available in social work accounts based on personal entitlements, morals and facts are not easily separated. It is rather narrativity and literary features which can be heard as the site for investigating constructing activities. How characters in stories are made available to be read involves interlocking moral and factual attributions.

NOTES

[1] Shuman (1986:144) says referring to adolescent fight stories:
A central warranty of retellings is interpretation. In the case of the stabbing story, the outcome was known by most listeners.. Listeners wanted to hear interpretations that would account for how such a thing could happen.

[2] Atkinson (1990:26) quotes a number of studies of authority being displayed in anthropological texts through a mixture of 'personal narrative' and 'objectified description'.

[3] Such an accusation was at the centre of the criticism of the social worker in the Beckford inquiry (1985:85).

[4] This is an inappropriate answer to the question since the list (lines 10-12) is hearable as educational categories, requiring assessment by an educational psychologist (they were also replaced several years before this document was written). The category is, however, appropriated to contribute to Donna's character assessment.

[5] Perhaps talking to Angela earlier about K may have resulted in an account organised around the category 'odd behaviour' rather than mental illness.

[6] It could be argued that this opening is not part of the narrative. It is slightly set apart from the first paragraph and could be an answer to the request for information in lines 34-5. However, it has the effect of setting up the story for the reader.

[7] The 'narrative puzzle' is not the same as Smith's concept of 'proper puzzle' (1993:30). The latter is a wider formulation, 'a collection of items, which provides a proper puzzle to the solution becoming mentally ill'. Here the narrative puzzle is not resolved yet.

FACTS AND CLAIMING ENTITLEMENT: *Appendix* 141

APPENDIX 5.1

DIRECTORATE OF SOCIAL SERVICES
CASE—HISTORY (SUMMARY) SHEET

[RECEIVED I. CHILDRENS HOM... SECTION]

FROM [SOCIAL WORKER] Social Services
(State Borough or Establishment name and address)

TO.. [PRINCIPAL SOCIAL WORKER]

Child's name ... [DONNA] 5
(Surname in caps)

Date of birth . [D.O.B.] .... Religion .Methodist.........
              Date

Care order   Circumstances (brief) in which child came into care, with dates :—
S.1 without R. & P.
S.1 with R. & P.   [Donna] received into after Police
called to get mother to take her
back on the 2nd September.   10

Maladjusted
~~E.S.N.~~
Other category (please state) ....
*Delete as necessary

Mother saying [Donna] maladjusted ie steals
lies, rude + abusive. Poor relationship with teachers
confirmed by EWO... 15

Name of Social Worker now dealing with child and family [Social Worker]

Names of any previous S.W. or other social workers who may have relevant information :—
................................None..

Child's present address. [Address]
Child has been there since 2nd of September...........................

School the child attends or place and nature of employment (if any). [School]........... 20

Any other basic information about child ▮▮▮▮▮▮▮▮▮▮▮▮

I have only met [Donna] on two occasions. Both
times she hardly spoke. However impressions gained
were of a very unhappy withdrawn child, who
was totally devoid of auturally.

                    Mother. [Mother]
Parent's names and address
                    ~~Father~~. [Address]   25

Name of any other social service dealing with family ....

Comments on relatives (e.g., stepfather/mother, good or bad, interested or indifferent, domestic troubles, siblings
in care or not) Mother received into care when she was
same age as [Donna]. No history available.   30
Mother never had good relationship with child, has now
totally rejected her on basis that she might have had sex

P.T.O.

SOCIAL WORK AS NARRATIVE

REPORT and case-history (brief outline)

[Please begin with a chronological outline of placings (particularly moves in pre-school period where known).
(a) before in care
(b) while in care]

35

[Donna] has never been received into care before.

There have been many problems with [Donna's] behaviour according to mother. Mother requested RIC after she discovered that [Donna] had had some sexual contact 40 with a 37 yr old pimp. Mother reluctant to inform police also to accept social work intervention. She agreed to discuss problems but when it did not get results re [Donna]. received into care, and [Donna] ran away she refused to have her back. Mother 45 saying [Donna's] completely bad and she never wants her back.

RECOMMENDATIONS (if any) Full Assessment   (Continue on separate sheet if necessary)

[Social Worker]

Agreed [Principal Social Worker]

[Team Leader]

File is attached
File is not attached   Delete as necessary

6 Retellings: following the social work story

Bruno Latour (1987:15) recommends that in order to understand how claims are turned into facts, it is necessary to follow a text through the history of its encounters. He suggests that the fate of a claim depends on the action of later readers. They can accept the texts as stable and use them as a basis for further claims or they can ignore them. Through such trials and the scrutiny of powerful audiences, a conjecture can become a claim and then a fact. Eventually, it may become silent, a part of tacit knowledge.

In chapter 5, we investigated the strength of claims by considering the construction of the ratified reader in the organisation of a single text. Here, we follow the 'assessment story' of Donna's admission to care, as told in the Case-History (Summary) Sheet in appendix 5.1, through other texts and reading situations. It was noted in the last chapter that social work accounts are concerned less with merely creating entities as facts, than with telling persuasive accounts by deploying narrative and rhetorical features: the intrigue of the 'narrative puzzle' as opposed to the strength of the 'facts'. Furthermore, the 'facticity' of the clients of social workers is not just who they are and what they do, but how should social workers react to them. As social workers have increased contact with families, do their categorisations and responses change and stabilise, or remain contested and elusive? A further problem for social work accounts is that definitive formulations of character and strategy do not necessarily guarantee a successful outcome.[1] Assessment, prediction, action and evaluation are intimately intertwined.

Our analysis in chapter 3 considered how different (but concurrent) documents about ostensibly the same events constructed different audiences and different reading relations. This chapter investigates the sequential performances of the 'same' story in several related texts and reading occasions. The question is to what extent are events and characters stabilised into institutionalised stories as later texts retell the story for different audiences? Each retelling involves local and occasioned features of performance and persuasion but, at the same time, the authority of earlier reading occasions influences the agenda of present concerns. We first discuss theoretical approaches which consider links between texts and occasions and then follow the 'assessment story' of Donna.[2]

Theoretical approaches

Two theoretical concepts inform this analysis—'intertextuality' and 'blackboxing'. The former is used widely to investigate the relationship between texts. An example is reported speech (discussed in chapters 5 and 7) as stories enter texts, offering strength through the words of others. Blackboxing is a related concept, following how entities are shaped into texts which become closed and no longer available for scrutiny. Narrative as the focus of this analysis involves following how a story becomes the story. The institutionalised version of events and characters is rehearsed, the rough edges smoothed off and prepared for further scrutiny from wider audiences.

Intertextuality

This is a major concept in literary and cultural theory but is approached here in a specific way. Barthes (1977:126) is concerned with the way that novels incorporated references, themes and genre from other texts.

> We know that a text is not a line of words releasing a single 'theological' meaning (the 'message' of the Author-God) but a multi-dimensional space in which a variety of writings, none of them original, blend and clash. The text is a tissue of quotations drawn from the innumerable centres of culture.

Novels are seen as the ultimate arena for texts linking to one another. The author is no longer a focus for interpretation; instead, there is a concern to uncover structural features beyond the individual reading, notably the form. In contrast to formalism, recent approaches to intertextuality are less interested in formal structures than in reading relations between text and context. There is a recognition that all texts are constituted not merely by 'quotations' from other texts but from many historical, social and institutional discourses, genres and reading conventions. Such reading conventions are made available on the occasion of the reading through the interaction between the writer, reader, text and context. Thibault (1989:184) notes:

> All texts, whether spoken or written, have the meanings they do in relation to other texts within a given speech community as well as historically prior texts. However, it is not quite exact to say that a given text is meaningful in relation to a background of other texts. Texts do not stand in given static or neutral relationships with other texts. Instead, the relationships between texts are always constructed by text users.

Similarly, Bennett and Woolacott (1987:45) contrast their approach with Kristeva's concept of intertextuality which:

> ... refers to other texts which can be discerned within the internal composition of a specific individual text [whereas] we intend the concept of inter-textuality to refer to the social organisation of the relations between texts within the specific conditions of reading.

Texts refer to other texts, but also to other occasions of the use of texts and relations between texts and readers. When a social worker's court report sits in a filing cabinet, it may have certain features of style of writing or form similar to other social work reports. But as soon as it is read, it becomes a part of the social relations of the occasion of the reading. In chapter 3, it was suggested that features of a social work account, when read as a text, restrict readings by constructing the ratified reader and performing the social work community. Reading a social work report both anticipates and constitutes the reading occasion. In the Case-History (Summary) Sheet in chapter 5, the ratified reader was constituted as the Principal Social Worker, restricting appropriate reading to a specific context.

When the 'same' events and characters appear in other accounts at other reading occasions, in what way is a similar or different story performed? It might be anticipated that different reading relations are constructed and thus the story of Donna changes. Without the need to persuade the Principal Social Worker that a Full Assessment is the only way to proceed, the story of Donna may take on different features. However, whilst different occasions do indeed suggest different constructions and audiences, the intertextual relations of other occasions include and react to the previous texts and reading occasions. We can ask in what way the first text sets up the reading relations of later versions of the story of Donna. How far are subsequent texts read through the relations configured in the first report? Donna's admission to care is one story amongst others which constitute future versions of the case of Donna. However, we are suggesting that social work accounting practices require a stable reading of the 'assessment story' in order for a case to be processed through the appropriate administrative channels. She must become blackboxed.

Intertextuality is thus approached in a restricted sense, investigating the relations between performances of the 'same' story in different accounts on different occasions.[3] At the same time, the wider use of intertextuality, where words and genres enable the reader to make connections between texts, is located in community-established reading conventions.

Blackboxing

This concept has been developed in the sociology of science and is applied here to the sequential reading of social work documents. Social work accounting requires that depictions of characters, plot and strategies are stabilised to convince important audiences and enable appropriate action. Decisions, plans, meetings, forms, reports are organised around the display of the process of gathering facts, assessing alternatives and choosing strategy. Blackboxing is essential, but also provisional, as new information is gathered and interventions tried.

For Latour, the strength of a claim depends on later users. Claims set up later occasions and texts but, at the same time, a successful claim is dependent on it becoming unquestioned in its use and eventually silenced. Black boxes must not be reopened, since this would force readers to revisit the site of previous controversies, threatening the claim. Latour (1987:1-17) notes how scientists unquestioningly handle entities, like a computer or the structure of DNA, which on previous occasions were controversial and uncertain. How an entity moves from unconnected fragments to unquestioned building blocks involves following scientists' claims through the many trials and struggles of a wide politico-scientific world. Claims are not only constructed through 'normal' scientific activity at the lab bench or in the scientific journal, but also the deployment of bigger machines and the enrolling of many diverse interests (funding bodies, political patronage). For Latour, a scientific fact is dependent for its strength, not only on textual construction in reports, articles and research proposals (as discussed in chapter 5), but how it is used by the next generation.

> A sentence may be made more of a fact or more of an artefact depending on how it is inserted into other sentences. By itself a given sentence is neither a fact nor a fiction; it is made so by others, later on. (1987:25)

The link with the concept of intertextuality is clear. The movement towards a fact or artefact involves a period when a claim is undermined and threatened, its very basis questioned, even ridiculed. As more and powerful entities are enrolled, the facticity of a (successful) claim becomes accepted, appropriated by others and no longer a source of debate—the box is closing. Eventually, the claim is no longer associated with the writer and becomes part of the tacit knowledge of the group of users, leading to its incorporation in the claims of others. A successful journey can be outlined, based on Latour figure 1.6 (1987:44)

Original statement (A is B): Donna is in need of a children's home.

Negative modalities M-(A is B): No! Donna needs to sort out her relationship with her mother and should stay at home.

Positive and negative modalities M-+(A is B): Various contested voices on the appropriate intervention with Donna, some more powerful than others.

So and so has shown that (A is B): The case conference agreed that Donna's needs are best met by a children's home.

No modality at all (A is B): Request to children's homes for vacancy.

Tacit Knowledge (silence): Donna, the children's home resident.

Incorporation (instruments): Susan is like Donna (so she should be placed in a children's home).

In social work, however, challenges to 'facts' as building blocks can come from a number of sources. First, categorical claims (girls like Donna are appropriately placed in children's homes) can be undermined by different character formulations. A counter claim, 'but Susan is different from Donna in various ways', is acceptable. Second, whilst claims are dependent on later users, they are also dependent on evaluations of outcome, increasingly in the hands of others. There may not be a vacancy in the 'right' children's home; Donna might not settle in the children's home, despite everyone agreeing that it is an appropriate place. Social workers' formulations are provisional since the trials through which claims must pass become increasingly outside their control. Success or failure could be attributed to a wide range of contingent factors outside those which substantiated the original claim. Furthermore, such trials are immediate, since social work facts must be quickly operationalised into strategies. At the same time, unenrolled entities are inevitably resisting such blackboxing. Claims, then, are hedged with provisos. In summary, by treating social worker accounts as intertextual and sequential stories, we are able to follow the stabilising or subverting of social workers' claims.

Retellings

Two studies have looked at several occasions of telling of the 'same' story.[4] Bauman (1986) looks at 'tall stories' performed by a folk storyteller. The occasions of the retelling were for small groups of tourists, at public folk festivals and performances for the author. Shuman (1986) investigates different people telling the same story about the same fight between adolescents. Whilst there are important differences from the documents concerning Donna, both studies investigate the proposition that the 'same' story is being retold.

Bauman shows that the 'tall story' increased in length and detail over the three performances. He compares the different versions using a modified version of the structural schema of Labov and Waletsky (1967) and considers that the additions to the first telling are produced by taking advantage of the "structural opportunity afforded by the ellipsis already established in the first telling" (1986:92). The additions increase the cohesion of the story and different codas in particular "enhance the performative efficacy of the narration" (p.93). Bauman suggests that the additional features comment on the story and are important instructions to new audiences unfamiliar with background features understood by earlier listeners.

> All of these, like the more extended metanarrational statements, have the effect of bridging the gap between the narrated event and the storytelling event by reaching out phatically to the audience, giving identificational and participatory immediacy to the story. (p.100)

Bauman discusses the distinction between the narrated events and the narration event, noting how features were developed for less knowledgeable audiences. The extension must not go too far since it may lose the tension of the story, as the storyteller told Bauman:

> I like to make it a little longer because it keeps 'em from hearin' the end of it all at once, you know, keeps 'em in suspense a little bit longer. (Bauman, 1986:104)

The storyteller can be heard to create context, not only by the instructions to the audience, but managing their reaction. Even so features of content, plot and style remain across different retellings. In the private version for Bauman, the storyteller begins 'well folks'. As Bauman (1986:105) notes: "he is a public storyteller now, whether or not the public is present".

Shuman (1986) considered several versions of the 'same' event told by different people on different occasions about a fight between two adolescent girls in a high school. Like Bauman, she is concerned about the relationship between narrated events and narration event, which is developed through Young's distinction between the 'story realm' and the 'tale world' (p.140). The former refers to the occasion of the telling and the latter to the world inhabited by the characters in the tale. Shuman considers that entitlement and contextualisation are linked to the ability of the storyteller to justify his/her right to represent the 'tale world' in the 'story realm'. Some 'tale worlds' have almost universal access, fairy tales or detective stories; others are more restricted.

For the adolescents who witnessed the fight, the version in the newspaper told the facts but misrepresented the 'tale world'. It made inferences about violence in the school without understanding the context of the school and the relations between those involved. Stories told immediately after the fight were concerned with how the authorities were or should be reacting. When the incident was over, the point of the telling was to make claims to listeners about the importance of the incident and its implications, Labov's 'evaluation':

> ...the significance of stories told after a dispute was resolved was not a matter of currency or immediate relevance to the listeners, but had to be demonstrated in the telling. (Shuman, 1986:48)

In such stories, the evaluation is more important than suspense. Most of those who heard the fight story already know the outcome, but it is the explanation of the significance of the characters and events upon which the retelling is assessed.

The concept of evaluating significance seems particularly appropriate to an investigation of social work accounts. However, this should not underscore the importance of suspense in hearing social work stories. It suggests two different extremes of ratified audiences. 'First-time hearers' are unfamiliar with events and characters and must be given 'the facts', as well as their significance. They might include the judge, the researcher or when it is a new case. 'Informed hearers' are similar to those discussed by Shuman–they already know the 'facts' and are interested in their evaluation. This would be the old case, the colleague, other professionals and especially case planning meetings and reviews. There are a wide range of potential listeners between these extremes, not only informed about 'this case', but with differing access to commonly known scenarios amongst competent listeners. In the case of Donna, the ratified reader of Document 1 (appendix 5.1), the Principal Social Worker, would not know 'the facts' about Donna, but would be familiar with the type of case and their potential categorisation and significance. He may need to be held in suspense, in order to bring off appropriate categorisation, as was suggested with the 'narrative puzzle'.

Bauman and Shuman agree that retelling the 'same' story includes similarities and differences. The audience determines the nature of the telling, the 'story realm', but the 'tale world' or narrated events bears a relationship to other tellings. Indeed, each telling adds to the story. For Bauman, the storyteller expands later versions by emphasising the performance of the story. In contrast, blackboxing suggests reducing the story. As it becomes more of 'a fact', a précis of the story is enough to outline the situation, to remind ratified and informed listeners of the circumstances they all know. Shuman also notes the closure or resolved aspect of stories which are retold. When told outside the 'tale world', stories are less likely to be challenged and more likely to become 'blackboxed'.

> Stories told following the resolution of a conflict were often recounted to people removed from the situation described. When the situations had no direct consequences for the listeners, entitlement was less likely to be challenged. In contrast, stories told during an ongoing dispute often had immediate consequences for both listeners and tellers. (1986:50)

Retelling the 'same' story involves a complex range of processes which sets agendas and displays styles, genres and conventions for later versions. At the same time, reading occasions attend to a variety of informed and first-time readers. How later readers retell and re-write the story determines its success, as categorisation and closure enable an institutional, if provisional, story to emerge.

Following the 'assessment story' of Donna

The account of the 'Case-History (Summary) Report' (Document 1, appendix 5.1) is discussed in chapter 5. It is the first report of the case of Donna and the request for Full Assessment was accepted by the Principal Social Worker. In following the 'assessment story' we consider how it sets the scene for later retellings and to what extent it becomes 'blackboxed'. New story realms revisit and appropriate the tale world of Donna.

The features of the 'assessment story' are as follows. First, the plot was that this was a case of a 'serious' dispute between mother and daughter; problems had been developing over a long period. Second, work with the daughter remaining at home was unsuccessful, resulting in Donna running away and Mother refusing to have her back. Third, the characters were portrayed as a rejecting mother and an unhappy daughter. Fourth, Mother's reaction to Donna's sexual activity was considered the key feature with a hint at teenage prostitution. How do later texts retell the events of the admission? Later reading occasions construct different ratified readers, some informed, others first-time readers. Of particular interest is the handling of the key claims of the story—Mother's complete rejection of her daughter and Donna's sexual behaviour, described in chapter 5 as 'the narrative puzzle'.

Document 2: 'Report of Assessment Conference', 23 October

The 'Report of an Assessment Conference' (appendix 6.1) is the minutes of a case conference bringing together all those involved in the assessment process at the end of the Full Assessment. Six weeks after Document 1, Document 2 does not offer a persuasive imperative, (merely) reporting the key points of the discussion of the meeting. It is produced by a minute taker with an audience of informed readers who attended the meeting and contributed to the assessment process.[5] Being informed and ratified, these readers look to the report for description and evaluation rather than suspense or persuasion. The report makes available a structure which follows what can be heard by competent readers as a typical case conference—reports from the social worker, the school and the children's home followed by recommendations for action. The report draws together the 'bricolage' of the meeting into an institutional narrative.

Document 1 made the case for a Full Assessment on the basis of a serious breakdown between mother and daughter and the second document reaffirms that state of affairs. Between lines 1-9, the mother's rejection is made available through described speech and social worker evaluation:

> Donna's social worker reported that [mother] has indicated that she thinks she can manage one daughter (i.e. sister) at home. She wishes to keep her daughters apart. Donna is seen as immoral and badly behaved ... [social worker] did not think that [sister] would be home for long as [mother] does not have the emotional capacity to cope with adolescents.

The opening can be heard as oriented to the 'assessment story'. There is no explanation of the events of the admission to care with an audience of informed hearers to whom such events are well known. The state of affairs reaffirmed Mother's rejection because of Donna's sexual behaviour, but it is now supported by the social worker's assessment, giving it more factual status. Whereas Mother's voice in Document 1 implied her rejection, here the authority of the social worker changes it to a professional explanation of a character fault: she cannot cope with adolescents. The 'narrative puzzle' is beginning to be solved: it is mother's fault. Another witness also blames Mother: "[Grandmother] sees the problems as [mother's] responsibility" (line 10). Mother's 'preoccupation' with Donna's promiscuity is turned from self reporting to a character flaw, indeed hypocrisy:

> Donna's mother is preoccupied with the idea of Donna's sexual promiscuity. [Mother] does not see the birth of her two illegitimate daughters in the same light as Donna's behaviour. (lines 20-24)

The claim that Mother is overreacting is backed up by 'objective' evidence, since in the children's home there had been no sign of the "provocative behaviour described by her mother" (line 24-5). This is extended at lines 55-

60. The long term nature of the problem is displayed at line 31 with a description of earlier contact with a child guidance clinic. Overall, Document 2 can be heard to reaffirm the key features of the 'assessment story', displaying further evidence that amplifies the original assertions. Where Document 1 uses the mother's voice to tell the story and make the claim of 'serious rejection because of sexual behaviour', in Document 2 the social workers are the main speakers. The mother is constructed in an unsympathetic way and strong notions of blame attributed to her, thereby answering the 'narrative puzzle'. The events of the admission to care have been silenced, 'blackboxed' and the claims of the 'assessment story' have been reaffirmed and extended.

Further stories are made available offering the reader evidence that mother's rejection can be displayed rather than merely asserted. A second story can be heard as a 'synecdoche' (Atkinson, 1990:51), describing Mother's attendance at a psychiatric appointment:

> Since her admission Donna has had no contact with her mother. They met in Dr.__'s office on the 21 of October but [mother] was late for the appointment and did not acknowledge her daughter. Donna was extremely upset by this encounter. (line 61-65)

The extent of Mother's rejection is illustrated, confirming the impossibility of reconciliation. As with the admission to care, this story becomes definitive of the case of Donna: an event which dramatically displays the realities of the case of Donna that a mere professional assertion could not achieve. The tension of the event can be heard by initially asserting "no contact" (line 61), but then describing a meeting where the mother did not acknowledge her daughter's existence. Not just as no contact but complete rejection; mother was in the same room as her daughter but denied her presence. Such a formulation does more than illustrate rejection, it constitutes it.

A third story revisits the 'narrative puzzle' of Donna's sexual activity. Whilst at the children's home, there is no problem (lines 24-5 and 56-60). An incident outside the home suggests there may have been trouble in the past:

> However, [the previous social worker] walked through [town centre] with Donna one day and it became apparent that Donna is very well known by her peers, and they were subjected to a series of cat calls and obscene suggestions by various groups of boys. (lines 25-29)

Another definitive story is made available about Donna, also an event observed by a social worker.[6] This synecdoche revisits the dark and worrying aspect of the case, is she promiscuous? The 'narrative puzzle' is resolved by implying that there may have been trouble in the past but it is now being handled better in the children's home than by her mother:

> It was felt she may be benefiting by being able to stand back at [children's home] and form better relationships with boys rather than granting sexual favours as alleged by her mother. (lines 56-60)

Document 2 uses observed events to turn Donna's behaviour to a condemnation of Mother's handling of her daughter. The report of the children's home manager describes Donna's willingness to be "more forthcoming with information about herself and her situation" (lines 51-2). It can be heard as a sign that she is co-operative and entering into the helping process.

In summary, Document 2 can be heard to confirm and develop features of the 'assessment story'. Where Document 1 uses the mother's voice, Document 2 instructs the reader through social worker commentary and evidence. There is indeed a major breakdown in the mother-daughter relationship but the mother's depiction of Donna as "immoral and badly behaved" (line 4) is ironicised and turned into a blaming. Donna is now depicted as co-operative, reflective, vulnerable, yet beginning to deal with her problems; Mother is rejecting, emotionally lacking and hypocritical. 'The narrative puzzle' is partly resolved: mother is to blame for the rejection because of her own incapacities, but the fact of Donna's sexual past remains. The recommendation of the case conference is described with no discussion of alternative courses of action—a children's home is being sought with possibly a family placement later.

The strength of this position can be heard in two assertions about the future. First, "She should understand that she is not being prepared to return home" (lines 100-1) confirms Mother's rejection with no return home considered. Second, social services' control over Donna's future is displayed at the end. Even if Mother changes her mind, social services will stop her reclaiming Donna:

> If Donna's mother interferes and attempts to prevent action by Social Services a section 3 resolution should be implemented. (lines 103-5)

To threaten the use of a section 3 resolution[7] in this situation, can be heard by a competent hearer as indicating extreme resolve and certainty of direction. The 'assessment story' has become 'blackboxed', being revisited, reaffirmed and a basis for strong assertions. Such a claim relies on a direct link between the 'tale world' and 'story realm', the world of Donna is resolved by social services intervention and control. There is no suspense in the text but considerable evaluation.

Document 3: 'Profile', 5 November

This document (appendix 6.2) is sent to the managers of children's homes who may admit Donna and is written by a residential social worker at the children's home where the assessment is taking place. The audience are first-time readers and may scrutinise the report for suspense, (oh, what problem are they sending now?). It is a more comprehensive document, providing considerable information and evaluation about Donna. It can be heard to 'sell' her as a potential resident: how the 'tale world' of Donna might fit into the 'story realm' of a children's home. Her appearance, interests and relationships with her peers and staff are described, all hearable as no problem:

> She maintains a good standard of personal hygiene and takes considerable pride in her appearance and dress. (lines 4-6)

> Donna's interests are listening to music, watching television, collecting foreign currency, some reading and will participate in whatever activities are on offer. (lines 40-43)

> Recently Donna has formed one close relationship with a 13 year old girl here at [children's home] who she shares a room with. This relationship is one of confidence. Her relationship with other girls is of an easy friendship. Donna takes an active interest in boys and enjoys their company, and can be found at times holding 'court'. (lines 44-50)

> Staff here at [children's home] have found Donna to be quite forthcoming with information regarding her personal life and feelings ... She tends to somewhat kick against authority, but realises that when in need of support and advice that these are the people she needs to seek out. (lines 51-59)

Donna can be heard by the audience of children's home managers as a reasonable, almost perfect candidate for their children's home. Many of the features displayed are not merely descriptions of Donna but outline the hazards of managing children in a residential home—personal hygiene, arguments between children, threats to authority, co-operation in facing problems. In all of these, Donna can be heard as no problem. She is not perfect, but there appear to be enough positives to justify taking her on. School attendance is also depicted in this vein: it was a problem when she was at home, but has got better since admission to care and she is bright enough to make it a worthwhile enterprise (line 33-9). There may be problems with Donna but in the last analysis, she will not put up too much resistance to successful social work help. To work with Donna can be heard as potentially rewarding, with little disruption and possible success in educational and therapeutic terms.

Much of this information has not appeared in earlier documents, the character described is Donna, the children's home resident. Documents 1 and 2 construct Donna as the rejected daughter and develop her character as a victim of a hard-hearted mother. The 'assessment story' reappears in Document 3 but is less closed. In Document 2, there are no details of the admission. Here, the admission to care (lines 8-15) makes available a reasonable history of how Donna came into care and answers the question why social services has become involved. Furthermore, it can be heard to offer a description of the 'non existent relationship' between mother and daughter (lines 16-22). Such 'facts' provide a 'proper puzzle' (Smith, 1993) to the solution: this family has split up and a children's home can feel able to work with the young person without the interference of the mother. The mother's 'rejection' can be heard as completed rather than concurrent as with the earlier documents. Donna also concurs with the state of relations:

> According to [mother] she wants no dealings with Donna, nor to have her return home. Donna's feelings also coincides with mum in that she has no wish to return home, or resume her relationship with mother. (lines 18-22)

There are no modalities in the description of relations. It is heard as an unquestioned state of affairs, but not silent, as it offers the children's home a job to do.

Having access to earlier documents, the reader might ask why certain information is omitted. There is no mention of 'the narrative puzzle', the concerns of sexual activity and possible prostitution which dominated Document 1. It might be suggested that such 'deception' avoids scaring off the children's homes. Describing Donna as "beyond her (mother's) control and having a bad influence on her sister" (lines 10-11) is read as Mother's formulation. None of the "maladjusted" descriptions of Document 1 are available. 'Deception' might also be interpreted in the way the children's home is seen as the preferred option, supported by Donna not wanting fostering (lines 69-70). This is not what Document 2, the conference minutes, reports:

> ... a children's home is being sought but not necessarily for the next 3 years. She could still be prepared for a family as she might benefit from the challenge to form relationships in such an environment. (Document 2, line 96-100)

It is suggested, then, that Document 3 makes available aspects of the 'assessment story', both to frame a typical admission to care and to link Donna's problems to the job of residential social work. Document 3 can be heard to both describe the task of a children's home and to celebrate its potential, in contrast to a rejecting mother or a foster home. Unlike Document 2, where the 'assessment story' is revisited to substantiate mother's rejection, it is appropriated here to reaffirm the positive nature of the job. The rejection of

Donna is heard as an unquestioned state of affairs which attempts to enrol children's home managers. It is no longer controversial nor replete with recriminations; instead, it offers a closed past and directs the reader to the potential future in a children's home.[8] The link between the 'tale world' of Donna and the 'story realm' of the children's home is direct and persuasive, if deceptive.

Document 4: 'Progress Report', 18 November

This report (appendix 6.3) was written by the same residential social worker as Document 3 for the next review meeting. The audience are informed readers who probably attended the earlier meeting. Much of the detail is concerned with recent events in the children's home–absconding, relationships with staff and children, health and education updates. It is dated only two weeks after Document 3 but now Donna can be heard as a major management problem. There is a mixture of suspense and evaluation since an informed reader who attended the earlier meeting might be surprised at the range of new problems. Is she still that thoughtful girl whose sexual activity was her mother's preoccupation? She can be heard as absconding (lines 33-51), having 'fluctuating' relationships with staff (line 53) and having contacts with "friends of dubious reputation" (line 101).

The report begins with a reaffirmation of the state of the relationship between mother and daughter, using the same expression 'non existent' as Document 3:

> Since Donna's conference on 23 October up until the present, relations between (mother) and Donna have been non-existent. Donna has made no attempt to enquire about her mother nor has she shown any desire to do so. (lines 2-6)

Unlike document 3, the 'non-existent' relationship is not couched in the past, but in the ongoing present. Further illustration of the 'rejection' is offered by a detailed description of a telephone call to her sister:

> At no time during their conversation did Donna enquire about her mother, but stated that whenever she telephones again, she hopes her mother will not answer the 'phone because she does not want 'rejection' and the receiver hung up on her. Prior to Donna making this call, she had refused outrightly to talk to her mother if she did answer the telephone, and requested staff to remain with her just in case this should occur. (lines 11-19)

The 'rejection' of the 'assessment story' is made available. The reader can hear in a single incident the dynamics of how the state of affairs between Donna and her mother is constituted. Such a story illustrates the current state of relations through a description of action which stands for underlying feelings. At the same time, the 'rejection' of Donna can be heard as appropriated into the everyday life in a children's home: the telephone call home. There is no discussion of other conversations where Donna talks about her mother to residential staff nor professional assessment. Like the story of the walk through the town centre and the encounter at the psychiatric interview, these cameo stories have begun to take on mythical proportions, providing events which illustrate and constitute the definitive state of affairs.

The word 'rejection' (line 15) in inverted commas can be read as reported speech: Donna does not want a rejecting reaction from her mother on the phone. It is unlikely that the report writer heard or expects the reader to hear Donna use the word 'rejection'. Whatever Donna said, it is heard as performing the state of 'rejection' as opposed to hearing the word rejection. This is 'what she is really saying'. The reader can link the cameo with a psychological concept of 'rejection' which underpins the 'assessment story'. A small piece of action is again able to be heard as evidence for a wider claim.

Further evidence of the extreme nature of this 'rejection' is available in the contrast with Donna's harmonious relations with her sister and her grandmother. After a phone conversation with her sister she "sounded quite pleased to hear her voice" (lines 10-11). The contact with the grandmother is exuberant with upgraded terms and a building sense of achievement: phone call, weekend stay that went well, planned Christmas stay and alternate weekend stays in future (lines 20-29). Such a contrast can be heard to display Donna as hard at doing family work, whilst being rejected by her mother. The characters of a rejecting mother and harmed but family-centred daughter are reconfirmed.

A new state of affairs is made available. The sexual behaviour of Donna is no longer only the mother's version of events, but has become a management problem for the residential staff. The 'narrative puzzle' returns and is less resolved than in document 2. Her sexual activity is now made available as a feature which has been around for some time:

> Donna's interest in the opposite sex has not lessened, but has taken second place at the moment for some unknown reason. (lines 81-3)

Such a comment is in contrast to Document 2, where it is presented as no problem in the children's home but maybe outside and a preoccupation of Mother. Here, it can be heard as an ongoing concern which is temporarily quiet. Later, there is concern expressed about her wishing to make contact with an older woman who "used to be a prostitute" (line 104). Mother's picture of a promiscuous girl with contacts in prostitution can be seen to transfer from an (irrational) 'preoccupation' to a major concern for residential staff.

In summary, the 'assessment story' is being appropriated, added to, but also modified. The key features of relationship breakdown and mother's rejection have been revisited and reaffirmed. Donna's sexual behaviour and absconding have become a major management issue, hearable as an ongoing concern. Donna is summarised thus:

> Donna continues to need firm and consistent control. In saying this it has been noted that Donna tends to be more accepting of certain points and comments where her attitude is concerned and it is felt that with this consistency that we might see some positive results. (lines 110-116)

Donna is still heard as appropriate for 'consistent' residential care but it is not so easy now. As the mother can be heard to move further away from everyday involvement in Donna's affairs, her sexual 'preoccupation' is less necessary to illustrate the source of the breakdown and can/must be taken over as the legitimate concern of the children's home. Document 4 reports on the 'tale world' of residential care, as the controversy of the entry into care is transferred into an ongoing task of control. The black box of the 'narrative puzzle' is reopened in the light of the current state of affairs. Furthermore, its retention legitimises why Donna is where she is and why social work with her is necessary. In reaffirming the 'puzzle', we reaffirm social work.

Document 5: 'Interview with the Social Worker', the following May

This is a long and complex account,[9] produced eight months after the events above, involving the second social worker and the researcher. This social worker had not written any of the previous documents but can be heard to revisit and reaffirm some of the stories made available there. Not only is the 'assessment story' heard, but also some of the other cameos—the walk through the town centre, the assessment interview where mother ignored her daughter, though not the telephone story. The characters of mother and daughter are presented with much greater information and evaluation. The mother is not merely depicted as hard-hearted but a detailed character assessment is offered. Information is made available about her history in care, family relations and an attitude of fatalism linked to Thomas Hardy, in order to explain her rejection of her daughter. Donna is also hearable as a more rounded character—bright, mature and "sexually very aware".

Whilst it might be expected that eight months of social worker contact has enabled further 'data collection' on the case, the 'assessment story' continues to be heard, both in an unaltered set of words and in the formulation of characters and states of affairs. Controversial features of the earlier documents are reaffirmed and enhanced but there is little in the way of 'silence'. If anything, there is more 'noise' as each feature of the 'assessment story' is repeated and accounted for. Such a deluge of information and opinion constructs the ratified reader, the research interviewer. A description of the case from the initial contact has been invited, allowing the social worker to revisit and recount eight months of stories and occasions of storytelling for a first-time hearer. Retellings have rehearsed and polished the story which can be heard as detailed, logical and coherent.

As with other interviews presented in these data, the opening description is long and largely uninterrupted, making available events and detailed descriptions of characters and states of affairs. The 'assessment story' can be heard at several points. First, the admission to care was because of long-standing problems:

> I first became involved because the children came into care there'd been child care problems for some time with mother complaining about Donna mostly (-) she's bad and [sister] is good

Mother as the complainant and Donna depicted as 'bad' can be heard again.[10] A similar formulation of Mother as someone not capable of looking after adolescents is made available:

> I met with Mother[11] and that in one way intransigence and intensity I thought the prospect of Donna going back very remote cos I don't think Mum is able to meet the needs of adolescent girls and she's held out on that but I didn't foresee Donna being placed back home and the thing was to get her in a place of safety and security cos she was heavily involved with sort of sexual activity ...

The opening of this document makes available mother's character, her 'intransigence/ fatalism', setting the scene for the story. The reader is able to discover her character as explaining how the events of the story unfolded, a 'psychological' narrative (Todorov, 1977). In the previous documents, we have heard events with little character development.

As with Document 4, Donna's sexual activity can now be heard to be appropriated by the professionals as the problem they face but it is also offered as a result of mother's character. The 'narrative puzzle' of whether mother was over-exaggerating or Donna's sexual behaviour existed independent of mother's 'preoccupation' is laid out:

> ...but her concern over Donna was that she was sexually acting out all over the place and this was shocking and terrible and monstrous and sex was (-) the way she talked they were both virgin births (-) sex just didn't exist...

> ...she's sexually very aware has had a great deal of experience (-) that I'm sure about (-) it has been mooted that it might be fantasy and because of the stuff she's written in her diaries it's extremely graphic and I think based on fact...

Donna's sexual activity is true and an overreaction by mother. The 'narrative puzzle' has been resolved by agreeing with both versions of the story. It is interesting to note how the comment "the way she talked they were both virgin births" appeared in Document 2 as "she does not see the birth of her two illegitimate daughters in the same light as Donna's behaviour", written by the minute taker. Such a rhetorical feature ironicises Mother's position and bears repeating, further confirming the interlinking of texts.

As things have moved on, so the 'narrative puzzle' is no longer controversial. Mother's rejection is no longer a proposition which is required to justify action, as it is available in the continuing non-contact. The need to lay all the blame on the mother for both the rejection and the 'preoccupation' is no longer necessary. A sympathetic depiction of mother's character can be made available. At the height of the crisis, such a view would not have been heard, as the justification for Full Assessment required categorised depictions—a rejecting mother and harmed daughter. Now the response can be softer. Shuman (1986:48) notes that at the end of a dispute:

> [a story] could be reported without exaggeration, often the triviality of the offence specifically mentioned.

It is not suggested that exaggeration or trivialising Donna's circumstances has occurred; the use of such terms suggests an objective level of reporting. With Woolgar (1980) and Smith (1993), we see events and their representation as inseparable. Even so, the force of the rhetoric can be seen to have altered, as the story is 'blackboxed' and no longer controversial. Character depictions are now relativised and complex. This sympathetic hearing of the mother can be contrasted with the moral condemnation of the mother in the 'failure to thrive' case in chapter 5 which was still disputed and controversial.

Another element of the 'assessment story' was the formulation that, as a result of the serious breakdown/rejection, it was no longer appropriate to attempt to work with the mother and daughter together. This is available in the work of the Documents 2 and 3, offering a role for residential social work. Similar conclusions are offered here but with a twist:

> ...I'm not doing any family work but there's no one else to take it on.

And later this is linked to a retelling of the psychiatric appointment story:

> ...so really it was from that point on that one felt there was no return home (-) and Donna herself didn't want to discuss returning home...

But it could have been otherwise. At the beginning of the description of mother's character, an alternative formulation of the nature of the case is offered:

> ...a few years ago if the case would come it would be in terms of having long term casework with Mum which I'm sure she would actually be able to benefit from but as there's no motivation from her at the moment at all I'm not investing my time in that...

and again near the end of the interview:

> ...as I said earlier if the clock went back ten years I would probably be working avidly in building up a relationship and all that with mother and I would see that as a tool [unclear] piece of work to do that but I can't be bothered to make the investment now...

At the beginning and end of the interview, it is now even possible to suggest that the last eight months of constructing the breakdown/rejection formulation as the basis of this case could have been done differently. Instead of responding to the crisis by admitting Donna into care and permanently separating her from her mother, an appropriate (if old fashioned) intervention could have aimed at counselling Mother. A competent hearer can hear words like "long term casework" and "building up a relationship" as suggesting an alternative intervention—working on Mother's problems, possibly looking to her becoming aware of why she was having problems with Donna, perhaps Donna going home—all unthinkable in mid-October. Such a direction is heard to be rejected because of time and interest and is contrasted at the end with a different way of working that this social worker now favours:

> ...I'm more interested in [mother] and Donna maintaining their family relationships their relationship systems rather than going into their internal world and start plucking around there...

This contrast can be heard as two conceptions of this case, but also two different approaches to social work, juxtaposed in a preferred/dispreferred comparison. Either way a different trajectory to the whole story is now being offered and rejected. Telling social work stories can be heard to manipulate and juxtapose versions of what constitutes events, characters and social work. Following the 'assessment story' has proved relatively straightforward. The story has been stabilised to some extent and on some occasions but not necessarily because it is accepted unquestioningly by all participants. It has been closed and opened as the occasion demands. At the same time, retelling occasions have reacted to the clarity and simple justification which the 'assessment' story made available and the crisis required. The 'assessment story' and the need to resolve the 'narrative puzzle' has played an important role in revisiting, affirming or modifying states of affairs. Document 2 can be heard as reaffirming much of 'the assessment story' and beginning to offer a strong view as to the resolution of the 'narrative puzzle': it was all mother's fault. Document 3 trades on this version of events whilst ignoring the 'narrative puzzle' which had set it up. It appears too concerned with its marketing role. Document 4 resists the possible resolution of Document 2, re-opening the 'narrative puzzle', Donna's sexual activity was real enough. Finally, with the controversy over and the long term future of Donna marked out, Document 5 can retell the story and be more circumspect in its claims and sympathetic in its blamings, even suggesting viable alternative versions.

The 'assessment story' did survive to some extent the various trials and reaffirmations. Throughout the eight months the state of affairs of the relationship between Donna and her mother was told in the same way–it was a rejection, a serious irrevocable breakdown. From an institutional viewpoint, it was unchanged, a placement away from home was needed. There were variations for different audiences with reformulations, modifications and things just generally calmed down. The controversy subsided, being strong and categorical did not matter so much now; until 'it could have been otherwise'.

Is the 'assessment story' a 'basic story' on which are based all the other versions, as Chatman (1978) might suggest? The 'assessment story' has become an institutionalised version of events. At retelling occasions, familiar features are available. All the documents can be read to affirm that there is a serious breakdown in the mother-child relationship, all but the last blame this on the mother, all but Document 3 have a 'narrative puzzle' about Donna's sexual behaviour. Whilst there are similarities, locating the 'assessment story' needs investigative work on the part of the reader. Furthermore, the additions and modifications are such that the 'assessment story' is placed in differing relations with newer stories. They could be heard to support it as long as there is an informed reader. For example, to see the 'telephone call' story as extending and adding to the 'assessment story' requires a ratified reading that 'rejection' is being demonstrated.

This suggests that 'blackboxing' takes place on at least two levels: the story and the reading. In the first, groups of events, experiences and descriptions are formed into stories which float around social workers' storytelling performances. Second, to be made available for reading, such stories need to be appropriated and turned into synecdoche. They are added to the stock of available stories which are read as supporting the accepted state of affairs. Hence, the 'telephone story' can be read to support the institutionally accepted 'assessment story'. Although the 'assessment story' is not challenged until

Document 5, its relations with the newer stories alters. Eventually, it becomes silenced because it is no longer relevant. Other stories take over: Donna as the children's home resident, Donna as the absconder, Mother as a fatalist. By Document 5, the silenced story is even available to be reopened, altered and seen as a version. Newer stories are strong enough and caught up in other concerns; no one need worry about its demise.

This chapter has confirmed that features discussed in chapters 4 and 5, moral characterisations and fact construction, when combined with 'narrative puzzles', are able to form strong and ratified versions of events. Through a series of constructions of informed and first-time reading situations, the 'tale world' of Donna is made available in the 'story realm' of a variety of institutionalised reading occasions. A network of interconnected stories and storytelling encounters can be heard to set up alliances and strong formations, which, for a time, appear so strong as to be tacitly accepted. Actor network theory studies the construction of associations, alliances and networks, where entities are brought together and temporarily form apparently unassailable formations. Law (1986:70) describes a process of 'interessment':

> [interessment] may be defined as the action of interesting, enrolling and translating. It will be recalled that to translate is to speak for others, to make oneself indispensable and thereby determine and allocate roles and to decide what may be exchanged between the occupants of those roles. It is, in short, to impose a structure upon others.

Could a different network of characters and entities have been configured? Just suppose that the social worker did have time and belief in the alternative version, could he have interested, enrolled and translated the residential social workers and the case conference? Suppose that the then department policy of placing children in families was insisted on by the Principal Social Worker, would a strong story have constructed Donna, the foster child? Suppose that the new stipulation in the *Children Act,* 1989 was in force to require the investigation of placement with the extended family. Suppose the recent discourses to stress family responsibility had been interpreted to refuse a placement in care in the first place, suppose... suppose... so many alternative versions but the child care assessment system can only cope with one at a time and tries hard to 'blackbox' a strong story to direct future action.

Coda: 'It could have been otherwise'

Much has been made of 'it could have been otherwise', the social worker's formulation, identified in Document 5. What if it is turned round on the author?

The reader has so far heard the case told in a chronological way, starting with the first report of September and moving through various documents up to the following May. The author, however, did not approach the material in that way, as his entry to the case was via the interview. He looked at the documents later and he was not so surprised by the changes in the story. Does this suggest that his retelling has manufactured the suspense in order to support a contention of 'narrative puzzle'? The interview can be read as juxtaposing versions as the social worker introduces the idea that he could have read the situation in another way. Heard in isolation from the other documents, such a formulation does not trade on a 'narrative puzzle', but as a justification for one version of events rather than another. There is no surprise in the resolution, as the author has attempted with the reader. Instead, there is a construction of one version of events by contrasting it with another.

The social worker in the interview also offers a justification of why his role was carried out a particular and possibly unconventional way. After re-emphasising his decision not to offer long term casework with the mother, he outlines his current role with Donna:

... similarly with Donna my contact with her is not the traditional child care officer role (-) I see her every three to four weeks (-) I see the primary caring unit is (new children's home) doing their work and I'm involved peripheral to that (-) but any negotiations that it's helpful to do then I'll do them (-) but I'm not in to activating things because I have the responsibility (-) rather it's the other way round isn't it they've got the day to day care they should have the responsibility rather than me saying this that or the other.

Has the reader been misled? Has the narrative puzzle been manufactured to ironicise the strength of the early texts which the author knew from the beginning could have been read differently?

Rather than tricking the reader, the narrative puzzle has surely re-emphasised the temporary configuration of reading relations, but which, on occasion, replay earlier motifs in a fix manner. We have seen that the early documents when read in isolation offer a strong and 'blackboxed' institutionalised story, so strong that they keep reappearing. But there are so many reading relations with these texts. Document 5, a laid-back chat with a researcher about a case that is no longer causing much trouble and where uncertainties do not matter, should not be seen as any more definitive than the others. For example, the children's home manager who received Document 3 may not see Document 4 and may be said to have heard half the story. A case conference participant from Document 2 may be surprised by the change in recommendation in Document 3; what happened to the family placement suggestion? Each reader has part of the story. This analysis has tried to present the ratified reading occasions around these documents, but each occasion is required to revisit earlier ones. We are privileged readers, not ratified readers We still do not have the definitive story, just a wider range of stories and reading relations around these texts which produce versions and versions of versions. That a strong story and a narrative puzzle was available across at least some texts and reading occasions is all the more remarkable.

But 'it could have been otherwise' theoretically as well. The description of rhetorical features and the overall metaphor of 'blackboxing' has made use of theories which, whilst not concerned with realist versions of events, do attempt to suggest a certain version of events privileges a particular reading of data. The construction of facts, the allocation of blame and the 'narrative puzzle' have been pointed out to the reader as being available, can't you read them, look, there as well? Isn't this a pretty convincing theoretical approach to reading versions. Or is it one amongst many?

I lied earlier. There is another attempt to trace a story through several texts. Hak (1989) considers several texts concerning a psychiatric case, consisting of transcripts of interviews and a final report. He approaches the data differently to Bauman and Shuman, concerned less with the story, as with the 'transformation' of one phrase 'sex(ual) life'. He is also concerned with imputing into the report the use of 'psychiatric knowledge'. His conclusion is that:

> Thus, the report is an interaction of two simultaneous 'reading processes'. On the one hand, a situation is read for 'findings' and on the other hand psychiatric 'knowledge' is at the same time consulted for diagnoses. 'Psychiatric practice' apparently consists in the ability to have both processes simultaneously resulting in a common product: a case that represents the situation of a particular person and a 'knowledge' all in one. (Hak 1989:87-8)

Why the deceit? Why the worry about this approach? Isn't the conclusion in line with the approach here–that events are presented as hearable in terms of a professionally competent reader and, hence, construct competent professional work?

The formulation 'it could have been otherwise' can be heard to raise a potentially undermining alternative and then reject it. The concern about Hak is less with the conclusion than the methods. He is concerned with seeing one phrase as 'transforming' through the texts to produce a particular reading. With the help of Hodge's (1989) criticism of Hak, I will now attempt to reject this alternative version and reinstate the version so far presented, thereby using the 'it could have been otherwise' formulation.

Hak attempts to offer a 'formal method' of analysis, in particular a 'transformational method'. His aim is to 'describe literally' (1989:76) rather than interpret. To do this, Hak makes use of Foucault's idea of genealogy. He considers Foucault developed this in order to "relate unique events with underlying structures", not as identical but 'difference'.

> The relation between two utterances is not located any more in their common origin in an underlying structure but instead in the transformative mechanism that produces the one (the paraphrase or reading) from the other (the origin) ... It is my contention that this literal description of reading processes provides a sociological description of social practice. (1989:78)

Hak establishes 'genealogical chains', whereby the final text is considered to be the product of transformations of utterances from the earlier texts. Drawing on

Pecheux and Harris, he is interested in a formal method, where utterances are considered for their form and positioning in a text; the placement of identical words. He considers, quoting Pecheux, that such transformations offer an 'objective' analysis:

> ... without using any knowledge of the meaning of its morphemes or the intentions of its author ... the use of effective algorithmic procedures (is) free of any 'subjective' addition. (p.77)

As Hodge (1989:101) notes, the core of Hak's claim is to be "objective, formal and scientific". Hak considers the transformation sequence which he follows, 'sex(ual) life', is changed from a denial by the father, to a discovery of incest in his own words and to a cover up by the psychiatrist. However, as Hodge notes, Hak is not clear about the attribution of utterances to utterer:

> In fact it is clear that in the interview the girl did give descriptions of activities which could legitimately be labelled 'her sex(ual) life'. It is difficult to justify that the father has any monopoly of the term. So the transposition Hak notes (from "(my = the father's) sexual life" into "her (=Anna-Lize's) sex life") has as its primary agent not the psychiatric assistant nor psychiatry itself, but Hak the analyst. (1989:103)

Hodge goes on to offer another analysis of the text. The use of 'objective and scientific' by Hak suggests a lack of the scepticism which has been a feature of the approach here. Nor is there a conception of the reader, whether ratified or privileged. To read Hak's 'sex(ual) life' statements as representing formal relations outside the occasion of the reading is contrary to an approach which is concerned with reading made available through many possible relations between writer, reading, text and context. Blackboxing has been demonstrated in Donna's story as less the transformation of particular statements through the five texts, since the 'same' words were not necessarily used or transformed in a formal way. It is the concerns of readers and writers to respond to and interact with other significant occasions of the telling the 'same' story. In particular, the telling of the 'same' story is a feature which is attended to and revisited in each occasion of the reading. It is this which is the institutionalised version, the occasion of re-reading the 'same' story when it is (re)constructed, not when a particular utterance reappears or is transformed.

Conclusion of Conclusion

This chapter has offered an extended coda, in which it has been suggested that storytellers use the formulation 'It could have been otherwise' to offer up alternative versions, but also to reject them. It can be heard as a strong feature to demonstrate to the reader that the storyteller is aware of how things may have been different, to offer a twist in the story, but also to confirm the original formulation. For the social worker, the formulation is able to demonstrate that an alternative was available and professionally acceptable, but would not work here. For the author, it has been used to revisit the problem of attributing meaning from 'scattered expressions of members' (Hak 1989:76).

Rather than look to formal methods, which offer 'objective' readings of texts or external knowledge schemas, this project has re-affirmed a focus on reading occasions of the factual and moral narrative by competent and ratified professional readers. Both the social worker and author are displayed as fair-minded, open to other ideas, eclectic, but confident of their position.

NOTES

[1] Pithouse and Atkinson (1988:187) consider that in social work:
> Occupational failure is rarely looked for in the worker's own abilities or in the occupational mission itself. Demoralising failure is attributed to others. Frequently it is the clients themselves who are seen as the main cause of an intervention with little prospect of success.

It was noted in chapter 4 how blaming as a feature of moral storytelling was not attributable to particular social workers. As with other texts concerned with unpredictable entities like people, using formulations to justify and recommend action, making definitive claims and attributing causes and effect, involves accounting practices littered with provisos and conjecture.

[2] The 'assessment story' refers to the events of the admission to care and how they should be interpreted. The 'case of Donna' refers to the subsequent accumulation of information on and categorisation of Donna and what to do next. The former is considered to be a key feature of the latter: who she is depends on what happened, at least in the first instance. Or to use narrative terms, plot determines character.

[3] Studies of conversational storytelling have investigated the powerful but also precarious nature of 'he said she said' stories, as the words of other storytellers are used to support claims (Shuman 1986, Goodwin 1990).

[4] I will continue to place 'same' in inverted commas, as depicting events as the 'same' is an interactional and rhetorical task, and not an *a priori*.

[5] Minutes of meetings record only particular contributions and, perhaps, reflect the views of certain key participants, especially the Chair. In other research, we observed how unwelcome points of view were left out of the minutes (Packman and Hall, forthcoming).

[6] Isn't it surprising that in the six weeks since the admission to care, social workers, who have seen Donna for perhaps an hour once a week, have observed the quintessential events of this case!

[7] A section 3 resolution was the method of dispensing with a parents' 'rights and duties'. It provided social services with similar power to a care order but without going to court. It was seen as controversial and used only if parents were considered to be sabotaging plans which were considered in the child's best interests. It is no longer available following the *Children Act*, 1989.

[8] Since the late 1970s, a strong view in social work has seen residential care as damaging to children. Wherever possible, children should be placed with foster parents,

adopted or returned home quickly. This has been called the 'permanency planning movement' (Maluccio et al, 1986) although it is less clear how far this approach can be applied to adolescents.

[9] This interview is referred to but not presented in full, as it amounts to some 14 pages of transcript.

[10] Note the new information–the sister came into care earlier than Donna for a weekend and returned home quickly–odd that hasn't appeared before. There will probably be a file on Jane somewhere, but a strange example of 'non -intertextuality' all the same.

[11] Note that both the text writers and the author have moved between 'Mother' and 'the mother' or 'her mother'. The first implies a character, the second a role. In Documents 1 and 2, Mother was more prominent perhaps reflecting the social worker writer's work with her, whilst Documents 3 and 4 are written by residential staff who have less contact. Note the familiarity now extends to 'Mum'. Furthermore, by using a capital letter in interview transcripts the author has departed from his convention of avoiding punctuation since it imposes an order on the text. In making such a move here, he has imposed on this text that Mother is to be read as a character.

APPENDIX 6.1 DOCUMENT 2
Report of an assessment conference

Re: Donna
Present: Principal Social Worker (Chair)
            Education Welfare Officer
            Residential Social worker
            Placement Officer
            Social Worker
            Educational Psychologist
            Children's home manager

Minutes

Donna's social worker reported that [mother] has indicated that she thinks she can manage with one daughter (i.e. Donna's sister) at home. She wishes to keep her daughters apart. Donna is seen as immoral and badly behaved and if sister misbehaves it is invariably seen as Donna's fault. [Social worker] did not think that [sister] would be at home for long as [mother] does not have the emotional capacity to cope with adolescents.

[Grandmother] sees the problems as mother's responsibility. She does not wish to interfere or influence any decisions taken concerning Donna. [Grandmother] has telephoned Donna since her admission to [children's home] but has not visited her. Donna has not expressed any particular desire to see her grandmother. Donna's mother and grandmother fear an inevitable permanent breach in the family so they always 'agree to disagree' rather than co-operating and trying to find a solution to their problems.

Donna's mother is preoccupied with the idea of Donna's sexual promiscuity. [Mother] does not see the birth of her two illegitimate daughters in the same light as Donna's behaviour. At [children's home] Donna has not shown any signs of the kind of provocative behaviour described by her mother. However, the previous social worker walked through [the town centre] with Donna one day and it became apparent that Donna is very well known to her peers, and they were subjected to a series of cat calls and obscene suggestions by various groups of boys.

Donna's mother referred her daughter to the local Child Guidance Clinic last year but only one interview took place and the conference did not have any information about the outcome of this visit.

Donna's father lives in the area near to her school. Apparently [father] is a [occupation] and on one occasion visits the school in a professional capacity. He met Donna and introduced himself as her father.

EDUCATION
Prior to coming to [children's home], Donna's attendance at school was very poor and she was often late. On several occasions she has been suspected of stealing at school but never challenged to her face. She was described as being 'a law unto herself' and not concerned with the school rules or her performance. Her attitude to school has improved since her admission to the children's home. She attends regularly and is more receptive to advice and reprimands.

[Children's home manager] reported that since coming to [children's home] Donna has become more articulate and is more forthcoming with information about herself and her situation. She has begun to realise that such information is not necessarily going to be 'used against her'. Contrary to the information supplied by her mother Donna's attitude to boys is to let them approach her rather than actively seek their attention. It was felt she may be benefiting by being able to stand back at [children's home] and form better relationships with boys rather than granting sexual favours as alleged by her mother.

Since her admission Donna has had no contact with her mother. They met in the psychiatrist's office on the 21st of October but [mother] was late for the appointment and did not acknowledge her daughter. Donna was extremely upset by this encounter. She had previously considered writing to her mother to make some kind of contact but neither seems ready to make the first move. Both mother and daughter like to have a sense of control and neither want to back down. Mother may feel uncomfortable visiting the children's home. On one occasion she wanted to send [sister] to visit Donna. It was felt by the conference that contact with [sister] should not be controlled by [mother]. She may be using the sister as a form of go-between to find out what is going on.

RECOMMENDATIONS

[Social worker] should attempt to contact [father] to inform him that Donna is in care and may possibly go into long term care.

[Social worker] should make a request to the school for a formal report as to how Donna is functioning at school at the moment.

Contact with Donna's grandmother should be encouraged if Donna expresses the desire to see her.

Donna should be encouraged to write to [sister] and possibly inquire after her mother.

[Mother] should be given positive feedback from the social worker about what is happening to her daughter at [children's home]. He should do this in the form of a letter and suggest that the 2 girls would benefit from contact.

Donna should be given positive feedback about herself by the children's home. Staff should reinforce the idea that it can be helpful to express one's feelings rather than harmful.

It should be made known to Donna that a children's home is being sought but not necessarily for the next 3 years. She could still be prepared for a family as she might benefit from the challenge to form relationships in such an environment. She should understand that she is not being prepared to return home.

Donna should be invited to the next review.

If Donna's mother interferes and attempts to prevent action by Social Services a section 3 resolution should be implemented.

Review 20/11

APPENDIX 6.2 DOCUMENT 3
Report from a children's home

Profile on Donna   (DOB   )

Donna is a pretty fourteen year old girl who is somewhat small for her age, being of slight build and height. She maintains a good standard of personal hygiene and takes considerable pride in her appearance and dress. Donna has been living at home with her mother and younger sister up until her admission to [children's home] on 2nd September. The reason surrounding her admission was because her mother felt Donna to be beyond her control and having a bad influence on her sister, subsequently Donna ran away from home on two occasions. The first stay being at her grandmother's, the most serious being three days on the run, this leading to her admission to [children's home].

Since admission, Donna's relationship with mother has been non existent. Neither Donna nor mother has made any attempt to bridge the gap between them. According to [mother] she wants no dealings with Donna, nor to have her return home. Donna's feelings also coincides with mum in that she has no wish to return home, or resume her relationship with mother. Donna retains a normal relationship with her sister, although according to Donna her social worker has passed on to her that mum does not wish for [sister] to visit Donna here.

[Father] has recently made contact with Donna at school and on two occasions has given her a lift home in his car. Donna has stated that she is unsure of her feelings towards him owing to the fact that she has had no contact with him for at least 7-8 years.

Whilst at [children's home] Donna has continued to attend [school] where there has been a great improvement in her attendance. She still has some difficulty in being punctual, but with the help from the staff at [children's home] and school this has somewhat lessened. Report from school is that Donna is an extremely bright girl, but fails to use her full potential, however, with the guidance of staff and liaison with [school], Donna has shown a marked improvement.

Donna's interests are listening to music, watching
television, collecting foreign currency, some reading
and will participate in whatever outside activities are
on offer, as she enjoys being out and about.

Recently Donna formed one close relationship with a 13
year old girl here at [children's home], who she shares
a room with. This relationship is one of confidence.
Her relationship with other girls is of an easy friendship. Donna takes an active interest in boys and enjoys
their company, and can be found at times holding
'court'.

Staff here at [children's home] have found Donna to be
quite forthcoming with information regarding her personal life and feelings. However, this has to be on a
one to one basis, as Donna tends to find in a group
setting, i.e. staff or girls, that most things in general 'are a big joke'. She tends to somewhat kick
against authority, but realises that when in need of
support and advice that these are the people she needs
to seek out.

The conference decision is for social worker to make an
attempt to contact [father] to inform of Donna's admission to care and the possibility of this being long
term, also to encourage contact between grandmother as
Donna has expressed a wish for this. Encouragement is
also given to her contact with her [sister] whereby she
can gain information on mother.

As well as conference recommendation for Donna to move
to a children's home, Donna has also expressed this
wish as she sees [Teenager Fostering Project] as not
being sufficient for her needs. She feels she will
benefit far more from an environment where she could
have recourse to a much larger number of adults of
differing personalities.

Donna has mixed feelings about what exactly she wants
from life. The staff at [children's home], through
close working with Donna realises she needs stability,
affection, coupled with strong authority, also self
esteem needs to be built up and for her to realise that
love can be gained through caring and not through ex-
ploration of herself.

APPENDIX 6.3 DOCUMENT 4

Progress report

NAME   Donna   DATE REVIEW

Feelings Concerning Parents and Siblings

Since Donna's conference on 23rd October, up until the present, relations between [mother] and Donna have been non-existent, Donna has made no attempt to enquire about her mother, nor has she shown any desire to do so. In addition, since Donna has become aware of her mother's feelings about her not wishing her sister to visit her at [children's home] there has been no contact between them; however, through constant encouragement, Donna has now telephoned [sister] and sounded quite pleased to hear her voice. At no time during their conversation did Donna enquire about her mother, but stated that whenever she telephones again, she hopes her mother will not answer the 'phone because she does not want 'rejection' and the receiver hung up on her. Prior to Donna making this call, she had refused outrightly to talk to her mother if she did answer the telephone, and requested staff to remain with her just in case this should occur.

On 8th November, Donna telephoned her grandmother. She was extremely pleased to hear from her, and was very willing to have Donna spend the weekend with her. On return from this visit, Donna let it be known that she had an enjoyable time and expressed a keen desire to spend her Christmas with both grandmother and great grandmother, as they live together. Furthermore, [grandmother] has extended the invitation for Donna to spend alternate weekends with her if the children's home is in agreement.

Donna has passed on to staff that her father works at [workplace] but had no further encounters with him since January/ February.

Absconded Details

On 25 October, Donna absconded from [children's home] accompanied by another young girl, who is also resident here. This came about after Donna had received a telephone call from someone claiming to be a friend, which we later found out was [resident]. Later on that evening, Donna was spoken to by two members of staff who informed her that they were under a strong impression that she has plans to abscond with [resident], also that we had knowledge that it was [resident] that she had received the telephone call from earlier in the day. Donna then confessed her plans for running with [resident] and they had planned to go to a party in [area]. She then went to say that she realised that this was wrong and had already changed her mind about accompanying [resident]. However, at 9.55p.m. it was realised that Donna was missing from her bedroom; a search for [resident] also proved the same. Donna had after all done exactly what she said she would not do!

Relations with staff

Donna's relationship with staff fluctuates from day to day depending on the circumstances she is in. It has been observed that whenever Donna is confronted and corrected about her general attitude she will agree to conform, but will continue to do exactly as she pleases. One such occasion was 12.11 when Donna failed to return home from school at the set time. She eventually waltzed in at 6.30p.m. stating that she had decided to visit her friend's home, having met her in the street, claiming she had not seen her for a month. On account of Donna's failure to return she was notified as an absconder to the police.

Relationship with other children

Donna maintains a good relationship with most of the girls, and her friendship accepted by them all. Recently Donna has formed a close friendship here at [children's home] with another girl of the same age, but unfortunately their friendship has suffered on account of another girl who has caused much disharmony amongst all the girls, claiming a powerful hold over their lives in [children's home]. Donna has shown at times that she can hold her own against this girl, nor can be influenced by her actions.

Recently, [children's home] admitted two little emergency girls and during their stay, Donna demonstrated a caring and helpful nature towards them and expressed an interest in caring for children when she is older.

Donna's interest in the opposite sex has not lessened, but has taken second place at the moment for some unknown reason.

Health and Mannerisms
Donna has complained on several occasions of feeling unwell and of sore throat - a course of anti-biotics were prescribed which she is still taking. In addition, Donna had contracted chickenpox which is now clear.

Education
Regular contacts are still maintained with [school] and the teachers have reported that Donna is an extremely bright girl, but fails to use her full potential. Up until recently there has been a marked improvement in Donna's punctuality, whereby she was taken off report. However, since last week they have reported concern regarding her time keeping, and therefore put her back on report.

Further remarks or suggestions
During the last couple of weeks Donna has made several requests to visit a couple of friends of 'dubious reputation'. Donna stated her reasons for wanting to visit one of them as "she may not see her again." The other lady Donna stated 'used to be a prostitute, but is now going straight' furthermore she contracted the NSPCC when she was having problems with the mother. Donna went on to say how responsible this lady is and she would encourage her against rather than into it.

1) A profile on Donna has been circulated to a number of the homes, and we are still awaiting their replies.

2) In the meantime Donna continues to need firm and consistent control. In saying this it has been noted that Donna tends to be more accepting of certain points and comments where her attitude is concerned, and it is felt that with this consistency that we might see some positive results.

7 Reported speech: hearing the words of the client

This chapter marks something of a change of direction from the approach in chapters 3 to 6. It is, then, an appropriate place to pause briefly and review the direction of the argument so far and to set a context for the discussion in chapters 7 and 8. It is not suggested that chapters 7 and 8 invalidate the approach thus far but a different role for the reader is envisaged. We saw at the end of chapter 6 that there are potentially many readings of a social work account. No definitive interpretation has been offered of what really happened or who Donna really is since each reading occasion configures different reading relations. Whilst it is not proposed to consider a wide range of other readers, unratified and unaddressed, we can investigate the possibility of a more active reading.

The persuasive text and the passive reader

Social work accounts have been approached as stories. Social workers have been seen to make use of narrative methods of plot, character and point of view, deploying rhetorical features such as moral and fact construction. However, social work accounts have not been seen as stories defined by particular structures but as available in the performance of reading occasions and relations. When a social work document is read, certain relations are available to be invoked and attended to by different readers on specific occasions. When read by ratified and addressed readers, social work accounts can offer persuasive and convincing portrayals. Culler (1981) investigates such literary methods as verisimilitude or 'vraisemblance', as truth-like rather than truthful. Chapters 3 to 6 have demonstrated some methods by which persuasive narrative performances are made available.

In spite of these strong and persuasive performances, the texts were not entirely successful. In chapter 3, it was shown that by attending to the ratified reader, a competent and shared performance of social work reading conventions was displayed. Characters and events are made available and understandable by locating them in a story. To read a change from one state of affairs to another, to hear illustrations of events as signifying underlying conditions, to be drawn into an interpretation by joining a shared community of readers constrains the ratified reader from doubting the social worker's formulation. And yet the 'broken nose' story failed to persuade the judge and the interviewer started to desert.

In chapter 4, persuasion was located in the moral construction of reading relations. Contrasts between a culpable client and a flexible professional, acceptable and unacceptable behaviour, enabled the reader to draw the only possible conclusion: that the social worker's intervention was morally correct. Following stories of unfolding patterns and predispositions, blame was always located elsewhere and intervention was inevitable, a last resort. The 'warrant' instructed the reader it could not have been otherwise. And yet again a judge did not agree, he said that the intervention had been too much.

In chapters 5 and 6, social work accounts were read as strong and factual stories. The social worker was not easily removed from the construction of account but, by drawing in allies, claiming entitlement and eye-witness reporting, authority was displayed. And yet, whilst in the crisis the story was unquestioned and blackboxed, later we hear that it could all have been otherwise.

By binding entities in a narrative performance, the reader is morally persuaded, factually convinced and bound to the community of ratified and competent social work listeners. A large range of rhetorical features could be heard to support such constructions—three part lists, extreme case formulations, contrast structures, pathing devices. Yet examples of gaps and slippage have emerged.

It is not merely that particular readers, like the judge, are not convinced. The text offers opportunities for critical and subversive readings. In concentrating on the benign building of texts, the investigation so far has constructed a passive reader. Such a reader has accepted the reading conventions and is easily persuaded by the moral and factual nature of the formulations and relationships set up—a supportive colleague, a sympathetic manager, an 'understanding' research interviewer. However, readers, even ratified readers, are liable to find gaps in logic and configurations which do not stand up to various tests. Latour (1987) has shown how scientists attempt to bind actors and entities into a strong network, persuading them that their interests coincide with those of the storyteller. But the strength of the network can evaporate as new actors fail to be drawn in and associations begin to unravel. As Callon (1986:25) comments on the failure of the development of the electric car: "Translation becomes treason." The police did not charge the father in the 'broken nose' case (chapter 3), the scales did not support the social worker's concern in the 'failure to thrive' case (chapter 4) and later tellings of the 'assessment story' of Donna (chapter 6) are subverted as other events take over.

Given the constructedness of benign text building, are there opportunities for a critical, though still ratified, reader to recognise and subvert such constructions? Can the reader step briefly outside his/her enrolment and recognise narrative features and rhetorical formulations as tricks to deceive the reader? Tyler (1990:297) illustrates the 'tricks' of rhetoric:

> Obscured here beneath these purple robes of sanctimony is rhetoric, the dark twin of sweet reason, whose black instrumentality is the means of the speaker's domination of the hearer. Not through reason, but by stirring emotions, the trickster's bent and twisted truth persuades and convinces without belief in order to gain some illegitimate advantage over unwary listeners.

Whilst not supporting 'reason above rhetoric', we might ask what are the implications of the reader recognising such tricks and asking questions about his/her constructed position. Is an alternative approach to consider processes of deconstructing the text? London (1990:7) comments that recognising a text's "constructedness" also suggests acknowledging its "fictionality". We can thus consider what can be gained by investigating the way in which texts are available to be undermined, as well as constructed. How can they be seen to disintegrate from within and from outside; entities no longer in control, strength evaporates, friends desert and knots untie. As Eagleton (1983:133-4) says:

> The tactic of deconstructive criticism is to show how texts come to embarrass their own ruling systems of logic; and deconstruction shows this by fastening on to the 'symptomatic' points, the aporia or impasses of meaning, where texts get into trouble, come unstuck, offer to contradict themselves.

It is not suggested that the constructed, persuasive efforts of the text writer should be overthrown. Reading social work accounting as stories, which construct a ratified reader, first requires an openness to be persuaded by truth-like and moral claims. A ratified reader is after all constructed in order to facilitate appropriate interpretation. The analysis so far has offered important insights into the performance of social work accounting practices. Has not the reader of this thesis been convinced that social work accounts 'make sense' when treated as stories? Persuasion is what the enterprise of text writing and reading is all about. However, it is incumbent on this investigation to interrupt the cosy construction of preferred readings since subversion is commonplace in the everyday reception of social work texts. Subversion is, after all, what the storyteller is expecting and trying to guard against.[1]

The reader of the next two chapters is attended to as critical and informed. S/he is not an unratified nor unaddressed reader–social work texts will not be read as shopping lists. Nor is the aim to offer a platform for the client, his/her barrister or the Daily Express. Rather as with Eagleton (1983) quoted above, we remain within the "ruling systems of logic" of the text. We have already seen occasions where things do not seem quite right–the 'deception' of Document 3 in chapter 7, the contrast between the formulation of a united welfare network in the 'failure to thrive' case in chapter 4 and the health visitor's phone call. As privileged readers, you and I have been able to delve into restricted texts and make ironic contrasts. We have placed versions next to one another and, in so doing, have demonstrated the local and temporary nature of their formulation. It is thus incumbent on us to go further with such questioning and explore the subversive potential available in reading texts. By allowing the reader to be critical but remain within the logic of the text, we can investigate not only the preferred reading but the dispreferred versions which the writer tries to suppress. We no longer merely marvel at the 'artful practices' of the storyteller but seek out gaps and slippage.

'The other'

Otherness, 'the other' or alterity is an important concept in recent philosophy although it is not planned to offer a synthesis of these approaches.[1] This section reviews the concept of 'the other' and sets up questions for chapters 7 and 8; how far can seeking out 'the other' help uncover subverting and undermining voices available in the reading of social work texts? Such an approach is investigated in this chapter through reported speech: what are the implications of bringing the voice of 'the other' into the text? In chapter 8, 'the other' is located in the reading of adequate/inadequate representations of character in social work accounts.

Otherness recognises that for every representation or knowledge claim, alternative and competing versions are available which the text attempts to counter and suppress. In the work of Lyotard, discussed in chapter 1, otherness is central to the distrust of the metanarrative which aims to subsume or suppress voices and narratives. Carroll (1983:66) comments:

For Lyotard, a justice of the postmodern condition can no longer be conceived in terms of universal laws that resolve diversity, difference or contradiction; rather it demands that the alterity of 'the other' be respected and that the conflictual diversity of social space itself, which can then no longer be determined in terms of history, a theory or a model, be maintained.

Otherness suggests offering space for alternative voices and interpretations, and avoiding finalised claims or definitive representations. It opposes the authoritative and the monologic text which tries to tie down meaning and interpretation. Bakhtin (1984:292-3) writes:

> Monologism, at its extreme, denies the existence outside itself of another consciousness with equal rights and equal responsibilities, another I with equal rights (thou)... Monologue is finalised and deaf to the other's response, does not expect it and does not acknowledge in it any decisive force. Monologue manages without the other, and therefore to some degree materialises all reality. Monologue pretends to be the ultimate word. It closes down the represented world and represented persons.[2]

How far is a social work account a monologic text, aspiring to be the official word on and definitive representation of the client? It has been demonstrated in the moral and factual stories of chapters 4 to 6 that social work accounts aim (indeed, are required) to provide official versions of inexplicable and deviant family life. Whilst not always successful in their strategic ambitions, social work accounts were seen representing people and their circumstances in reports, files and conversations, aiming to become fixed and authoritative. By seeking out 'the other' of social work accounts in alternative depictions of the client, authoritative readings of clients can be undermined. One way to locate 'the other' is to approach representation as appropriation.

Appropriation

Representation seeks to display characters as categorisable entities. By constructing facts and deploying moral formulations, characters are turned into rejecting mothers or promiscuous teenagers. Appropriation shows how the words of 'the other' are taken over by the official text in constructing a definitive version, what s/he is really saying. In literary theory, for example, attempts to discover the 'real voice' of the author and his/her characters are manifest in claims to present the authentic and legitimate interpretation of the work. Marcus (1987:xi) notes, in discussing the conflict over versions of Virginia Woolf, that appropriations are "a kind of custodial battle for her reputation". Any claim to represent authors, texts or characters is an attempt to appropriate, capture and finalise. In contrast, theories of 'heteroglossia' or multiple voices resist final versions and question the basis of such authority. London (1990:12) discusses appropriations of Conrad, Forster and Woolf:

> ... the competing critical voices cannot be easily reconciled; engaged in a struggle for meaning, ownership and authority, they call into question the integrity of authorship—the possibility of a single voice, however expansive, we can rely upon.

The problem of depicting and representing 'the other' is also an issue in recent anthropology (Gidley, 1992). Reacting against the scientific ethnography of Malinowski or Mead, there is a concern about claims to speak for the indigenous person. Criticism centres on the anthropological enterprise as Eurocentric, attempting to represent 'the native' through Western eyes. Clifford (1988:25) notes:

> If ethnography produces cultural interpretations through intense research experiences, how is unruly experience transformed into an authoritative written account? How, precisely, is a garrulous, overdetermined cross-cultural encounter shot through with power relations and personal cross-purposes circumscribed as an adequate version of a more or less discrete 'other world' composed by an individual author?

A number of writers have returned to classic anthropological texts in order to uncover the techniques used, for example, Stocking (1983) on Malinowski and Clifford (1988) on Evans-Pritchard. They note some of the literary and rhetorical devices we discussed in earlier chapters—narrative constructs, use of active voice, illustrative dramatisations of the author's discovery process. These early anthropologists approached 'the other' by producing fixed and stable versions of their world as culture. They attempted to explain away the strangeness of 'the other', but did so from the standpoint of the western culture, thereby contributing to the struggle to control the indigenous people (Gidley, 1992:2). To represent 'the other' is thus to exclude (Kauffmann, 1990:187). 'The other' is not spoken to but spoken of, an object of the discourse.

Appropriation is an attempt to represent 'the other' by claiming to speak on her/his behalf. How do social workers authoritatively and definitively represent the behaviour and strangeness of their clients in order to appropriate and control? In this chapter, appropriation is investigated through a study of reported speech; how the very words of 'the other' are plucked from encounters, to represent and finalise. At the same time, studying processes of appropriation offers a chance to exploit gaps and slippage in order to see how using the words of 'the other' are available to be heard as unsettling official versions.

Approaches to reported speech[3]

Reported speech in literary and everyday texts offers an important opportunity to investigate the words of 'the other'. Voloshinov (1973) considers that any act of understanding resembles reported speech. It involves taking in an utterance and preparing a reply to it, as Morson and Emerson (1990:163) say "like a citation and commentary". In chapter 3, it was noted that reported speech can be heard to add strength to an assertion, as developed in conversation analysis (Holt 1992, Wooffitt 1992). However, a wider view of reported speech necessitates an investigation of the potential unstable reactions of telling stories, using the words of another. The reader can hear the claims of 'the other' and judge if the quoted words are incorrect, were not said, are out of context or meant something else. There is, then, an opportunity to subvert the claim.

Wooffitt (1992) investigates paranormal stories deploying conversation analysis. He is interested in the methods used by the storytellers to warrant claims that the events they are describing could only be supernatural. He sees the use of reported speech as "powerful inferential devices" (p.186) to corroborate the claims of the storyteller. The words of others are brought in to add credibility to claims that entities and experiences can only be paranormal. Holt (1992) looks at the introduction of reported speech in newspaper articles. She suggests that they appear immediately preceding the main claim of the report, adding authoritative support. However, do the words of another speaker necessarily support a claim, particularly when the quotation is depicted as self condemning? Is a gap offered for using the reported speech to challenge the formulation?

Other writers outline more complex varieties of reported speech. There is first a distinction between reported and described speech. Shuman (1986) notes in adolescents' stories how reported speech attempts to reproduce the sense of the performance by, for instance, mimicking the dialect or style of speech. Described speech does not insist on the repeating the exact words used. She observes that this creates important differences in entitlement:

> Reported speech was used to exaggerate the insult or to confirm or substantiate a described accusation. The person who reported an insult could herself be challenged for interfering in someone else's business, and such challenges often rested on inaccurate reports. Described speech was often considered inaccurate since it was not what the person had actually said...[the adolescents] understood the potential consequences of using different forms. (1986:160)

The use of reported or described speech makes an important difference; if contemporary and local, the right to report the other's exact words is examinable and open to challenge. Described speech is less contentious but also less authoritative. Reporting 'the other' can be attended to as highly contestable, depending on the circumstances of the encounter and whose words are being reported. It offers an opportunity to challenge the use of reported speech as misappropriation.

Bakhtin (1984) develops complex notions of the reported speech of characters in Dostoevsky, what he calls a typology of 'Discourse Types'.[4] Reported speech not only presents the words of another, but also their intonation or style, the appreciation of which is shared by readers. Bakhtin makes a distinction between 'single- and double-voiced words'. In 'single-voiced words', the words of 'the other' are offered as unproblematic, assumed to be representative and typical of a character or group. This is monologic discourse, as Morson and Emerson (1990:149) comment:

> ... no dialogic relations exist between the author and his character; they do not lie on the same plane and so they can neither dispute nor disagree with each other.

In double-voiced discourse, the author includes in the speech of characters the intonation and position of others. According to Bakhtin, this creates new forms of speech as received truths are questioned. In some cases, the author uses the words of another for her/his own purpose. For example, in parody another style is introduced and criticised or ridiculed, but retaining the author's speech is in some way superior. In active double-voiced speech, the reported speech resists the purposes of the author.

> In such discourse the author's thought no longer oppressively dominates the other's thought, discourse loses its composure and confidence, becomes agitated, internally undecided and two-faced. (Bakhtin 1984:198)

Bakhtin looks at the way that characters in Dostoevsky appear to talk in one kind of speech but, at the same time, allude to another which is never articulated. Such discourse, by remaining uncertain and at the mercy of the characters, is out of the control of the author and caught up with defending itself against possible hostile unspoken voices.

In the analysis which follows, we examine a number of examples where the words of 'the other' appear in social work accounts both to support and subvert positions and knowledge claims. Reported speech is considered as a site of appropriation of the words of 'the other'. It is introduced to represent, picture, categorise and finalise the client but, at the same time, offers gaps for criticising and undermining such portrayals. The problem of how to represent another are located in the encounter between critic and author, ethnographer and native, social worker and client. It is cut across with complex relations of appropriation and representation. The questions to be asked are: how far does depicting 'the other', the client, by the social worker, mean speaking from an official and monologic standpoint? Can such formulations be challenged by seeking out the disruptive voices of 'the other'?

Hearing the voice of the client

How is the voice of the client made available in social work accounts as reported and described speech? When presented with reported speech, the reader has the opportunity to hear the clients' words, point of view and style of speech. We look at a number of extracts mainly from interviews between a social worker and research interviewer and consider the consequences of allowing the client to be heard.

The client's words support the social worker's claim ... or do they?

We have already come across examples of reported speech in the interview and the court report of chapter 3, the 'broken nose' case. In lines 91 to 96 of the interview (appendix 3.1), direct speech (underlined) is used to present the mother's view of the situation:

> ... and because we talked to E and she seemed to think <u>well it's ok for dad to see the children I'm not really bothered</u> er and because of that attitude the fact that she hadn't been honest with us (-) we felt that the children's sort of long term future was at risk ...

This section forms part of the social worker's formulation of a second and unsatisfactory state of affairs, as discussed in chapter 3. The mother's direct speech is made available to be read as portraying her point of view that the father is not a risk to the children. Such a view is counter to how the case is initially presented, where social work intervention has been build around the father as a threat. The mother's words, then, are heard as self condemning. However, by line 105, the social worker's claim has been relativised to the extent that it is "our side of the story" and the judge subsequently endorses the mother's version. Given this twist in the story, the words of the mother can be heard to take on a new significance since an alternative version of events has been allowed into the story: "fathers should be able to see their children". The reported speech, which is initially heard as ironic; "that attitude" which is clearly unacceptable, is now available to be re-interpreted as possibly reasonable, indeed the successful proposition at court. The irony of "that attitude" is available to be reversed, a not-what-it-seems formulation is perhaps what it seems. The reported speech offers clarity and simplicity which lingers over the performance, hinting at an alternative formulation.

In the affidavit, direct reported speech is explicitly marked and can be heard as bringing the words from another occasion to illustrate the problems of this occasion, what Shuman (1986:168) calls 'recontextualisation'. On several occasions, the mother's words appear in direct quotation marks. For example:

"Get her out of my house" (referring to myself)...
"No no no, tell me what I've done"...

In chapter 3, it was suggested that this direct speech is heard to support the social work position, offering condemning words hearable in a mock cross examination. The lack of relativity in this document is nearer to Wooffitt's view of reported speech as supporting a claim. Furthermore, the content of these extracts can be heard as hysterical outbursts rather than stated positions; the mother's point of view is not being represented but her (unacceptable) behaviour is displayed. However, as later informed readers of this text, we know the outcome of the court case and have the opportunity to revisit the reported speech as a source of an alternative and now possibly believable formulation. Can an alternative reading allow the mother's words to be heard as reasonable, even protective of her children? Later in the interview, the social worker provides an explanation as to why the case failed:

I think basically because the judge felt that there is no better place really for the children to be than with their mother unless we can come up with some better reasons as to what is you know (-) can the mother harm them.

The ratified reader of the affidavit does not have access to such later rationalisations. We are privileged readers with access to later texts and outcomes. Such readings are not ratified nor addressed by the affidavit. But a later reader, approaching the file for what went wrong at court, might re-formulate the reported speech as a possible legitimate version of mother's fight for her children and an inadequate presentation at court. The condemning words may have offered a portrayal of a deceitful client and unprotecting mother but she was not harming them. We can, then, question whether the reported speech supports or undermines the social worker's formulation and it is suggested that such support is discoverable only in terms of the reading occasion. When read as by passive reader and in terms of rhetorical moves, reported speech can be seen to be supportive; when read by a critical reader and in terms of possible gaps in the text, it is available as subversive.

What the client is really saying?

Wooffitt (1992:161) considers that some speech is reported as direct speech when "in fact it is unlikely, or, in some cases, impossible, that the words so reported were actually said in that way". He considers that the storyteller is designing utterances 'as if' they are said. This is a more complex notion than Wooffitt suggests since he does not investigate whether the hearer might react critically to such deception. If the hearer agrees that the words were unlikely to have been said, although they are reported as such, they are now heard as a construction of the narrator and no longer objective. They cannot be heard to 'confirm objectivity' (Wooffitt, 1992:159).

There is a formulation available in some of these social work accounts, where speech is reported as spoken by the client but the source of the formulation (if read critically) can be heard as that of the social worker. In an interview, the social worker is reporting how a young man, Ray, is uncertain about moving into a hostel:

INTERVIEW EXTRACT 7.1

> Social Worker: …Ray at that time didn't seem able to commit himself to not smoking dope which says quite a lot about whether he was committed to the hostel or not and basically he was saying <u>you won't be able to tell if I smoke outside</u>…
>
> (He is asked to leave a hostel because of a number of rule infractions)
>
> Interviewer: so what went wrong
>
> Social Worker: I think Ray jeopardised it more than anything else when he actually got evicted from the hostel (-) it wasn't so much that he was drunk the night before (-) that they would have contained and handled (-) it was that the next day he actually sat on the bed and openly smoked dope in front of them and that was the final thing and the hostel actually clearly says that the young person has got to want to work with us and <u>Ray was clearly stating to them that he didn't want to work with them</u>…

In these utterances, it is not clear if the reported speech of the client is heard as his/her words or the social worker's assessment of what the young person is 'really' saying. In the first interview extract, the social worker's description of Ray's words can be heard as an affirmation of his position over the hostel, supported by reported speech. Ray's words are not set in the context of, for example, a dialogue 'I asked him if he would abide by the hostel rules to stop smoking dope and he said 'well you won't be able to tell if I smoke outside'. The use of 'he was saying' implies a position rather than what he actually said. The second extract is indirect speech and uses 'state' rather than 'say'.[5] Again, the words seem unlikely to be Ray's, but what he would say if they knew himself as the social worker does. The formulation 'what they are really saying' is heard as the social worker interpreting from behaviour to deeper feelings and intentions. A critical reading of such reported speech might wonder about the ownership of the client's words.

Other examples of reported speech can be heard as formulating a state of affairs in which it is not clear whose words are being reported. In an interview, Mandy has been asked to leave her older sister's home and the social worker is considering where she might go. The clients' words are offered to justify the decision taken to place her in a children's home rather than a foster home.

INTERVIEW EXTRACT 7.2

> Interviewer: you'd never considered fostering at this stage
>
> Social worker: well Mandy was dead against fostering because she said <u>I've been in so many family experiences</u> (-) we were talking about a year really because when she reached 16 and left school we would like her to move to an independent unit which was what she wanted as well and she said <u>I've had so many families I can't really give my loyalties to somebody else</u>... I think our aims were very clear when she went to [children's home] what we wanted and also there was consensus on these aims.
>
> Interviewer: ok so she went to [children's home]...

Are these the words of the client brought in to support the social worker's formulation as Holt and Wooffitt might suggest? Throughout this account, Mandy can be heard as a character who is depicted as capable and independent—"she has coped well with moves (between care and home)", "(at the sister's) she spent helluva lot of time actually alone and she'd coped with that and never abused it". Her thoughts and feelings are regularly made available as the determining factor. Despite hearing a story apparently directed by the client, a critical reader may wonder about the justification of the decision not to pursue fostering.[6] The formulation in 7.2 "dead against fostering" is available as a counter description of fostering for teenagers. The use of the phrase "so many family experiences" can be heard as a direct rebuttal to an unheard charge 'Mandy needs to experience family life'. The inappropriateness of fostering is further supported by the time available "we are talking of about a year really", being heard to solicit the support of a competent social worker hearer who is aware of the time it takes to find an appropriate placement. The utterance, then, is not merely the words of Mandy since it includes versions of professional knowledge about fostering within the reported speech.

In both these extracts, words are offered as if they were the words of the client but a critical reading can reformulate them as the words of the storyteller. The reader is being deceived into thinking the social worker's formulation is supported by the expressed words of the client. Instead, there is an overt formulation of 'what the client is really saying' which is heard as social work assessment.

The client sets the agenda

The account of Mandy is heard as apparently directed by her own wishes but, on reading critically, the social worker's point of view can be heard to direct Mandy's words. In extracts 7.3 and 7.4, we investigate the implications of using reported speech, where the words of the client are heard as the strongest voice in legitimating the claim, thereby weakening the authority of the storyteller.

Extract 7.3 displays the social worker describing the process of court procedure and negotiations with the parents. The children have been admitted into care on an emergency order after the police found them unattended and the parents drunk. It was decided to institute proceedings for a full care order, but set up a rehabilitation programme aimed at discharging the order. The narrative is told through reading out entries from the case file as well as the social worker's recollections. This extract appears towards the end of the interview when the main narrative has been completed. The interviewer queries the decision to ask for an interim care order after the emergency order had run out, given that the aim was rehabilitation. This might be heard as inviting an 'evaluation' (Labov and Waletsky, 1967), where the storyteller is encouraged by the interviewer to reflect back on the implication of the story.

INTERVIEW EXTRACT 7.3

>Interviewer:why therefore did [Melchester SSD][7] suggest care proceedings and not return the children home after eight days
>
>Social worker:your guess is as good as mine
>
>Interviewer:oh (laugh) right
>
>Social worker:er (18 secs looking at the file) er hang on though the children were actually removed on the twelfth which meant that we had to go to court on the (-) nineteenth (-) er I am sure that we went to court on the nineteenth and obtained an interim care order this is all as a result of work done afterwards after the first interim was obtained ok so [Melchester SSD] came to that conclusion [to institute care proceedings] after after some thought
>
>Interviewer: oh I see their initial response was really to say ...
>
>Social worker: protect the child now ...
>
>Interviewer: go for an interim order ...
>
>Social worker: protect the child now whilst we think about this (8 secs)

> er all the evidence from the children's home and the foster home indicated that these children were wonderful that they had a strong bond with their parents parents were visiting regularly in fact they were coming collecting the children and taking them home and bringing them back at night there was very very regular access and the parents were doing brilliantly with the children so that was all very positive (turns the page and 6 second pause)
>
> Interviewer: it is er (-) it's not for me to say but ... sorry go on
>
> Social worker: the other issue was <u>the parents were stating categorically that they were prepared to co-operate</u>
>
> Interviewer: yeah
>
> Social worker: that they were prepared to co-operate with social services and in the face of a parent saying that you have very little grounds for insisting on an order **especially** when you are proposing to return the children home
>
> Interviewer: yes
>
> Social worker: er (8 seconds turning pages) and the guardian *ad litem* was also saying er (15 seconds reading file entry) the guardian *ad litem* actually asked for an adjournment for three months to test their behaviour she was sufficiently concerned to ask for an adjournment er the family were very opposed to this and court heard from the guardian *ad litem* er in court but wouldn't agree to an adjournment so the care proceedings were dropped we didn't offer any evidence and the children went home after that court hearing
>
> Interviewer: right
>
> Social worker: on the eleventh of August...

There is an unusually disrupted flow to this exchange. The social worker is reading the file and the interviewer is unsure if the gaps are an opportunity to ask questions. Throughout the dialogue, it seems that the interviewer is wanting, in a so far unspecified way, to question the appropriateness of the action taken. He had already queried the initial decision to institute care proceedings. In anticipating such an intervention, the social worker is telling the story by relating the file entries but, at the same time, interrupting the interviewer's interventions and answering the questions she assumes he is trying to ask. As with Bakhtin above, an unspecified possibly critical discourse is being attended to, while the chronology of the file entries is made available.

In responding to the initial query, the social worker agrees with the interviewer and then searches the file for an explanation. In the first paragraph, the procedure of dates of court hearings shows that it could not have proceeded otherwise. Next, the interviewer's acceptance is met with what can be heard as a 'put down'. Where the interviewer is merely talking procedures:

"response", "orders", the social worker is talking principles: "protect the child". This silences him temporarily. As Bakhtin notes (1981:342), the use of direct 'sacred' speech is monologic and authoritative and cannot be questioned.[8] In the third paragraph, the depiction of the children as "wonderful" and the success of the parents is described in upgraded terms, with no pause and with a list of three–evidence from the carers of a strong parental bond, regular visiting and even taking them home. This is further upgraded with "very very regular", "doing brilliantly" and the summary "all very positive".

A long pause gives the interviewer an opportunity to begin what sounds like it will be a strong criticism–"it's not for me to say but ...". This is immediately rebuffed by the use of indirect speech and the voice of the client: "the other issue was the parents were stating categorically that they were prepared to co-operate". This comment is unlikely to be available by reading a file entry but is heard as providing an evaluation of the state of affairs. It can be heard to establish both a fact and a principle: co-operation and the positive voice of the parents cannot be resisted. It is delivered with upgraded terms "categorically" and with emphasis "especially". It determines all other action. The repeat of "they were prepared to co-operate" with the interviewer's "yeah" in between, further enlists his support. After this explication of the principle of parental co-operation, the interviewer is silenced, even though other chances to intervene are available with several long gaps. This formulation is further supported by outlining the position of the guardian *ad litem*, who had an opportunity to present an alternative version of the case, perhaps similar to that of the interviewer's unheard complaint. This alternative version was heard by the court and rejected, as it was opposed by the family.

It is suggested, then, that in this exchange the social worker is heard to use 'double-voiced discourse' of both relating a story and undermining an unheard alternative. It is only with the appropriation of the voice of the client, through indirect speech, that the impossibility of the alternative version of the state of affairs or action is demonstrated. The use of indirect speech, backed up with upgraded terms and sacred principles can be heard as the strong formulation that finally silences the critic, the ultimate persuasion, the trump card. From that point, the 'categorical' words of the parents hover throughout the rest of the story, appearing to determine the outcome. It suggests that the indirect speech be heard as the ultimate rebuttal to silence an unheard criticism.

This formulation used a mass of rhetorical features, principles and allies but the words of the client are pivotal. Without the indirect speech, would it be strong enough to counter criticism? The social worker's description and assessment in the early part of the formulation does not stop the questions, only the unequivocal words of the parents can silence the unheard critic. Throughout the rest of the interview, the reader awaits the words of the client to direct and legitimate any claim.

In another case, the reported speech is similarly heard to determine the direction of events but in a way that the social worker did not want. After the social worker has described the events of the admission to care, the interviewer summarises the role of mother and social worker and asks about subsequent activity:

INTERVIEW EXTRACT 7.4

> Interviewer: right er so it was essentially (mother) who asked for reception into care but you wanted to see how things were going you wanted to do all the assessments and so on (-) right did you work out a particular contract with her
>
> Social worker: at that time no but then I saw her within say three days of the children going into care because (sigh) and and you know I had to really chase her to get that and I saw her and we worked out that the children it was then <u>that she started saying I don't want them back ever</u>
>
> Interviewer: ah
>
> Social worker: and then <u>we started saying well no this was not the plan</u>
>
> Interviewer: right but three days afterwards you right...
>
> (The interview continues to discuss placement and school arrangements and five minutes later, the interviewer returns to overall plans)
>
> Interviewer: so (6 secs) ok so after oh so how what was your initial view of what the likely stay would be
>
> Social Worker: we actually thought that we would be doing a rehabilitation programme with mum (-) and getting them back home
>
> Interviewer: within a few
>
> Social worker: well I think we would say like within four five months that would be the longest we would want that would be by then sort of mum having a new house cos we had to wait for mum to be offered new accommodation...
>
> (Social worker describes the rehabilitation programme and mum's non-co-operation for two minutes)
>
> Social worker: ...and so it was sort of doomed to failure I think
>
> Interviewer: and so at what point did you realise that it sort of...
>
> Social worker: (sigh) well I think that mum as I said at the beginning had been oscillating between you know first of all she didn't want

to see them again (-) then wanted them and she wanted them adopted and then she didn't want them adopted then she wanted them back home and we said right if you are saying back home that's it so we quickly throw in a rehabilitation programme (sigh) and then mum just never played ball with it and you know it was like never give up hope and even after five months she was still saying I want them I want them you see right you know we'll try again (-) so I think now you know we're in a situation Mum is expecting again and these children have been in care since then

Interviewer: oh really

Social worker: and you know they have not been home and the visits have been very rare so I think adoption is now

Interviewer: right

Social worker: right for these children

(Discussion continues around where they are currently living)

These three extracts can be heard as the points at which story evaluations are asked of the social worker, the rest being descriptions of placements, transport, visits. As with extract 7.3, they are invitations for evaluation after the events of the narrative have been presented. Again, the words of the mother are heard to set the direction of the case but here they are resisted by the social worker. The first picture of the social worker's approach to the mother has her 'chasing' the mother; already the mother is seen to be calling the tune. The utterance is confused and hesitant: "because (sigh) and and you know ... we worked out that the children it was then that ..." as the social worker struggles to outline the direction of her work. Abruptly, this is resolved by the mother's words, sounding clear and unarguable. The direct speech "I don't want them back ever" is presented as a 'categorical assertion' (Lyons 1977:809), with added emphasis "ever". The interviewer's response "ah" can be heard to acknowledge this as the definitive state of affairs. In contrast, the social worker's position is now introduced as tentative: "we started saying...". She uses direct speech "well no", then indirect speech "this was not the plan": hearable as a drop in emphasis. It can be heard as a retort rather than an assertion, after a strong position has been set by the mother's words.

In the second extract, the rehabilitation programme is set up and plans for a return home envisaged: the social worker's position. Again, it is introduced with reservation: "we thought that...". A critical reader might question the mother's affirmation to give up her children, as not what she 'really' thought or see it as unacceptable to want to give up one's children so soon. No social worker should act on it. However, such a position is not made explicit. In the six minutes since mother's categorical statement of her position, the social worker's position has not been reasserted nor a change in the mother's position described. A description of the failure of the rehabilitation programme ends with the assertion that it was "doomed to failure", re-emphasising perhaps that the mother had never accepted it.

In the third extract, the interviewer invites the realisation of the ultimate state of affairs. In response, the social worker refers back to the mother's words, though differently. In the first extract, the mother's words indicated only one direction, not wanting the children back. She is now described as "oscillating". Yet no such change of mind has been made available to the hearer, the mother's position has remained unequivocal until now. The section describing the changes is complex and rushed, not merely describing 'oscillation', but performing it. Could it be that it is the social worker who has been "oscillating", not the mother, imposing on a reluctant mother a programme with which she was never in agreement? It was social services who "never give up hope"; their plan that was "doomed to failure", a weak and contradictory position.

It has been suggested that by bringing in the mother's words as categorical and unchallenged, a state of affairs is made available in which the voice of 'the other' is heard to direct and legitimate the plot of the story. The strong words of the mother are in contrast with a confused, reactive and 'oscillating' social worker. The reported speech of 'the other' can be heard not to support the social work storyteller's position but to subvert it. The critical reader looks to 'the other' for a sense of direction; the storyteller is merely a reporter of events with the characters out of her control.

Social Worker: Hang on isn't this going a bit too far? Characters out of control of the storyteller? Surely the social worker is merely describing an ambivalent mother. I mean, you seem to think that by inventing this 'critical reader' you can come along and make all these criticisms of social work. In the previous chapters, you have merely pointed out how a social work description is produced. I don't object to that bit. I can see that building up descriptions does involve a thoughtful presentation. But now you seem to be very critical, rather arrogant, I might say.

Author: Wait a minute, I think you have misunderstood me. I'm not trying to question whether particular social work interventions were appropriate or say that descriptions were wrong. I am listening as an informed reader to the storytelling of the social worker and anticipating possible responses which reading occasions suggest. And the character of the mother in extract 7.4 appears to me to be out of the control of the author, in that her words and position can be read as clear and unequivocal compared to the storyteller's confused words and position. The mother's words can be heard as more authoritative, so her character appears to determine the direction of the story. I think this is what Bakhtin suggests of Dostoevsky's characters.

Social Worker: Well, you can hardly compare Dostoevsky to a social worker's description of a client. And all this reliance on storytelling, as if the story is more important than the actual social work.

Author: I'm not sure of whether we can easily separate the account from the action, as Garfinkel would say. And yes, you are correct that there are important differences between characters in novels from those in social work descriptions, but that does not mean that similar storytelling features are not part of the reading relations. That is the whole point of this study and the depiction of character is one of the most important aspects. I'd be very worried if this line of inquiry is challenged.

Social Worker: But my main point is how do you justify your criticisms, how is your critical reader's point of view any more valid than anyone else's? If you are a critic of social work, then you need to show your credentials, your entitlement as you outlined in chapter 5–you don't know very much about social work nowadays do you? You seem to have forgotten the difficulties there are in working with people's ambivalence.

Author: Well, I hope that I am pointing out conventions in the text that any informed reader can read in the same way as I do. Haven't I convinced you that social work talk and writing requires careful construction with rhetorical features, rehearsed performances etc. I have moved on from that to suggest that these constructions don't always work; that an informed critic, like you and me, can find gaps and slippage. Now, if you want my entitlement, I have been a social worker, team manager and researcher of social work for 24 years, so I think I can hear when social work conventions are being deployed…

Social Worker: Yes, yes we have all had lots of experience but …

Author: But you are right of course, when you say that other interpretations of the storytelling of social workers are equally valid, as long as they come from informed readers. I am happy to listen to your interpretation.

Social Worker: Ok. In that last case, I did not read what the social worker said in extract 7.4 as a weak or inappropriate interpretation of the situation. If a mother says she wants to give up her children, there are likely to be all sorts of ambivalent feelings floating around. It is obvious to try out a rehabilitation programme and allow her the opportunity to think carefully about it.

Social Worker 2: Well no, I don't agree. You are just one of those 'Kinship Defenders' [9] aren't you.

Social Worker 1: Who are you ?

Social Worker 2: I suppose I'm a 'Society-as-Parent Protagonist'. I happen to believe that children's needs come before the prevarications of parents. If a mother is that rejecting, that clear so soon after her children are taken away, then there is very little hope for a successful rehabilitation. My complaint is that things didn't move quicker, I mean 5 months waiting is a long time in young children's lives …

Social Worker 1: And you think you can come up with a satisfactory permanent family for these children, all four together …

Author Hey, now stop, this is getting out of hand. I did not intend to question that what was done was appropriate or inappropriate and not in terms of such metanarratives. It is quite possible that the mother (in other texts, on other occasions, to other audiences) said different things. I am not suggesting that mother or social worker had a consistent position outside the text ...

Social Worker 1: It was a very consistent position, allow the mother to sort herself out, although I'm not sure if she was given enough help with that difficult process. There could have been more input.

Social Worker 2: Well, I think the consistent position was the mother. She said from the beginning she did not want her children, ever. That's what Author said as well didn't you?

Author: Don't pull me into this. Haven't you both provided support for my suggestion that there are many available positions, all equally valid. What my critical reader does is try to question those that s/he reads, without supporting either the position or its alternative. My aim has been to take what appears to be the preferred version of the storyteller and inquire how that can be subverted, not to produce a correct version.

Social Worker: Ok, myself and my colleague have different views. But you talk about weak and strong positions, don't you, as if some versions, with which you seem to have privileged access, are more valid than others?

Discourse Analyst: Yes, I have my doubts about your version of the social worker's version. You have said several times that you are interested in constructing and reading alternative versions and meanings, yet you seem to have constructed a definitive version yourself. I know that in yours the client's version apparently is 'stronger', but what is your warrant for showing 'strength'?

Author: I was worried that you might show up. Well, I have tried to be guided by you to some extent. I have pointed out strong features of texts–three part lists, extreme case formulations, positive modalities.

Discourse Analyst: Yes, that is true, but we have not pointed to weak texts so much. We have mainly been interested in showing how particular utterances can be read as strong. Neither have we tried to go beyond the utterance to some overall strong or weak reading of the whole story. Where do you get your justification for this overall definitive reading of how the story should really be read?

Author: Oh hell. This is very difficult. I am not saying 'should' be read, but 'can' be read. Look how often Wooffitt uses 'is', for example, "is therefore a resolution" (1992:179). I have tried to suggest that my readings whether critical and/or ratified are only one alternative–how many times have I said 'can be heard', 'are available' to avoid saying 'is'.

Discourse Analyst: Yes, that has become very boring.

Author: I am sorry about that, but I made a deal with an elusive character called 'Sceptic' back in chapter 3. I haven't invited him back since. But I really want to move away from being stuck with analysis merely at the level of the sentence. That is why I think stories are a more appropriate approach, because we read stories as a whole, how they hang together, how they are convincing or not, why characters and plots are intriguing. I am sure that this is more than each reader, on each reading occasion, having a different version. Some readings are more 'robust' than others, and yet there are always gaps and slippage, allowing alternative versions.

Discourse Analyst: What do you mean 'gaps'; by whose assertion is it a gap?

Author: The critical reader who understands the reading conventions and can see them being challenged. They offer pathways for alternative readings, which make available subversion of the storyteller's version. Not all readers are likely to follow such gaps, the interviewer clearly missed most of them. But I have tried to show that they are ratified readings and yet subversive. Surely you agree that in reading texts, we get an overall sense of strong and weak voices, characters whose point of view we are more likely to listen to than others. In extract 7.4, the mother's words did seem so clear, whereas the social worker's were heard as confused. The storyteller was able to use that clarity to shape and justify her story but, in doing so, has lost authority in her own assessment. The reader is only convinced when s/he hears the client's words.

Literary Theorist: I agree with that. Characters in narratives are strong or weak, believable or not. We have developed lots of ideas about this ...

Author: Have you really, perhaps we can discuss them in the next chapter.

This chapter has begun to seek out 'the other' through an analysis of reported speech. Wooffitt's view that reported speech supports the "objectivity" of the storyteller needs to be reassessed. The contention here is that it depends on the nature of the reading occasion and undermining readings of reported speech have been explored. In this chapter, a variety of story features enable a critical reading of reported speech as appropriation of the words of 'the other'.

In the discussion of an extract from the 'broken nose' case, we saw how the mere appearance of the words of 'the other' offer the reader an alternative version of events. Although depicted as dispreferred, different reading relations can offer the opportunity to formulate alternative versions, for example, after hearing the outcome of the court case. In extracts 7.1 and 7.2, it became difficult to recognise whether the reported speech was that of the client or was heard as the assessment of the storyteller. At what point does the critical reader question the reported speech as not the voice of 'the other', but a deceptive concealment of the social worker's views in the client's voice? In extracts 7.3 and 7.4, the words of 'the other' can be heard as the strongest voice in the text, setting the direction of the story and determining action. The storyteller appears to lose control, her assessment works only when supported by the stronger words of 'the other'.

It has been suggested that the strength of the other's version is linked to the use of categorical assertions or emphasised features. The other's speech is not relativised or modalised (Palmer, 1986). The storyteller does not provide evidence nor commitment to the formulation, the other's words are strong enough and the narrator loses control. Furthermore, the position of the reported speech in the sequence of the story is important. In examples 7.3 and 7.4, they can be heard as the evaluation stage of the story, where events have been outlined and comment invited. In contrast, in examples 7.1 and 7.2 they are part of the claim formulation and less evaluative. The words of 'the other' initially appear to support the proposition and only subvert through a later, critical reading.

The implication for this analysis is that reading reported speech can set up alternative relations and responses. Here is an opportunity to seek out 'the other'. Following Bakhtin, it has been demonstrated that a story is 'double-voiced'; putting forward a position and, at the same time, rebutting an alternative position. By presenting the words of 'the other', even if they are depicted as condemning, gaps and slippage are made available. An opportunity is made available for a sympathetic reading of the unheard alternative story. Perhaps more serious for the storyteller, the appropriation of the words of 'the other' can be heard as deceptive and offer a potential challenge to the veracity of the storyteller. "I've had so many family experiences" (extract 7.2). should be read as "I've had so many 'family experiences'". Mandy's words are appropriated to challenge the authoritative words of departmental policy (see footnote 6).

To seek out 'the other' in reported speech is an occasion on which an alternative depiction is made available for re-reading. In the next chapter, we investigate how alternative readings are offered by reading character depictions.

NOTES

[1] For example, otherness is discussed in postmodernism (Lyotard), existentialism (Sartre), phenomenology (Husserl and Merleau-Ponty) and symbolic interaction (Mead).
[2] This 'same' passage is translated rather differently in Todorov (1984:107). Without attempting to suggest the significance of using 'ultimately' for 'at its extreme' or 'objectivizes all reality' for 'materialises all reality', it is interesting that there is not a definitive version of Bakhtin challenging definitive versions.
[3] Reported speech is used to denote the insertion into an utterance of the words of another. This is commonly split into direct speech, using a personal pronoun and quotation marks, and indirect speech, which describes the other's words. For example, direct speech would be

He said, "I am coming after the meeting."

Indirect speech would be :

He said he would come after the meeting.

Shuman (1986:160) refers to reported and described speech. There are occasions where the two are merged.

He said he would "pull out all the stops this time".

Without the personal pronoun, it is not clear whether these words were used or whether the reporter is interpreting the intentions of 'the other': what he meant rather than what he said.
[4] This a rather confusing typology and my description is guided by Morson and Emerson (1990:146-171).
[5] A similar example of the formulation 'what the client is really saying' was noted in chapter 6, document 4, when Donna is reported as 'stating' that she does not want to face her mother's 'rejection', a term Donna is unlikely to have used.
[6] A Policy Statement of the Social Services Department at the time included the following:

A local authority cannot perform all the functions of a parent. Therefore care in a local authority establishment should be viewed wherever possible as a channel towards the provision of a permanent family home— either the child's natural home or a substitute home.

[7] Some of the children were already in care to a neighbouring authority, Melchester SSD, and this department was acting on their behalf. Decisions were dependent on negotiations with Melchester.
[8] The use of 'sacred' words like 'protect the child' or 'in his best interests' are also reported speech from legislation or professional texts, but this analysis concentrates on direct speech by the client, the other.
[9] Fox (1982) discusses two value positions in child care. The 'kinship defender' sees "the natural biological family [as] being of unique value to the child ... state intervention should therefore be directed to preserving, supporting and strengthening the family unit." In contrast, the 'society-as-parent protagonist' places "greater faith in the possibility of beneficent State intervention ... The responsibility and necessity to defend children against mistreatment is strongly emphasised" (1982:272).

8 Depicting character: reading adequate representations of the client

Having outlined an approach to critical reading in the last chapter, we now investigate the construction of characters in social work accounts. The aim is to explore how the client is portrayed and what reading relations are available to enable the ratified reader to understand what sort of person this is. It also provides us with a further opportunity to seek out 'the other' by investigating alternative readings of the character of the client: is the representation adequate or believable? are there opportunities for gaps and slippage in the characterisation?

Depicting the character of the client through reading social work accounts has already been shown to be an important feature of their construction and reception. In chapter 4, the moral construction of character was explored through depictions of good and bad, culpable and blameless. In chapter 5, the factual construction of clients and their attributes showed how displays of entitlement and the support of witnesses enabled characters to be depicted as independent of the construction of the storyteller. The 'narrative puzzle' in chapters 5 and 6 provided uncertainty in characterisation, encouraging the reader to investigate further. In chapter 7, the words of the client offered an opportunity for alternative interpretations of the account and a distrust of the author.

A critical reading explores what depiction of character the story advocates and resists. How is the characterisation made available? Is it adequate? Are we convinced? Rather than exploring a benign construction of character through rhetorical features, critical reading assesses overall narrative reception. What is the critical reader's overall reaction to how the character is depicted? Smith (1993:47) notes how "local weaknesses... are obscured by the [progressive] cumulation of items". Critical readers can, however, investigate such gaps and slippage. Investigating the reading of character depiction in social work texts is an important way of questioning the adequacy of social work representation.

Adequacy of representation in social work and literary theory

Adequacy of character representation is a concept associated with literary criticism, not a sociological study. It is not intended to adopt conventions from literary criticism which debate whether an author has created a believable character whom a reader can recognise and react to. This is a study of how social workers attempt to depict 'real' people to specific audiences on certain occasions. By developing a theory of narrative, we are concerned with reading relations and 'adequacy' of representation, but we are assuming that both reader and writer believe there is a 'real' person to be characterised. The ratified reader is faced with specific tasks in certain contexts. S/he has to decide if the writer has provided an adequate depiction of the person, which enables him/her to locate in the character certain attributes, ways of behaving which require specific interventions. Such interpretation is a literary activity, involving recognising types of characters and locating these characters in a story. However, this is not the same as criticising novelists for producing inadequate characters in their stories, since the novelist is not attempting to represent real people. An inadequate character for the novelist is a criticism of poor style; for the social worker it is being wrong. In a wide range of professional encounters social workers are expected to be able to depict a 'real' person adequately and accurately.

A number of writers have considered that constructing the real world involves portraying and interpreting characters. Goffman (1959) has developed a dramaturgical model of the everyday world and notes the importance of performing adequate characterisation.

> When an individual plays a part he implicitly requests his observers to take seriously the impression that is fostered before them. They are asked to believe that the character they see actually possesses the attributes he appears to suggest, that the task he performs will have the consequences that are implicitly claimed for it, and that, in general, matters are what they appear to be. (p.17)

Bakhtin approaches the study of literature from the basis of everyday speech (Holquist, 1990:72). He argues that in literature before Dostoevsky, the author created a monologic character, easily categorisable and within the control of the writer. As noted in chapter 7, Bakhtin sees Dostoevsky's characters as unfinalised.

> Dostoevsky creates not voiceless slaves but free people, capable of standing alongside their creator, capable of not agreeing with him and even of rebelling against him. A plurality of independent and unmerged voices and consciousnesses, a genuine polyphony of fully valid voices ... (Bakhtin, 1984:6-7)

Dostoevsky creates characters who are able to resist the control of the author, just as 'real' people might argue against how they are portrayed. Morson and Emerson (1990:263) note Bakhtin's distinction between character and personality, the latter suggesting the characterisation of 'real' people.

> Monologic writers represent their heroes as 'characters', Dostoevsky represented them as true 'personalities.' As Bakhtin uses these terms, a character is a bundle of psychological and social traits. A character's psychology may be immensely complex, but it is in essence something 'objectivised' and finalised. By contrast, a 'personality' is a genuine other person, capable, as real people are, of changing his or her essential identity. To represent a hero as a personality is to portray him as truly unfinalisable.

Novelists have continued to explore the relationship between author and character, often with dialogues between the author and character and with unfinalised and ambiguous portrayals of characters.[1]

This approach to character is complex. It suggests that in portraying their clients, social workers are in a similar situation to authors creating characters in narrative. They are caught between, on the one hand, wanting to finalise and categorise their depictions of clients as the definitive portrayal but, on the other hand, they are open to criticism from various audiences for being monologic and wrong. The occasions of reading social work accounts involve potential challenges to monologic characterisation. Cuff (1980:32) suggests that situations like courts involve a "principled position of doubt", with participants expecting accounts to be scrutinised. Furthermore, rapidly changing depictions of clients demonstrate how fragile social work constructions are easily overthrown by new requirements and new audiences, as with Donna in chapter 6. Opportunities exist for the critical reader to investigate character depictions as adequate and/or believable. We are now in a position to put such formulations through various 'trials' before we believe the author (Latour, 1987:53) but from within the reading relations of social work texts. Adequacy should be approached carefully, unpretentiously. After a discussion of theoretical approaches to character, the analysis will explore the character depiction of three clients in social work texts: Mr King, Sarah and Stuart.

Theoretical approaches to depicting character

This section assesses the usefulness of some approaches to character depiction in literary theory and sociology. We have discussed how 'character' in literary theory suggests monologic and fixed versions which Bakhtin contrasts with 'personality'. It is not intended to use the term 'personality' because of its association with psychology and we will see how some recent approaches to character are more wide-ranging.

Character and plot in narrative

In formalist approaches, character is merely a product of plot. For Propp (1968), the character does what the fairy tale requires. Chatman (1978:112) sums up such an approach: "characters are means rather than ends of the story". Recent approaches see the attribution of traits to characters in novels as an important feature of literary analysis. Todorov's (1977) distinction between psychological and a-psychological stories was noted in chapter 3, where character or plot is seen as structuring the story. Barthes (1975) stresses a psychological understanding of character. This 'process of nomination' of personality traits is recognised as open to reader interpretation.

> To read is to struggle to name, to subject the sentences of the text to a semantic formation. This transformation is erratic; it consists in hesitating among several names: if we are told that Sarrasine has 'one of those strong wills that know no obstacle' what are we to read? will, energy, obstinacy, stubbornness etc. (p.92)

For the reader to name and categorise traits of characters in social work accounts equally leaves room for uncertainty and reader choice. Social work accounts are likely to make available a wide range of attributes: how are they portrayed as important and what are the consequences of such selection for the reader?

Another important feature of social work accounts is the link between characterisations and intervention. What characteristics warrant particular social work responses? An important reader, the judge, may not dispute the character depiction but may consider the social worker's suggested action is unwarranted. The judge in the 'broken nose case' (chapter 3) may have accepted that the father was violent and the mother unpredictable, but perhaps did not consider that the children remained in danger and they were returned home. Reading plot and character are intimately bound together in performing social work accounts, since action inevitably follows (or precedes) the depiction and reading of characters and their attributes.

Round and flat characters

The question to consider is how social work texts handle uncertain and changing character depictions and what opportunities exist for critical and informed readings to locate alternative depictions. Literary theory offers an interesting distinction between 'round' and 'flat' character:

> Flat characters ... are sometimes called types and sometimes caricatures. In their purest form, they are constructed round a single idea or quality: when there is more than one factor in them, we get the beginning of the curve towards the round. The really flat character can be expressed in one sentence ... (Forster, 1974:46-7)

Flat character depictions are easily recognisable and categorisable, whereas round characters are more complex, displaying a variety of traits, not always consistent nor predictable. Forster does not suggest that flat characters are incapable of making an important contribution to the story, they are simply less easy to remember. Round characters, on the other hand, inspire a strong sense of intimacy, even though they are more puzzling. As Chatman (1978:132) notes:

> We remember them as real people. They seem strangely familiar. Like real-life friends and enemies it is hard to describe what they are exactly like.

Such a distinction has important consequences for reading character in social work stories. Forster (1974:48-9) quotes Norman Douglas in criticising 'flat' characterisations in biography:

> ... it selects for literary purposes two or three facts of man or woman generally the most spectacular and therefore 'useful' ingredients of their character, and disregards others. Whatever fails to fit in with these specially chosen traits is eliminated; must be eliminated, for otherwise the description would not hold water ... The facts may be correct so far as they go, but there are too few of them: what the author says may be true, and yet by no means the truth.

If characters are depicted as 'flat', easily categorised but limited, a critical reader has an opportunity to question their authenticity.

Chatman (1978:119) suggests a similar 'open theory of character', the reader being encouraged to construct the character from more than is available in the text.

> A viable theory of character should preserve openness and treat characters as autonomous beings, not as mere plot functions. It should argue that character is reconstructed by the audience from evidence

announced or implicit in an original construction and communicated by the discourse.

This concept is important for this project, since speculating about the character's actions in situations outside those made available by the account is precisely the concern of the ratified reader of a social work account: which placement and what court order is suitable for a young person with particular attributes? In court, case conferences or with supervisors, decisions and plans are likely to be performed on the basis of characterisations and what can be done, with various versions of the client available to be negotiated.

In summary, reading social work accounts offers ratified readers (the judge or the manager) and critical readers (you and I) an opportunity to speculate about characters, their attributes and the future. Whilst social workers may wish them flat and definitive, it is likely that characters in social work stories are round, unfinalised and temporary, shifting as new occasions require, anticipating critical reading and negotiating re-appraisal.

Versions and categories

A literary approach to unfinalised and contested character depiction has much in common with sociological concepts of versions and categories. Both concepts are concerned with investigating how people and entities are represented and how typical characteristics are attributed. As with the reading of character discussed above, sociologists have rejected the stable psychological trait of categorisation as representing objective, cognitive processes. Instead, the manipulation of categories and versions is approached as an interactional and occasioned accomplishment.

Categories and their discursive manipulation have been discussed at length in sociology.[2] An interactional approach sees categorisation as a method of depicting people and entities, but as also negotiating that depiction. Attributes associated with categories can be negotiated and provide opportunities for subverting that categorisation. Particularisation involves the active relativising of categories, where instances are separated from the overall formulations, thereby generating endless subcategories (Billig, 1985).

Constructing alternative versions is discussed by Smith (1993:49). She identifies how the storyteller provides for an authorised version of K as mentally ill but in uncovering these features, the reader is able to question the authenticity of that version. She suggests that it is possible to construct a version of K as being frozen out by her friends and not mentally ill:

> ... the construction of an alternative account in which K is not mentally ill is not possible on the basis of what is available. But I can briefly show for some parts how it might be done. It would involve

finding rules or contexts for K's behaviour which would properly provide for the behaviour to the same effect. If the enterprise were successful it would result in a description which would lack any systematic procedure for bringing these items together. The pieces of behaviour would simply be fitted back into various contexts. This present account would disintegrate. The reader/hearer would be unable to recover from them a rule under which he could see what the account 'was all about'.

Cuff (1980:31) criticises Smith for moving from a member's to an analyst's reading and for suggesting that her version of K is "equally plausible and possibly more convincing". He points instead to the importance of establishing how reading occasions routinely make available subversion, if accounts are suspected of being biased. As mentioned earlier, he suggests that there are situations, like courts, which scrutinise what is being said from a 'principled position of doubt'. This supports the possibility of informed and critical reading as a key feature of social work accounting since such scrutiny is part of the task of constructing the ratified and addressed reader. The reading relations of social work accounts expect and anticipate scrutiny and doubt.

A critical reader can take the scrutiny of social work accounting further. Not all features of the social work account are likely to be examined by the ratified reader in court or case conference. The social worker provides 'information' as well as 'analysis' and 'recommendation'. 'Information' is less likely to be contested; it is the step to 'analysis' and 'recommendation' which is available for scrutiny.[3] For the ratified reader, it is the hearing of the overall performance of the narrative to which the reader looks in order to be persuaded, passing over 'mere' details. Critical readers are able to question the detailed display of 'information' as a rhetorical process, as well as the overall story. A range of positions of doubt and acceptance is available in reading social work accounts.

In summary, it is suggested that reading character in social work accounts can be developed further than the benign construction of character offered in chapters 4 to 6. If the client is approached as 'the other' of social work stories, then undermining and alternative character depictions are already a part of the reading relations of the text. A range of concepts enables an investigation of alternative depictions. First, characters can be read as unfinalised and changing, 'round' and 'open'. Second, categorisation and naming enables typifications of characters, fitting them into routine responses. In contrast, particularisation offers the possibility of endless sub-categories. Third, social work reading occasions and ratified readers already attend to scrutiny and doubt.

Character in social work texts

Texts from three social work cases are examined for how the character of the client is depicted, attended to and how such depictions are linked to rhetorical activity. In line with the theoretical discussion above, we address three key questions of how clients are depicted as characters in social work stories: how are depictions heard as adequate, how does categorisation warrant action and how does the critical reader go beyond the scrutiny of the ratified reader? The main part of the analysis considers texts concerning two young people, Sarah and Stuart. First, we study briefly an example of the direct link between character categorisation and action in a case conference.

Characterising Mr King as a child abuser

The interrelation of character depiction and action can be observed in a radio programme about a child protection case conference.[4] The question is whether Mr King has sexually abused his partner's daughter, Jane, and what to do about it. Having agreed that Mr King probably has abused Jane, possible action is now discussed.

RADIO EXTRACT 8.1

> Chair: why would you rule out the possibility of Mr King coming back to the family and er there being some therapeutic work with them all to try and unpackage all of this I mean would you rule that out absolutely
>
> First Social Worker: yes I would Stewart because basically you can't er do therapy with someone who is not acknowledging that there's a problem
>
> Second Social Worker: yes
>
> First Social Worker: and that is the problem with Mr King er all that's going to happen if he goes back is that er the pressure will be placed on Jane to retract her story and she'll do it
>
> Second Social Worker: and the abuse will start again
>
> Chair: ok ok that's a view expressed
>
> Playgroup Leader: but do you feel that if Mr King has a chance to see the video he may then come clean he may then realise what a terrible thing he has done and with help he could be allowed back within the family
>
> First Social Worker: call me a twisted old cynic if you like but er er I I've come across very few men that have confessed to these things
>
> Playgroup Leader: it does seem a shame though that the child has got

such a lot other than the sexual part obviously from Mr King that
she's going to lose everything

Second Social worker: I think that's preferable to being abused again
and since the sexual abuse is addictive behaviour and I agree with
John it must be acknowledged by the perpetrator before it can be
worked with and I feel it's inappropriate for this child to be living
in the same house as Raymond King.

This complex interchange is towards the end of the meeting, rather like the evaluation in interviews discussed in chapter 7. It displays the strong link in social work meetings between character depictions, categorisation and action. How Mr King is negotiated and finalised will determine official attempts to control the relationships amongst these people. The problem the conference faces is that, as there is not enough evidence to prosecute Mr King, there is no legal way of removing him from the family.[5] Just before the extract above, the descriptions of Mr King are positive. The health visitor[6] and the playgroup leader[7] both describe how he appeared to have helped Jane's development, although this is immediately underscored by the chair, as "not a lot of background information". Next, Mr King is described as a support to Jane's mother by the family social worker,[8] but the social worker assumes that Mr King cannot return to the family under any circumstances. Such an assumption is ruled as premature by the chair, but it sets up the discussion of appropriate action.

Despite there being little information on Mr King amongst the speakers, his behaviour is used to depict his character and hence, what to do. The category being attributed to him is 'child abuser', with all the outrage of that ascription. However, he is a child abuser who has provided support to both mother and child. A subcategory of 'child abuser' is negotiated: 'abuser-unsupportive' as opposed to 'abuser-supportive', with speakers agreeing on the latter. This is an action as well as a character problem, since mother will not welcome his departure,[9] whereas she may have agreed to evict an 'unsupportive abuser'. A further subcategory is offered: is he the kind of 'supportive-abuser' who can be treated, reformed and return to the family? Both the chair and the playgroup leader can be heard to suggest a therapeutic subcategory: 'supportive child abuser who might be reformed'. Two social workers reject such a subcategory with a further subcategory: 'abuser who confesses may be reformed.' However, in the next two utterances, they deny such a subcategory. The first social worker considers such men do not normally confess and the second social worker denies the possibility of reform, and anyway it is too much of a risk.

In extract 8.1, negotiation over appropriate categorisation displays both agreement and dispute in the depiction of the client. Offering subcategories can be heard to relativise the main category, but this is resisted by other speakers. All speakers agree that Mr King is a child abuser and that he is supportive. Some think he can be reformed. The two social workers acknowledge the 'supportive' attribution, but reject this as a valid sub-category given the impossibility of reform; he is a child abuser, and hence a danger to Jane. Undermining the 'reform' position is achieved both rhetorically and through appeals to entitlement: depicting the character of child abusers and their right to speak affirmatively. The first social worker starts his utterance with what can be heard as a stand—"yes I would [rule out therapy]". Using "basically", a categorical statement is made about the character of all child abusers—therapy is impossible unless they confess and they don't normally confess. The "twisted old cynic" depiction of himself plus "I've come across very few ..." portrays this social worker as someone who knows about child abusers through long experience and numerous contacts.

The second social worker starts her utterance with a strong 'contrast rebuttal' to the playgroup leader—it is better to lose Mr King than be abused again. This is followed by another categorical statement about child abusers: "sexual abuse is addictive behaviour ..." Next, a more relative comment about agreement to therapy forms an alliance with the first social worker. The three comments, in descending strength, are rounded off by a personal statement about what should happen. Both social workers can be heard to use a variety of strong rhetorical devices in countering therapy.

This analysis of the negotiation of the character of a child abuser has demonstrated the manipulation of categories and their associated attributes. Subcategories are seen to emerge which attempt to resist the main category. Such resistance is undermined, as rhetorically strong statements about the main category are heard to neutralise attempts at relativity. Categorical, monologic and flat characterisations appear to enable straightforward action, and in the rest of the case conference there is no longer any consideration of Mr King being allowed to return to the family. Complex, relativised attributions have no place in an arena where competent, professional assessment and decisive action are required. We now consider examples of categorisation and relativity across different texts and contexts.

Sarah—'the angry child'

Sarah is depicted in two accounts 17 months apart. The first is the beginning of a research interview and the second a report to the Director of Social Services (appendix 8.1). In chapter 6, the character of Donna's mother changed from an unsympathetic categorisation of a rejecting and unco-operative mother to being heard as a more sympathetic character, with the potential for "long term casework". The character depiction moved from a monologic, 'flat' categorisation to being more complex, diverse and 'round'. It was suggested there that the change was related to distance from the crisis and a less strategic, more relaxed storytelling occasion in the interview. With Sarah, this is reversed; the relativised depiction heard in the research interview was prior to the categorical depiction in the report.

The interview

The first account of Sarah is a research interview and took place with her social worker in March when Sarah was aged 16. The interviewer's initial question offered an opportunity for a character depiction and two apparently conflicting versions of Sarah are made available:

> Interviewer: how would you sum up Sarah in a sentence
>
> Social Worker: oh god (-) there's two sides one is a fiery character gets angry very very quickly and feels deprived whatever you do you're always unfair in some way (-) that's accompanied with a very shy side and as she's got older she is fairly (-) I'm a bit surprised that she is keen on talking about boyfriends jobs school dreams which is really quite surprising and she'll allow me to talk with her what it might mean or not mean (-) she can say it's rubbish but she is creating a space in which we can talk which is quite interesting

In this characterisation, Sarah can be heard as complex, 'two sided' and unpredictable. She is depicted through her dealings with the social worker, in which she is "fiery" or "shy", argumentative or discussive. Both "sides" are rhetorically matched, with three line lists, but with an addition. In the first, she is "a fiery character", "angry very very quickly", "feels deprived" plus "you're always unfair". The second version lists the subjects she talks to the social worker about—"boyfriends jobs school dreams". The fourth item in each list moves the depiction on to opposing planes. The first uses direct speech to locate the hearer in an argument; the second takes us to her fantasy world. Both additions can be heard to picture Sarah and the social worker in a variety of discursive encounters, thereby reinforcing the social worker's entitlement to depict her. The use of "accompanied with" indicates that these traits appear together, although there is a temporal aspect, linking this development to her growing up—"as she's got older" and becoming more co-operative "she'll allow me...". Sarah is heard as moving from one characterisation to the other, deploying professional and everyday concepts of maturation and adolescence. That it surprises the social worker can be heard to add a note of unpredictability. Such a depiction is thus heard as complex, round and unfinalised, but competent and authorised by long term contact with Sarah.[10]

Report to the Director

The second account, Report on Sarah (appendix 8.1) is written by a social work manager. It is 17 months after the interview; the social worker has left the department and Sarah has gone through a series of crises. Sarah is portrayed in a report to the Director, asking agreement for payment of a bill at a bed and breakfast hotel (B&B) and a criticism might be anticipated.[11] A defence of poor practice is made available through a characterisation of Sarah. This depiction is categorical and finalised, and trades on contingencies outside anyone's control.

The character depiction can be read as categorical and negative—she presented "numerous problems", a list of three and an unmodalised categorisation "she remained an angry child" and "at best a handful" (lines 8-11). That a foster placement breakdown is now reported (line 12) can be heard to suggest that her character and behaviour caused this. The depiction of Sarah is offered as a partial explanation of the events which follow. It is juxtaposed with another list of three contingencies related to staffing problems—the social worker left, then the team leader and the residential unit had staffing shortages. These two sets of problems can be heard to trade on one another—the "angry" and "increasingly difficult to engage" adolescent, and the inability of social services to respond because of staff shortage. The staffing problems are presented as secondary to Sarah's behaviour since they "exacerbated" the situation. Furthermore, that Sarah's categorisation is presented in three and a half lines, whereas the staffing problems take up eight lines, indicates the apparent necessity to make available staffing problems to bolster the excuse. The third paragraph relates the move to the 'last resort' placement through Sarah's absconding and inability to make her own arrangements successfully. The B&B is "finally" achieved (line 28) confirming its last resort status, everything else had been tried.

The depiction of Sarah as a difficult character, staffing problems and Sarah's increasing non-co-operation has brought the reader to the request for payment. Woolgar (1980:252) has suggested that the framing of a report in the title or the opening utterance, instructs the reader how to read what follows. Here, the request for payment first appears in the last sentence (line 36). The reader has heard a story of an increasingly difficult child and staffing problems, not a request for payment. The structure of this story can be heard to instruct the Director about the problems of managing difficult young people in a situation of staff shortages.

A sympathetic, uncritical reading of the report might accept the categorical depiction of Sarah, the extra staff shortages, and see the B&B bill as unfortunate, but no-one's fault. The Director agreed to the payment which suggests he endorsed such a reading. However, on an accompanying form he writes: "Jim, Please do not place teenagers and families at [this B&B] hotel". This comment can be heard as an extra criticism of the episode beyond the request for payment—not only is the request bad practice, but the hotel used is in some unspecified way inappropriate.

A critical reading of the text, however, suggests major weaknesses in the formulation, not merely because of contingencies, but due to the instability of the categorisation of Sarah. Not only is the professionals' action acknowledged as bad practice; the storytelling can be heard as deficient. With the case of Mr King above and Donna in Document 3 (chapter 6), categorical character depictions seem to be linked to action formulations. Here, only difficult, uncooperative adolescents are heard to end up in last resort placements. Having access to the earlier unfinalised, round depiction, we may wonder what happened to the maturing, discussive Sarah. A number of further uncertainties can be pointed out by a critical reading of the structure of the story and character depiction.

First, the narrative provides for a chronological before and after formulation—before the foster placement breakdown and after the crisis of the period of homelessness. Most of the report is concerned with the crisis (lines 12 to 28), and yet we read that it lasted only about eight weeks, from Christmas to late February. The use of "eventually" and "finally" implies a long period of crisis and struggle. Is this extreme case formulation heard as too strong for a relatively short period of disruption?

Second, is the character formulation too negative? The period of disruption was short and the foster placement breakdown had only just occurred. When a foster placement breaks down, social workers often expect a sad and angry reaction, so a subsequent disruptive period would not be surprising. Furthermore, the apparent stability of the next five months in the B&B hotel suggests a young person who can survive in what is considered by many social workers (politicians, journalists) to be a difficult environment. Here is a 17 year old, until recently in a foster family, having stayed for five apparently uneventful months in a hotel, where (according to common knowledge) there are poor facilities, no support, inhabited by all sorts of misfits. Even the Director thinks it should not be used for teenagers nor families. Is not the reader wondering about Sarah's apparent tenacity and powers of self preservation?

Third, where is she when the report is written in August? We are not told this. Given the categorical character depiction, any subsequent disaster might have been imported to confirm the inevitability of the formulation. That nothing is mentioned suggests to the critical reader that perhaps things are not so bad as we have been told. Indeed, six months later the case was considered less of a priority.[12]

A critical reading of this report can challenge the categorical formulation of Sarah's character. Presenting her as unco-operative, angry and disruptive may have been strategically successful for the task of getting the Director's signature and a mild rebuke. However, as an adequate character formulation in the telling of a competent story, it is a categorical, monologic and finalised depiction which can be heard as weak and misleading by a critical reading. Such a superficial character formulation glosses over complex events and traits available to depict Sarah. If examined by a critical audience—her solicitor, the previous social worker, Sarah herself—the depiction could be easily challenged. Does it matter? After all, the important audience was convinced. We, critical and privileged readers, cannot forget hearing the optimism of 17 months previously. An alternative formulation might have been to depict Sarah as a complex character, who was making the difficult move to independence. This she achieved unconventionally through a break with traditional routes and a period of radical self preservation in a B&B hotel. She is an heroic figure, not a victim whom social services has helped on her way to independence. Such a formulation has no more credibility than the categorical depiction. However, it demonstrates that, as with the alternative depiction of K by Smith (1978:51), a critical reader is able to reorganise the 'facts' to produce an alternative characterisation. In the next section, we follow Stuart through more complex character depictions.

Stuart—an ambiguous character

This section investigates character depictions which are unfinalised and uncertain, but far from producing 'round' characters, can be heard to display an ambiguous character. With Stuart, the different traits attributed to him are not heard as elaborating his character depiction, but can be heard to confuse it and do not appear to guide action. In the analyses of Sarah and Mr King, weak and strong, categorical and relative, round and flat depictions are made available to justify a course of action. With Stuart, categorisation is heard as less straightforward, since depictions, actions and events appear to undermine one another. In short, Stuart's character, events and social work action are not adequately and consistently depicted nor interrelated, and the reader is left uncertain of what sort of person and course of action is being suggested. Material is drawn from three texts: an interview with Stuart's social worker in April, case file entries on Stuart between April and July and a court report in December.

The interview

As with other interviews, the researcher starts the interview with an invitation for a brief characterisation of Stuart:

> Interviewer: how would you sum up Stuart in a sentence
>
> Social Worker: oh it's going to be very biased actually I like Stuart a helluva lot I think he's a really nice kid on top of that I think some of Stuart's behaviour patterns which sets him into a circle of needing special placements has a lot to do with his background how he was brought up and a lot of it is also a cock up on our part because certain things were made quite clear at the early stages of his care history and for various reasons didn't take off (-) so Stuart is nice but has had difficulties and I don't think we have helped to make those difficulties any better

The opening, "oh this is going to be biased", can be heard to instruct the hearer that the storyteller's version of Stuart will be personal and subjective. This raises the possibility that an alternative, unheard version of Stuart is available which might be heard as 'objective'. In this opening statement and throughout the interview, Stuart is characterised by ironicising and relativising categorical depictions. At the same time, the problem of how to handle Stuart can be heard as woven into the depiction.

Elements of personal reaction, behaviour problems and failed action are made available in the opening utterance. First, the "biased" reaction is positive towards Stuart. It is bolstered with upgraded terms, "a helluva lot", "a really nice kid", suggesting to the reader that the 'objective' version might be less sympathetic. Second, the personal reaction is contrasted with Stuart's "behaviour patterns" needing "special placements". This aspect of his character is "on top of" him being really nice. It is extra to the positive characterisation, not instead of it, as with the two sides of Sarah in the interview. The repeat/summary at the end of the utterance reiterates the two aspects and uses "but" to signify the unstable link between them. With Sarah, the "two sides" were linked temporarily with one seen as (hopefully) replacing the other. With Stuart, however, the two characterisations occur together and can be heard as an uneasy balance. This "nice but has difficulties" formulation might be maintained, but is identified as "biased". With which attributes should the reader align him/herself: the 'objective' unheard version, which would acknowledge the "behaviour patterns" and "special placements", or the subjective reaction to "a really nice kid"? Third, explanation and blame for Stuart's "behaviour patterns" are located in his background and upbringing and in inadequate social services intervention. Stuart can be heard as not primarily to blame for his behaviour patterns; the unheard version may not realise this.

The two versions of Stuart's character are not merely opposites, as the 'biased' version depicts him as "nice", but also acknowledges his "difficulties". This character depiction is developed through a series of 'ambiguity contrasts'. Stuart conforms to a category and yet does not. A category is presented but then relativised. This pattern of 'X yet not really X'[13] is heard as the storyteller instructing the listener that her 'biased', unfinalised, relativised version is more appropriate than an objective, monologic, categorical version of Stuart and events. This pattern is demonstrated through Stuart's character and his behaviour and how to handle him.

Stuart as 'X yet not really X' Stuart can be heard as depicted through a number of attributes which are presented and then relativised. Throughout the interview, a categorisation is made but its universality is challenged by linking it to a particular audience or occasion. 'X but not really X' is displayed in his "mixed race":

> ...he's got this image of himself I know that sounds social worky I don't mean it in that sense (-) Stuart wants to be the big macho and very much (-) he's of mixed race and I think that may be the source of confusion for him...

The problem of being black yet not black is presented as an important aspect of Stuart and a source of his problems.[14] Towards the end of the interview, when discussing him as appropriate for fostering, he is further described as nice but with 'these worrying periods', and also little yet big:

> ...he'll get a lot out of a family and I think he's a little boy he's nearly 16 and he's big but (-) he (-) it sounds soppy doesn't it but he's a nice kid (-) put it this way the last social worker felt that if her home circumstances were different she would be prepared to take Stuart home and I felt I'd be prepared to take Stuart home actually do that type of thing because he's just a nice playful kid (-) it's just these periods which are quite serious and quite worrying...

The struggle to handle him being 'little yet big' is attended to by bringing in a trusted witness, the last social worker and a personal position. Such an affirmation of potential personal commitment is unusual in these data and can be heard as an extreme case formulation. The "put it this way" (rather than another way) formulation is a further relativising construct, telling the reader that there are different ways to see things, and here is a personal one, linking back to her initial 'biased' positioning.

At other points in the interview, a categorisation is made of Stuart without a relativising contrast. When approaching a council committee to apply for admission to a youth treatment centre (YTC), a categorisation of "considerable risk" is made:

> ...we were saying that out of concern for Stuart we were saying that he is at considerable risk if he is left in the wrong place and getting into very serious trouble and other people were at risk because he could hurt them because when he blows (-) I don't think he realises what he is doing and we were saying that unless we take the necessary steps Stuart is going to end up in very serious trouble and we haven't offered any protection at all in trying to come to terms with the anger he is feeling (-) if you don't let him go (to the YTC) he's going to cause havoc.

Here the categorisation "at considerable risk" is oriented to a specific audience and to avoiding potential blame. Whilst it is not suggested that the "we were saying" formulation excludes a "we believe" element, the description is offered as strategic for the committee, warning them of potential criticism and "havoc" if they do not act. The categorisation is for a specific audience and thus relative. A few minutes later, when the interviewer asks about the violent outbursts, they are underscored by an alternative, categorical version of Stuart:

> when he was at (secure unit) I don't think they could understand why we were taking it all so seriously what a nice lad he didn't present much hassle so in that sense he just (-) Stuart can get annoyed at the simplest things ...

Another version of Stuart is presented from a different trusted witness, who can be heard to relativise the version offered to the committee. The use of reported speech "what a nice lad" is here used to provide a supporting voice. Another audience is, however, seen as reacting differently to a categorisation of violence:

> Interviewer: did the children's homes come up with anything
>
> Social worker: personally I don't think so 'cos you've got into wanting to see the report (-) this is a violent child (-) and a bit of me can cope with this ok I've not done residential work and a bit of me can cope with the staff feeling it's important wanting the kid they take in to mix with the group that's already there and there won't be too much violence but the other bit of me thinks damn it we've got to take the risk not put him outside to other risks...

The two 'bits' of the social worker can be heard to debate the two sides of Stuart, as the depiction of violence is related to local concerns of residential staff rather than an 'objective' categorisation. The audience is shown to be the warrant for a categorisation and the hearer is instructed not to use the reactions of residential staff as a basis for a categorical depiction.

In summary, Stuart can be seen as depicted in a variety of 'X but not X' formulations. He is nice but has difficulties, he is black but not black, he is little but big, he is depicted differently when negotiating with different audiences.

Stuart is difficult to handle but easy The 'X yet not really X' formulation is also made available in describing Stuart's violent behaviour and its handling. There are examples of his violence being acknowledged, with descriptions of him being out of control and unpredictable:

> ...[he needed] specialist help because when he blows he blows...

> ...on the whole I would say that you cannot be clear when it's going to happen it might be the slightest thing...

On other occasions, however, the violent behaviour can be heard as relative. The 'X yet not X' formulation is applied in three ways. First, his violence is not so bad as a categorical depiction implies. He has been involved in violent incidents but on closer study they can be seen as understandable, considering the context of his history:

> ...I think basically he came into care because he tried to strangle his little sister which sounds awful but she's an awful little kid do you understand me you've got to put it in those terms...

> ...he was also on a rape charge but he was involved in so far as he held down the girl whilst the others did what they had to do so he was very much on the periphery...

> Interviewer: were there a lot of offences

> Social worker: no I wouldn't say a lot (-) what he has done has been serious I think [looking at the file] I can't remember but not a lot considering what he has been through you'd have expected more...

The reader is given explicit instructions about how apparently violent or delinquent behaviour can be re-interpreted and not taken at face value.

Second, the social worker can be heard to suggest that his violent behaviour depends on how he is handled:

> ... if you say Stuart I'm not going to be perturbed because you know this is the situation there's reasonable bits to him...

> ...Stuart was causing problems at [residential school] and they were like it was on the balance but equally I was a bit concerned about the help that Stuart needed whether he was getting it there...

Third, Stuart is seen as in some way in control of the outbursts:

> ...he knows that people have an idea of how violent he can be and he will use it...

> Stuart responds to that sort of regime [a secure unit] he knows how far he can go and he knows the consequences...

> ...he's got this image of himself... Stuart wants to be the big macho

Thus, despite agreeing that Stuart exhibits violent and uncontrolled behaviour, the social worker relativises any categorical depiction as a violent character through deploying context, history, handling and Stuart's own manipulation of his violent reputation.

In this interview, the depiction of the character of Stuart and his behaviour is heard in various 'X but not really X' formulations. The storytelling frequently comments on its own use of 'X but not X'. This is an important formulation. The construction of depictions and categories, which see apparent contradictions as co-existing in the same characterisation, offers a way out of Gilbert and Mulkay's (1984:14) abandoning the search for consistency and definitive versions of events and people. People can exhibit opposing attributes of categorical oppositions. It suggests that the unfinalised characters in modern novels are commonplace in everyday character assessment. The more we know people, the less we are likely to be able to make categorical and finalised assessments of them. Is this formulation restricted to interviews?

Case files notes

Case file entries in which depictions of Stuart are made available are displayed in appendix 8.2. They cover the period around the time of the interview and the following three months. As discussed in chapter 3, case file entries can be read as a 'contract' recording 'normal transactions' between client and professional (Garfinkel, 1967:198). They record activities which are available to be pieced together by an 'entitled' file reader. Whilst files do not always record all activities, the many events of this period describe almost daily activity by a 'duty officer'.[15] Stuart stayed in the B&B hotel until the end of May and then embarked with a friend on a spree of burglary and car crime across the country. In July, he moved into a hostel where he stayed until a court case in December. Latour (1987:41) notes that the success of knowledge claims depends on later readers. Were the duty social workers guided by the team leader's X but not X character depiction? Did they characterise him as 'nice but with difficulties' in their dealings with other institutions and officials?

The file entries describe the work done by the duty officer, a telephone call, letter, office interview or visit. In a volatile case like Stuart's, such entries are an important record of action with clients or other professionals as they inform the next duty officer of what has been done and what needs to be done next. On occasion, messages to later readers of the file include not only details of action but also characterisations of Stuart. Appendix 8.2 presents those file entries between March and July which included such characterisations, assessments and hints as to the way that Stuart was being depicted by the duty officers.[16]

Unlike the interview, the duty officers' characterisations of Stuart make use of a straightforward and easily categorisable depiction: he has a history of disruption and is violent. Such a categorisation can be read to inform much of their activity. The depiction of his history of violence is attended to as matter-of-fact in dealings with potential placements and is reported as one of the main reasons for lack of success. In the entry of 6/3, a voluntary organisation reports that, along with his age, "his violence" is the reason for there being no placements. Similarly, in the 17/3 entry his "character" and "past history" are made available to account for the refusal of two children's homes.

These summations do not offer further explanation nor refinement since such categorisation is enough. In the first 17/3 entry, the existence of a vacancy in a children's home is invalidated by "Stuart's character" which is "a risk to other children and indeed staff". The latter comment adds an extra upgrading of the "risk", not merely to children but staff. It cannot be toned down or ignored. Even the remand unit in entry 5/6, which it might be assumed is used to young people in serious trouble, is made aware of "his previous history" and warns of a repetition of "previous behaviour of a violent sort". The term "past history" can be read as synonymous with his violence, as in the 17/3 entry concerning the second children's home. Whilst the social worker in the interview has depicted Stuart as complex and not easily categorisable, the duty officers respond to the violent attribute, apparently to the exclusion of the "nice bits".

The social worker in the interview had commented on and illustrated how Stuart should be handled. The instructions to carers and file readers are to handle with care. The 7/3 entry can be read as warning the B&B owners and justifying their capacity to cope: previous foster experience and school caretaker. The duty officers themselves report continual difficulties: not giving in to his mood 28/5, threatened to go thieving 16/6, extremely difficult and rude 18/6. These incidents are not depicted as beyond what the duty officer can handle but they are heard as typical when handling Stuart. Unlike in the interview, there is no implied criticism of those having to handle him. Furthermore, the overall social services intervention is doubted by one of the duty officers. Whilst the social worker in the interview had continued to seek treatment, the duty officer of 11/6 presents an alternative approach: let him sort out his own problems. This is reported not merely as a description of action taken but can be read to challenge the team manager to re-orientate social services' approach to her 'plan' and asks for support and comments. No reply is recorded.

The relativised depiction of Stuart made available in the interview has not informed the construction of character in the case file entries. A categorised depiction of Stuart as violent is attended to by the duty officers. It is deployed as the determining factor of events and responses, directly tied to the duty officers' action and their justification. Perhaps the 'violent' category is a particularly strong aspect of character in these sorts of situations and its mere suggestion warrants strong attention. The social worker in the interview does not deny his violence but attempts to explain, thereby underscoring it. No similar relativising of Stuart's behaviour is made available in the case file entries. The case of Donna in chapter 6 displays similar categorical and relativising reactions to her sexual behaviour. Indeed, most social work reports contain topics which could engender high moral panic: drugs, absconding, self harm, bizarre behaviour. Categorisation and particularisation are, therefore, important rhetorical resources. Differences of audience, reading occasions and topic can be heard to engender different degrees of relativity. For the duty officer finding a placement, their daily communication with unit managers depends on monologic character depictions and clear categorisations: what sort of person is this and, in particular, what sort of handling problems will they present?

Court report

In December, Stuart appeared in court for a range of offences committed during this period and later. From July to December, he had a more stable period in a hostel and a new social worker. However, the offences had mounted and he was asked to leave the hostel just before a court appearance. It was unlikely that he would receive anything other than a custodial sentence and the social worker's report does not suggest an alternative:

> Due to the seriousness of the offences in question, I feel I cannot make a recommendation. (line 34-36)

The absence of an explicit recommendation is unusual in court reports.[17]

The structure of the court report offers sections headed 'Social History', 'Background' and 'Stuart'. The last section is presented in appendix 8.3. The 'History' and 'Background' make available a chronology of his earlier childhood, his family relations and the range of unsuccessful social services interventions. 'Stuart' offers a character depiction. Unlike the categorical characterisations of the case file, Stuart is now hard to categorise and presented in a complex 'X but not really X' formulation. A clear recommendation can be heard as impossible given this complex character. Perhaps the apparent inevitability of the outcome allows the social worker the licence of an uncategorisable formulation. It can also be read as an excuse for the many previous failed interventions. A straightforward recommendation would have required a straightforward character depiction.

The section headed 'Stuart' is split into two paragraphs, the first of which makes available a depiction of Stuart and the second describes his behaviour. Such a split echoes the "nice but has had difficulties" summary which opened the interview. The person is separated from his difficult behaviour. The initial description as a "sturdy, energetic boy who immediately adopts an offensive nature" (lines 2-3) offers the reader a description of someone who could be capable of the history just described. However, this depiction is underscored as an unintentional reaction of someone scared by "new situations", not deliberate aggression. It is also caused by "his insecurity" which had been linked earlier to his relationship with his mother. Any aggression is thus read as not his fault; he is therefore X but not in all aspects of the category.

The not X description can now be heard as a contrast, signalled by "however" (line 6). Structuring the description in situational terms, reveals those occasions when he "relaxes and becomes more amicable and friendly", "pleasant and lovely" (lines 8-9): terms with a strong alternative depiction and contrasting with the aggressive depiction. However, the not X description is itself relativised since the pleasant/lovely aspects are only reserved for a few people. As these privileged/patient people are not identified, they are not able to speak on his behalf. Stuart remains an enigma, as not only are the categorisations 'aggressive/lovely' juxtaposed, but they are available in only limited situations. The reader is left wondering what he is like the rest of the time.

The second paragraph continues the pattern of setting up descriptions to undermine them. He looks older than he is but degenerates to be younger (lines 15-16). He requires intervention to place boundaries around his behaviour but is becoming too big for it (lines 16-19). The final sentence begins "on the other hand" as a hope against the abandonment of effort which the previous sentence implied. However, there is further undermining of any hopeful outcome: he craves affection but his response is only superficial (line 26-8). In summary, he requires treatment but is getting too big, he can respond sometimes, but only superficially. Every claim is relativised and hence undermined. At all points, the reader is stopped from making any categorical assessments.

The court report returns to and extends the 'X but not X' characterisation of Stuart. The monologic, categorical depictions in the case file enable the duty officers to justify their action on clear characterisations. Here, no course of action is legitimated, even the treatment approach of the interview is no longer a realistic option. The conclusion begins:

> Stuart has some very serious emotional problems that require expert help in unravelling over a long period of time. (lines 30-32)

There is, however, an unheard recommendation in the conclusion where he is depicted as responding "only to those (establishments) with a strict regime where boundaries have to be strictly adhered to". This is not merely a negative recommendation: I don't know what to do, do what you think? "Strict regime" echoed by "strictly adhered to" can be heard by the judge as a clear recommendation for a custodial sentence. There is no recommendation but then again there is.

This analysis of three texts which depict Stuart has suggested that they offer different versions of his character, behaviour and social work intervention. The 'X but not X' formulation can be heard as a rhetorical feature which continually categorises and relativises Stuart, his behaviour and what to do. The uncertainty for the reader is how to hear these characterisations. They can be heard to confuse rather than convince us that Stuart is being adequately represented. The ratified reader of the interview may accept the picture of conflicting attributes, but can they be resolved? The ratified reader of the case notes might also accept that the duty officer is constrained by many other audiences. The ratified reader of the court report may accept that there is no alternative to a custodial sentence, and concur with an opportunity to let the court know both how hard the department has tried and that not all has been a failure. But the critical reader is only confused. S/he might suspect that the unheard objective version of Stuart is overpowering any attempt to depict him sympathetically; he is really a pretty difficult character and, as one duty officer suggests, should be left to himself. 'X but not X' depictions of Stuart appear in two of the three texts, and far from building a round, complex depiction, the reader is likely to be more influenced by the unheard story.

This chapter has developed the search for 'the other' by considering how clients are depicted in social work accounts. The analysis of the three clients has offered different characterisations, in terms of a categorical/relativised depiction. Mr King was constructed in categorical terms: he is a child abuser. The negotiation of the case conference and display of rhetorical power by the social workers could be seen to dismiss attempts to relativise the category into subcategories. The outrage of the ascription, child abuser, was re-established. Future action was clear, the alternative version not given a chance. With Sarah, despite an earlier complex and 'round' character depiction, the later report aims to depict her in categorical terms. This can, however, be read as weak, defensive and possibly deceptive. A critical reading suggests gaps and an alternative heroic depiction of Sarah. The third case, Stuart, moves between relativised and categorical depiction in different texts in different contexts. However, the relativised depiction 'X but not X' is not heard as 'round' but as confusing. The character depiction and its unheard alternative are intertwined, the latter appearing to overpower the former.

Overall, reading these social work texts for adequacy of representation suggests that character depictions of clients can be undermined with gaps and slippage exploited by a critical reading. Alternative versions have been made available, suggesting that 'the other' is accessible. These alternative depictions, Mr King as potential for treatment, Sarah as a heroine, Stuart as a violent character, are not offered as superior to the preferred depictions and other depictions might be envisaged. The importance of this analysis is that social work representations of character face intense scrutiny in arenas of 'principled positions of doubt' (Cuff 1980:32). Unless the reader is tightly bound to the community of social work hearers and is a ratified reader, then doubt can be anticipated.

Another implication of this study is how the link between depiction and action is negotiated. It was suggested with Mr King that strong categorisation enabled strong action, whereas with Stuart confusing depiction produced uncertain action. Action and depiction are tied to one another; they mutually elaborate one another. Does this suggest that monologic, categorical depictions are a product of their being determined by the straightforward direction of action? Plot determines character, a-psychological stories. Mr King is constructed in categorical terms, as the action available requires a decisive decision: he is a child abuser and must be excluded from the house. The treatment possibilities are not available, hence the therapeutic categorisation is not acceptable. Where action is uncertain or multi-directional, then complex depictions can be made available. Character depictions are heard to overpower plot, justifying the uncertainty of action. Stuart's ambiguity is heard to render any action as inappropriate. The middle of these two extremes, where action is less contested, for example in the interview with Sarah, depictions can be heard as 'round'. There is less requirement to depict character in order to justify action. Action and depiction are separated, as they are less mutually accountable.

Has a critical reading been taken too far? Perhaps we should pull back from asserting that action determines depiction, or that social work depictions are weak and inadequate, easily replaced by the unheard story. The more modest claims of this chapter might be that depicting character in social work accounts is complex and variable with a variety of categorical and relativised formulations of clients being made available. Such formulations are likely to vary with audience and reading occasion. Chapters 7 and 8's search for 'the other' and a more critical reading are offered as possibilities for wider debate in a field of research, reluctant to go beyond describing benign construction.

NOTES

[1] For example, Pip in Peter Ackroyd's 'English Music' (1992:87) says to the stranger: "Why should I be trapped in the vision you have of me? There are other visions after all."

[2] Sacks (1972), Silverman (1987), Watson (1978) and Cuff (1980) discuss 'membership categorisation devices'. This is the interactional work involved in manipulating categories and their associated attributes. They show how categories are linked in collections, so that the use of a depiction in one collection can be subverted by attributes from related collections. In this way, apparent agreement about character depictions can still engender disputes about the appropriate attributes of that character.

[3] Toulmin's concept (1958) of the 'warrant' which enables data to lead to action is discussed in chapter 4.

[4] The radio programme 'Face the Facts' describes the case conference as taking place, but with "the names of participants and some circumstances altered for reasons of confidentiality."

[5] As the conference hears that the police cannot prosecute, the Doctor summarises the problem:
> There are two issues what to do with the child and what to do with Mr King and if there are no grounds for prosecuting Mr King er if that's what we are being told then what can we do legally to stop him living in the household.

[6] Health Visitor: since [Mr King] came on the scene things did seem to pick up a lot in her development er her speech was improving er she was lively and loving with Raymond and until [this suspicion] I had in fact ceased to worry about Jane's development as she was coming on in leaps and bounds it seemed to me.

[7] Playgroup Leader: we've noticed that Jane runs to er Mr King easier than what she runs to her Mum at home time always seems very happy when he picks her up
Chair: I mean essentially we haven't got a lot of background information have we.

[8] Family Social worker: [mother] has obviously found in Mr King a strong personality er a lot of control and order er that if we're going to consider Jane continuing to live with her that we've got to in some way provide because clearly er I think although we haven't got on to that decision Mr King won't be on the scene er well will not be allowed by the department to live with her (-) so I think we got to ...

Chair: there's John leading us in that direction, all right let's move back from that ...

Another social worker: I mean yes Mr King is quite a support to Mrs. Harris and we hear he collects the child from the playgroup he sits in two nights a week while she has a a little job and indeed that's quite likely when the abuse has taken place there is no indication that he has a job but if he is drawing benefit I mean there is additional money going into the household there is a financial reason for her wanting him back it would seem.

[9] Another social worker: I wondered if [family social worker] has put it to [mother] er that there may be a choice between having Jane living with her or having Raymond

Family social worker: yes I mean it certainly has been put to her that's one of the issues

Chair: and her response to that

Family social worker: really rather non committal.

[10] The rest of the interview charts a series of difficult episodes of parental rejection, disruption, but eventually a successful foster placement. The story can be heard to trade on the hero-social worker overcoming the odds.

[11] At the time, this particular budget was overspent and all payments were scrutinised by the Director. Use of B&B was seen as an unnecessary expense and as poor professional practice. This request is for a 'last resort' placement (see chapter 4), B&B payments over several months, and, as the placement was unplanned, there is further potential for criticism.

[12] When I last had access to the file six months later, it was not clear where Sarah was living. The case was unallocated and little recent contact. There was mention of her being missing from the B&B and in September spending time with her mother.

[13] The 'X but not X' formulation was first suggested to me by Steve Woolgar.

[14] The meta-utterance "that sounds social worky I don't mean it that way" further responds to and comments on the relativising work that is taking place: I am a social worker but I am not talking that way. Perhaps it is referring back to the personal v objective juxtaposition at the beginning.

[15] This case was not allocated to a specific social worker during this period and the social worker who was interviewed was 'holding' the case, that is, available for consultation but not available to do all the work. The work was generally carried out by a variety of social workers 'on duty', handling emergency work.

[16] Other case file entries describe action taken without commenting directly on Stuart's character or behaviour. For example:

2/6 Tried [Residential Admissions section and Remand Centre]. Neither can offer anything. No call from [hostel].

Such an entry merely describes action but when read as part of an ongoing sequence of similar descriptions, it can be heard as depicting Stuart as difficult to place.

[17] Spencer (1988:65) considers that information in a court report is selected to make a recommendation appear appropriate.

APPENDIX 8.1
Sarah: report to director

Sarah had been in care since 19_ following the divorce of her parents. After a period in [children's home] and an attempted reconciliation, Sarah stayed in [children's home]. A further reconciliation with mother failed and Sarah went to live at [children's home] in [date], where she remained until [date]. A family placement was then found with [foster parents].

Sarah presented numerous problems during this period – truancy, promiscuity, educational difficulties. Sarah has remained an angry child throughout this period and is described as a "handful". Unfortunately the placement with the [foster parents] broke down at Christmas. Plans had already been laid for Sarah to move towards independent living however, she became increasingly difficult to engage. This was exacerbated by her social worker [name] leaving, and our not being able because of the vacancy situation to allocate another worker. This was then further complicated by the Team Manager leaving, and resulted in our having to deal with Sarah on a duty basis. We attempted to find alternative residential placements for Sarah but with no success; the only establishment with vacancies was [children's home] but that attempt floundered because [children's home] was short-staffed.

Eventually Sarah moved to [hostel] in January. However, 30 minutes after being taken there she absconded. She then spent several uncomfortable weeks with friends, although refused to tell us where. Finally Sarah came into the office on [date] and we arranged for her stay at [B&B hotel]. This she did from March until July. We have written to [social security] asking for them to pay for this accommodation but the situation was complicated by Sarah refusing to sign on. In the meantime [B&B hotel] are asking us to meet the cost for 127 nights stay, and thus until [social security] make a decision I am asking for [cost] funding and then to look to [social security] for reimbursement.

APPENDIX 8.2
Stuart: Case Notes

The following are those file entries between March and July, which included characterisations and assessments of Stuart (see footnote 16).

In March, Stuart is asked to leave a hostel which considered that 'Stuart's violence is uncontainable'. The duty officer is asked to look for an alternative placement and on 4 March 14 phone calls are made to various institutions and officials seeking a placement in a secure unit, hostel or children's home. None is successful and Stuart "made his own arrangements". The search for a placement continued:

> 6/3. Overnight placement needed for Stuart. We are unable to provide anything from our [placements section]. Emergency overnight hostel needed - difficult as most hostels will not take under 16 years. Rang [Voluntary Organisation] for suggestions. They tried all suitable, possible placements and have come up with nothing - either because of his age or violence.

A B&B hotel was found for Stuart on 7/3 and the duty officer contacted the owner:

> I explained to [owner] about Stuart being in care and that he can be touchy and will need to be handled with care at times. Mr _ said that it was ok. His wife has done fostering and he has been a school keeper.

On 17/3, the team leader asked the duty officer to continue to try to find a placement in a children's home in the area:

> 17/3   I phoned [manager responsible for residential vacancies] and he had already had some details of Stuart's past. He said that there is only a place at [children's home] but Stuart's character would not be appropriate to be placed there as he might be a risk to other children and indeed staff. He suggested [another home] which he would contact himself....

> 17/3 Telephone call from [the second children's home]. Mr _ is saying that they were not able to accommodate him on two counts. 1. they are full. 2. that it was doubtful that with Stuart's past history they would be able to accommodate him.

Initially, there are no problems at the B&B hotel. However, the duty officer reports difficulties with Stuart wanting to transfer hotels at the end of May.

> 28/5 ..I advised Stuart to return to B&B hotel. This he has not accepted but told me to find a B&B somewhere else from [this area]. Thinking that it has taken all morning to ring around places for him unsuccessfully I don't think we should give into Stuart's mood.

A burglary spree now begins and he is remanded in care some 300 miles away. In a conversation with a unit in that area, Stuart is discussed:

> 5/6 [Area Manager] spoke to [headmaster] and explained the difficulties in placing Stuart both in relation to his previous history and to the current Court Case in [that area]. After receiving a potted history from me [headteacher] agreed to keep Stuart at [unit] for as long as necessary to complete his court case provided there are no repetitions of his previous behaviour of a violent sort which would warrant his removal..

Stuart returns to the area but is immediately arrested. The duty social worker visits him at police station and tries to sort out a placement with him:

> 11/6 ..I spoke with Stuart about the possibility of a place at [hostel]. He said that he is not interested because he is "sick of staff and other boys" and was not even prepared to entertain the idea of a visit and initial interview. We returned to the prospects of B&B and I said how we had been

unable to find anything. We discussed the
possibility of Stuart finding something for
himself in [another area] where all his
friends are. Stuart was keen on this idea.

[Note to Team Manager]
The above is the present situation with
Stuart are you able to support this plan? I
have organised it on the basis of Stuart
sorting out his own problems which is what he
wants to do.
Comments please - plus signature for money

16/6   Stuart to the office requesting
money.... he threatened to go thieving. I
felt discussing this with Stuart would make
him more likely to do this. He left refusing
to sign for money.

18/6   Telephone call from Night Duty social
worker. She had been called to police station
to collect Stuart who had been picked up
(burglary ?) but not charged. He was extremely difficult and rude with both police
and social worker.. when asked for an address
he refused to give it and became abusive. He
finally stormed off whereabouts unknown.

APPENDIX 8.3
Extract from Court Report

Stuart

Stuart presents himself as a sturdy, energetic boy who immediately adopts an offensive nature when he is approached with any new situation he does not feel in control of. This seems to be due to his insecurity. However, as he becomes more comfortable in a situation and ceases to feel threatened, he relaxes and becomes more amicable and friendly. He can be a pleasant and lovely boy, however, it takes a great deal of time, work and patience before Stuart will trust anyone, and therefore it is only the people who are closest to him that begin to understand this. He is of quite reasonable intelligence.

Stuart is a boy whose stature suggests him to be older than he actually is, but his behaviour is capable of degenerating below his age. Stuart has few, if any, internalised boundaries and is therefore a boy who needs definite external limits that must be clearly and persistently drawn. He is then capable of acting and reinforcing behaviour of a positive and constructive nature. Unfortunately, as he gets bigger it becomes more difficult for people (Social workers, care staff etc) to physically set those limits when necessary. On the other hand, he is a boy who thrives on individual attention and appears to be searching for a model to base his behaviour on. He craves affection and is capable of reciprocating it, although on a somewhat superficial basis.

Conclusion

Stuart has some very serious emotional problems that require expert help in unravelling over a long period of time. To date he has been placed in many establishments and responds only to those with a strict regime where boundaries have to be strictly adhered to. Due to the seriousness of the offences in question, I feel I cannot make a recommendation, but would respectfully ask the Court to make a decision as seen appropriate.

Conclusion

This study has located social work in the everyday written and spoken documents of professional activity which are treated as text, interaction and performance. In particular I have deployed theories of narrative to explore literary and rhetorical features which enable social work to be constructed. It is suggested that such textual and interactional work is central to the everyday accomplishment of social work; it is how the job gets done in the many discursive arenas of the profession.

In order to justify and display their work as legitimate and authoritative, social workers produce accounts which do not merely lay out facts, assessments and recommendations, but are made available as persuasive, surprising and crafted narrative performances for critical audiences on specific occasions. Such stories are heard to simplify the complexities of personal troubles and professional responsibilities into narratives of complex characters and social work plots. Characters in social work stories are portrayed as people with problems, attributes and histories, enabling events and behaviours to be rendered understandable. At the same time, strange or dangerous behaviour and extraordinary events form the basis for tales of alarm and action. In short, features like plot, character, denouement, point of view, moral assessment, synecdoche are central to the performance of social work.

The main feature of this approach to narrative has been to look at stories through audiences, the role of the reader and the identification of textual relations between writers and readers, speakers and listeners. This is important since it does not attempt to subscribe motives or intentions to social work writers and speakers, avoiding links between thought and action or the existence of a 'private language' so criticised by Wittgenstein. Rather, it sees language as a social activity in which meaning is a product of social interaction and context, with shifting interpretations and negotiated constructions of reality. It requires an interest in how texts are made available to be read and what characteristics of readers can be invoked. Stories only exist when they are read and reacted to: when the audience's attention is gripped, when the listener awaits the denouement, when the reader evaluates the morals or the force of the tale. Our concern has been, then, with the performance of stories to audiences, whether that performance is the joint accomplishment of a research interview, the reading of a report or the display of textual analysis.

There have been a number of readers. I have been mainly concerned to identify the reader that the text constructs, the 'ratified' or 'entitled' reader. In this way, it has been suggested that the appropriate reading of the story can be located through the conventions to which texts appear to subscribe. Thus, in the 'failure to thrive' story in chapter 4, the construction of reading conventions of poor mothering and competent professionals locates the characteristics of the reader and writer in hearing versions of proper parenting and good social work. By invoking such conventions the reader is drawn into a community of competent readers.

A second reader has been the 'superaddressee', the character before whom writers and readers may jointly have to appear (and appeal) for authority and legitimation: the judge, the senior manager, the social work academic, the press. In the 'broken nose' story in chapter 3, guessing how the judge would hear the facts and explanations of the mother's behaviour was suggested as a key feature of the construction of the story. In this way, the reader and writer can make agreements about how competent stories and justifiable formulations can be appropriately heard and closed.

A third reader was the critical reader of the later chapters. Here, we were invited to 'deconstruct' the texts by looking for gaps and slippage in the logic of the story. It offered an opportunity to note how speakers invoked power and authority with certain audiences, but in doing so that authority was seen to ignore inconsistencies and to silence other equally viable versions. In the case of Sarah in chapter 8, two texts appeared to invoke quite different versions of her character. Armed with the earlier text, such rhetorical moves could be read as deceitful, enabling the critical reader to question the authority of the writer.

The final reader is the you, the implied reader of this text. Here I shift my ground and await your judgement. How have you been approached, constructed and (hopefully) persuaded? Work on the persuasive strategies of sociologists (Ashmore 1989, Atkinson 1990, Woolgar and Ashmore 1988) has highlighted the importance of rhetorical and narrative practices. When investigating such practices, it is tempting to deploy them rather freely. There has been widespread use of three line lists, contrast devices and using 'we' to include you in my investigations, and the use of 'synecdoche'. Like the ethnographers described by Atkinson, I have tried to display to the reader something of the exotic world of the social worker and to invoke my authority and experience in talking about it. Like researchers of language, I have displayed large amounts of social work text[1] and given you the opportunity to disagree with my interpretation of what is going on. I have even tried to give some of you an opportunity to speak.[2]

Concern about the reader has been, in part, a persuasive device, to display the writer as someone open to possible disagreement. However, it is also an attempt at a different version of analytical writing; one that acknowledges the uncertainty of making claims and the possibility of alternative versions. The advantage of such an approach is to suggest that strong texts of any kind can be undermined. Perhaps this offers an opportunity at last for policy implications. In the rest of this chapter, I want to locate this study in wider debates about language, social construction, reflexivity and policy, and suggest that narrative approaches have a great deal to offer.

Language

This approach to social work has concentrated on an investigation of how social work is constructed through language. It is clearly in contrast to traditional descriptions of social work as developed by social work academics. Often associated with rational decision-making methods, such writers examined professional work in terms of formulations above everyday activity. Assessment or care planning, life story work or counselling are offered as ways of bundling what social workers do into overall concepts which give the work a direction or purpose. Usually these wider concepts are evaluated as successful or not, with conceptions of 'good practice' promoted. Social workers do not merely visit people, hold meetings, make phone calls or write letters, but such activities are given meaning through such wider labels.

To approach social work as available in and through language is to step back from the rational decision-making approach. Wider formulations are seen as problematic since they ignore the interactive nature of their construction. They are imposed on everyday activities by outsiders. Studies of such processes question whether decisions and plans are 'made' through the rational decision-making process. Instead, it is suggested that the rational decision-making process is used as a justification for action, not a guide. Brieland (1959) found that social workers judged the suitability of foster parents from information in the early part of the interview, using the rest of the meeting to seek evidence to justify the 'decision'. More fundamentally, Garfinkel's (1967:114) study of jurors reverses the process of decision-making:

> Jurors do not actually have an understanding of the conditions that defined a correct decision until after the decision had been made. Only in retrospect did they decide what they did that made their decisions correct ones. When the outcome was in hand they went back to find the 'why', the things that led to the outcome, and then in order to give the decisions some order, which namely is the 'officialness' of the decision ... the decision maker's task is justifying a course of action. The rules of decision making in daily life may be much more preoccupied with the problem of assigning outcomes their legitimate history than with the question of deciding before the actual occasion of choice the conditions under which one, among a set of alternative possible courses of action, will be elected.

Similarly, doing counselling or family therapy has been shown to be a complex negotiated task (Scheff 1966, Gubrium 1992). Clients are persuaded to conform to the process of therapy and workers actively construct assessments of family problems and solutions through interaction and language.

Taking language as the focus of research is now well established in the human sciences and cultural studies. The 'linguistic turn' associated with post modernism disguises a long tradition of studying language.

> The 'real world' is to a large extent unconsciously built upon the language habits of the group. (Sapir, 1929:209)

Communication between people is not merely swapping facts and opinions. Talk and writing are not like a glass through which an image passes unaffected; the glass at least distorts the message if not re-constitutes it. The process of communication becomes an integral part of what is transmitted and what is received. A better analogy is giving someone a birthday present. The giver anticipates what the receiver would like and what is appropriate to give. The receiver unwraps the parcel expecting to be delighted and to have a relationship with the receiver displayed. The present is much more than the object; it is the demonstration of a relationship, a special occasion, a series of obligations. Talk and writing are social interactions which in different ways aim to influence listeners and readers. Social actors have the capacity to anticipate reactions, build alliances, manipulate and deceive hearers, influence and entertain. There is also the potential for misunderstanding, embarrassment and stories which do not work.

Research on professionals which focuses on language has been wide-ranging but with little use of narrative theory.[3] Narrative as a focus of language research has certain advantages. First, the analysis is oriented towards large utterances, in contrast to research which focuses on sentences or turns. The whole thrust of a speaker's position can be traced as the story is introduced, told and its significance outlined. Second, through the story, speakers and hearers are able to grasp together into a single performance a wide range of facts, opinions, characters and events. Third, narrative is at the same time an everyday and analytic concept, enabling mundane and theoretical concepts to be linked together. Fourth, narrative is an interactive and textual entity enabling spoken and written documents to be compared. Finally, to repeat the comments of Herrnstein-Smith (1980:232) or Butler (1990:13), all texts have the potential to be read as a narrative.

Social construction

The study of reality as socially constructed rather than objectively available is also a well established tradition in sociology, particularly in social problems research. Again, social constructionism is not necessarily associated with scepticism or post modernism. Writers are divided over how social problems are viewed and what 'social construction' entails. There is a wide-ranging debate about the current status of social constructionism and social problems theory (Best 1989, Holstein and Miller 1993) and, whilst it is not proposed to summarise these arguments, a few observations are in order.

In this study, I have used 'social construction' in a rather unspecific manner, glossing over and borrowing from different approaches. This is partly because each 'school' makes interesting contributions, even though this can, as Bogen and Lynch (1993:214) comment, amount to 'internecine squabbles'. Using recent debates, we can locate where we have got to in our project and what aspects can be developed further. Much of the social construction literature is realist in approach. It was noted at the beginning of this chapter the difference between a deliberate, strategic approach to storytelling compared with interactive, reader orientation. This is mirrored in different approaches to social construction, with some researchers promoting 'claims-making' about social problems as deliberate, strategic action, aimed at influencing governmental and media discussions. This gives rise to metanarratives about social problems and rational action, privileging researchers' definitions of what counts as a social problem (Miller L., 1993). Other researchers stress the construction of social problems through interaction (Gubrium,1993).

Three approaches to social construction can be delineated. First, some writers are interested in the processes whereby various parties make 'claims' about a social problem, whilst acknowledging the objective status of the problem. For example, Spector and Kituse (1977) note that legislators' saw marijuana as addictive in the 1930s but by the 1960s it was no longer seen as addictive. However, during this time the substance remained the same. Actors interpret certain activities as social problems because of different histories, cultures or interests and such claims-making is an important arena for study, but the behaviour and conditions remain the same. Ultimately some versions of the problem are more accurate than others in assessing its objective status. Best (1993), for example, notes how investigating the social construction of AIDS inevitably entails a different approach to the social construction of satanism, although in both cases claims are made about widespread deaths. The researcher is likely to approach the claims in the latter case with more scepticism than the former, thereby asking different questions. For these researchers, social problems are social facts separate from their interpretation and it is possible to distinguish between 'true' and 'false' claims.

A second version sees the processes whereby social problems are constructed as integral to the nature of the social problem. How a social problem is constituted cannot be separated from how claims about it are made. There are thus no objective conditions to social problems and no distinction between 'real' and 'false' social problems. Unlike the above, such researchers are careful to avoid stating the true nature of the social problem, since it is located in the claims-making activity of interested parties. The problem is 'constitutive' of the claims made about it, the product of the work of various claims-makers.

A third approach develops the constitutive nature of social problems by acknowledging that analysts are also involved in constructing social problems. If researchers are engaged in the study of how various parties construct claims about social problems, how can their own claims-making more objectively delineate social processes? As Bogen and Lynch (1993:216) note, constructionists have made "a principled distinction between sociological and common-sense knowledge" and given privileged status to the latter. Even if the objective status of the social problem is questioned, the activities of claims-making has become the object of constructionist research. Schneider (1993:108) notes:

> For constructionists, as Ibarra and Kituse reiterate, our "objects" are (other) members' mundane idioms and activities. We take the ontological status of these objects seriously, never speaking of them as putative.

It requires a more self reflexive approach, engaging with rather than denying the facticity of the entity. Woolgar and Pawluch (1985:224) suggest that analysts should treat all claims-making in the same way and attempt to get beyond the "current impasse between proponents of objectivism and of relativism". Research should look at how claims are made and study the nature of all writing about social problems.

These approaches to social construction are not easily separated nor is a preferred version identifed. As Woolgar and Pawluch suggest, it is unavoidable to engage in social research without moving between various positions, even realism.

> Perhaps all attempts at accounting (explaining) depend upon presenting at least some state of affairs as objective. Perhaps there must always be some reliable dependable and not fluid determinant of the phenomenon to be explained. (1985:224)

How I have depicted (how anyone depicts) child abuse has continually moved between the three approaches of social construction since the consequences of leaving out one are so serious. We cannot say that there is not an activity whereby children are hurt, and worse, by adults. We cannot say that the activities of social workers and doctors, campaigners and legislators have not changed how we view the phenomenon. We cannot view our own writing about child abuse without worrying about how we depict the topic. And the word 'worrying' is right. If we make too bold a choice we leave out too much.

> We owe it to the children to help if we possess some knowledge or strategies which might alleviate their suffering. (Psychiatrist to students)

> [The aim of the paper] was to open a space for wondering why child beating is today most commonly read as a story of determinate pathology rather than, for instance, as the indeterminate effect of a bloody drama—a powerful play of violence behind the closed doors of privatised power—performed by people denied access to a script of public power and embedded in the text of corporate capitalism. (Pfohl 1985:230)

> Relativists may remark that some of the things called child abuse are seen only in a culture such as ours. But no one has yet had the pluck to suggest that our antipathy to child abuse itself is merely relative to our culture. (Hacking 1991:260)

These statements about child abuse all move between realism, constructivism and constitutiv-ism, and yet perhaps there are similarities in their claims. All want to do what is best for injured children, poor families, and worry about the state of professional power and knowledge. So do I. All are concerned about the status of knowledge: it is not good enough, it is controlled by interests, it asks the wrong questions. Perhaps by accepting the obvious nature of all these claims we can move further. Child abuse is obviously not merely a specific set of behaviours that can be identified; it is a malleable phenomenon (Hacking 1991:259, Parton 1991). Various parties are clearly committed to promoting their own interests (including me promoting the neglected importance of a narrative approach). Children are hurt, social workers have to do something about that and they need our support in making decisions. Perhaps we are obliged to be realist, constructivist and constitutive.

Approaching social construction as narrative has advantages. Reading stories involves recognising that the same facts can be interpreted differently, and how a story is constructed is integral to a successful narrative performance and to what the facts are. The social worker in the 'broken nose' story in Chapter 3 recognised this: "our side of the story". Readers and writers would accept that the boy was injured but different stories play out the nature, seriousness, intent and blameworthiness of the injury and in doing so the injury changes. The injury in narrative is real, actively constructed but also constituted and re-constituted in the performance.

Reflexivity

By considering the constructedness of social reality we accept the constructedness of all claims, including our own. All texts make representations about the world and, as all social reality is produced in texts, so this text is concerned with reality construction and claims-making. I have suggested that social workers tell stories to arrange an orderly world to display authoritative descriptions, assessments and programmes for action to critical audiences. Other writers describe other professional storytelling as concerned with creating their world in terms which enable them to set the agenda and become the mandatory rite of passage. Latour (1983) shows how Pasteur was able to persuade farmers that by passing through his laboratory anthrax could be cured. Loseke (1989) shows how wife abuse is constructed in terms of how it is to be dealt with, as a problem of police work. Now apply such claims to this text.

I have seen the social worker as a teller of complex and authoritative narratives, so how about the sociologist as a storyteller. Such a proposal is not new. Gale Miller (1993:269) notes the poststructuralist challenge to "serious" writing as "impartial, objective and privileged".

> Two ways in which privileged and mundane texts may be equalised is through deconstructive criticism, and reflexive writing practices that point to the partiality and constructedness of "serious" writers' stories.

Ashmore (1989) turns to formulations of sociologists of science on their own writing. So how can narrative and rhetorical analysis be turned on this text in a way that develops (and undermines) my claims about the centrality of narrative?

Strong ending

This study has presented a new approach to social work as narrative, focusing on text, interaction and performance. Drawing on ideas from sociolinguists, literary theory and anthropology, as well as social constructionism and micro sociology, a comprehensive approach to narrative has been outlined and applied to a wide range of social work documents. In doing so we have asked fundamental questions about professional work, the nature of research and social theory.

Conventional approaches see social work in terms of rational decision-making and positivist methods, which accept the objective nature of the data. This is challenged. Through a detailed analysis of these social work documents, we have seen how social work is made available through the use of rhetorical devices and narrative features which enable strong claims to be made and important audiences persuaded. Each document has been analysed for specific persuasive features and overall narrative structure. The characteristics of the ratified reader have been identified in the instructions made available to direct and construct the correct reading. It has been suggested that the application of narrative analysis has been a more appropriate way of understanding why social work texts are organised in the way they are.

This approach has linked social work

Weak ending

This study has attempted to investigate the extent to which social work talk and writing involve methods similar to storytelling. I have applied a variety of concepts of storytelling from socio-linguists and conversation analysis which shows that social workers make use of literary methods like stories in literature or everyday conversation. This offers new ways of applying other theoretical concepts to socialwork.

Such an approach is offered as an alternative approach which emphasises the social construction of social work talk. A sample of social workers were interviewed and some of their reports and case notes examined. An analysis of interview data and reports has shown how stories enabled the social workers to organise ideas and assessments into a coherent presentation. They were structured like other story structures, with an orientation, critical situation and resolution, and used persuasive speech devices. Many of the conventions used language features which would be familiar to other social work professionals. This approach which concentrated on the language used by social workers can shed a new light on the way that social work texts are constructed and can question the traditional ways of analysing those texts.

Studying professional activity by concentrating on the use of the language is becoming an increasingly importo debates in postmodernism, social constructionism and discourse theory. It has also promoted the application of narrative theory as a powerful analytic tool. It is suggested that further research in this area will offer fruitful insights into how professional work is accomplished and lead to an examination of how to research social work and the attendant policy implications.

tant new field of research. There is use of interesting new research methods of which storytelling is increasingly being developed. The study can help to develop this type of approach and thereby offer a better understanding of social work in particular and professional work in general.

These two endings attempt to show/powerfully demonstrate that rhetorical and narrative features can make a difference between/are integral to strong and weak claims. There are differences in a number of/three ways. First, the strong ending overuses to the point of saturation/makes widespread use of the rhetorical features I have discussed/we have seen—three line lists, contrasts, 'we' as opposed to 'I' etc. Second, the strong version links/locates the ambitions of the study to wider and more esoteric debates with strong allies and strong words—'fundamental' as opposed to 'alternative', 'powerful' as opposed to 'interesting'. Also/Third, the strong ending has more of a story/narrative structure since the complication-to-resolution move is/can be seen to be achieved by contrasting/challenging this approach with 'conventional approaches'. Finally, the weak ending remains more within itself and its own methods, an alternative view of social work (possibly alongside others) as opposed to the overblown/grand claims that narrative is the essence of social work.

> I rather like the weak ending, it is more modest in both its claims and its language, not so brash and claiming foundationalism.
> Yeah, but that undermines the whole thesis. If you can achieve reader approval by being modest and self effacing, perhaps that is more powerful than being strong.
> That sounds like another study.
> Perhaps the next book. Social work as mild and nice storytelling?
> Naargh.

Policy

Social Worker: You haven't really handled my questions about the abused child, have you? You have ignored them since chapter 4.

Author: Yes. That has been disappointing, I suppose. I did 'cop out' like other writers. I merely separated texts about child abuse as the construction of professionals, from the abusing behaviour, and said that it is impossible to move from one to the other without massive storytelling and rhetorical activity.

Social Worker: Well, that's not much help to me, is it? Can't you tell me anything about how I can get better at predicting and preventing child abuse? How can I know what is going on out there?

Author: You misunderstand me. At the beginning of this research, I had so hoped to come up with some answers which would help improve professional practice to help you ... and the children, of course! After struggling with 'data' and writing this book, I have only uncovered more questions and undermined more positions. But such scepticism is not aimed at social work, anymore than at social science or social policy. All attempts at representation are equally available to be scrutinised for their rhetoric and narrativity.

Social Worker: All this ivory tower academic angst just doesn't face the issues of the real world. Look, I'm getting really annoyed by this dialogue. You are doing myself and my colleagues an injustice by thinking that this voice can represent all the possible reactions of social workers. Besides you are only using me as a 'person of straw', a position which is simply presented to be easily rebutted.

Author: Oh heck. And here's me thinking I'm doing you a favour.

Relativism and reflexive writing do not easily lend themselves to suggestions about policy, at least comments in the British tradition of social policy writing, where it might be seen as social reform or 'social engineering.' This is summed up by Foucault (1981:12-3). When asked whether 'Discipline and Punish' stifled attempts at prison reform, he does not consider that the answer is in the hands of the social workers:

> My project is precisely to bring it about that they [social workers] no longer know what to do, so that the acts, gestures, discourse which up until then had seemed to go without saying become problematic, difficult and dangerous ... What is to be done ought not to be determined from above by reformers, be they prophetic or legislative, but by a long work of comings and goings, of exchanges, reflections, trials, different analyses ... The problem is one for the subject who acts.

I am not advocating that social workers should be put in a position to 'not know what to do'. However, locating the problem with 'the subject who acts' switches attention from the macro to the micro. It means a concern with processes not structures and with temporary and local rather than grand and definitive solutions.

Furthermore, there is considerable criticism of the apparently a-political nature of relativism, something referred to as 'quietism' or what Herrnstein Smith (1994:289) describes as:

> the (supposed) politically disabling consequences of a rejection of objectivism: the supposed refusal to make value judgements, the supposed disinclination to take sides on political issues, and, accordingly the supposed passive support of–or, in the current phase, "complicity" with–all or any present regimes.

These are major debates which can only be hinted at here. Suffice to say, it can be acknowledged that there is a wide variety of directions in which this discussion is proceeding, suggesting fruitful inquiry about how narrative might lead to policy and political debates. I will briefly discuss four here: Silverman's micro approach to policy, Roe's discussion of 'Narrative Policy Analysis', non-objectivist and postmodern conceptions. Whilst having different interests, they suggest a move towards policies and politics based on temporary formulations, uncovering hidden stories located in ongoing processes and open dialogue.

Policy implications of micro-analysis

David Silverman has made suggestions about the policy implications of his micro-sociology in a number of studies (1985, 1987, 1990). In his research in various clinics and counselling settings, he has observed how patients, carers, nurses and doctors interact with one another. He discusses the ways in which the analysis of these encounters can lead to 'policy implications'. He suggests that particular arrangements in clinics can give patients and carers more time to collect their thoughts and ask questions of the professionals (1985:175). He notes how AIDS counsellors are able to react to the disclosure of sensitive information (1990). These are suggestions based on close observation of everyday encounters and are careful to avoid overall policies or promote 'enlightened ways of working.' For example, he notes (1987:230) how attempts at reforming the clinic through changing consulting styles, broadening the care team or support groups appear inevitably to increase professional power and surveillance. His approach is rather to acknowledge that social control is endemic in medical encounters and such dilemmas cannot be easily resolved. His conclusion is that attempts at large scale social reform might be replaced by local action and awareness.

> It might lead in a very practical sense, to all parties deciding together that they have no need to defer to general moral forms but instead

can formulate together what seems appropriate for themselves, in this situation, at this particular time. (1987:263)

This project has not considered the professional-client encounter, but concentrated on the social workers' accounts to colleagues and other audiences as narrative. This does not deny the narrativity of professional-client encounters and in other work I have, with colleagues, explored the clash of alternative voices (Hall, Sarangi and Slembrouck 1997 b). What constitutes 'enlightened' practices in social work accounts is less straightforward. If we are concerned to promote strong performances and the persuasive power of the social worker in a variety of settings, then telling better stories does offer suggestions for practice.

The social worker can take what has been offered here to make her/his stories stronger and more persuasive to critical audiences. Following chapter 8, s/he may wish to make round, complex depictions of their clients, but should be aware that courts can only cope with categorical, monologic ones. Chapter 3 suggests the importance of story structure in reports and that recommendations are 'resolutions' to 'complications', whilst the narrative puzzles of chapter 6 can persuade by intriguing the reader. In chapter 4 we saw how bringing in witnesses is important, even if they might not agree with the way they are invoked. Contrasts are a way to make a point, but they can also be challenged. Above all, know your audience and seek to construct and instruct them at every opportunity... but don't think you are telling the truth nor be taken in by your own rhetoric. This promotes the deception of rhetoric; can there be more creative approaches to narrative as policy?

Policy narratives

A rather unusual source offers an interesting link between narratives and policy. Roe (1994) is a policy analyst in the field of economics and development. His thesis is that poststructuralist approaches to narrative offer a way of investigating policy-making and can be effectively deployed with intractable public policy problems. His argument is that many areas of policy are complex with alternative viewpoints and positions. Policy makers, as we have found with social workers, discuss their policy problems in terms of 'stories', which "conform to the common definition of 'story'" (1994:36). He defines policy narratives as:

> ...stories (scenarios and arguments) which underwrite and stabilise the assumptions for policymaking in situations that persist with many unknowns, a high degree of interdependence and little, if any, agreement. (1994:34)

As such, policy narratives offer policy makers a way of describing situations and making decisions by simplifying complexity into rules of thumb and 'common sense'. Even when these stories are not able to be proved empirically, they persist, providing their narrators with explanatory and descriptive power. Roe suggests that the persistence of 'discredited' narratives should not lead to a critique which generates uncertain conclusions and debilitates action. Rather, counter narratives should be explored and a metanarrative should be constructed which brings together competing narratives into a wider explanation which incorporates opposing positions.

Much of Roe's argument is couched in realist terms of 'evidence' and 'facts', and he admits that his approach is not relativist. His solution, located in inclusive metanarratives, appears rather idealistic. However, an approach that does not see policy dilemmas as resolvable by an appeal to objectivity and facts but based on socially constructed and reinforced positions is similar to an emerging approach to a 'non-objectivity' and postmodern policy. Offering professionals endless uncertainty is not helpful. However, if facts and evidence do not offer solutions since they are equally socially constructed, then perhaps the socially constructed nature of reality offers solutions. As Roe suggests, narratives are powerful and enduring. Since solutions cannot be found in definitive truths and overall explanations, then socially constructed truths may offer ways that actors can debate their positions and stories in a situation of tolerance and negotiation. As Silverman suggests, sensitivity to narrative features and rhetorical devices by participants can help each party acknowledge their persuasive moves and seek local and temporary solutions.

Non-objectivism

Barbara Herrnstein Smith promotes both relativism and a commitment to political action. She considers that values are always contingent, every claim about truth and falsehood necessarily involving local and preferential responses, not dependent on overall principles. Indeed, the greater danger is the authoritarianism of those who claim to be objective, riding rough-shod over the claims of those who oppose them.

> ...no judgement is or could be objective in the classic sense of justifiable on totally context-transcendent and subject-independent grounds ...such claims are always empirically dubious or logically hollow, depending either on questionable appeals to supposed pure facts or human universals and/or prior taken-for-granted but contestable and thus question-begging norms. For these reasons, objectivist claims may operate quite negatively under certain conditions and are in the long run perilous for the community at large. (1994:294)

This does not mean that all claims are equally valid or that it is impossible to make meaningful value judgements or be discriminating.[4] As Brown (1994:28) notes "relativism does not entail a society without standards". Judgements can be evaluated as something other than " 'truth-value' or 'validity' in the objective, essentialist sense" (Herrnstein Smith, 1988:98). Non-objectivist judgements and hence action depend on the situation.

> ... there is nothing in the non-objectivist's epistemology that obliges her to endure passively what she sees as peril or injustice to herself or to other people. How a non-objectivist *acts* under such conditions will depend, as always, on specific features of the situation as she perceives and evaluates them, and thus also on her general values and tendencies as shaped by her prior personal history within a particular culture. (1994:301)

Such an approach to analysis and action, then, is more flexible and responsive, engaging with others, trying to persuade them and respond to their persuasion. The non-objectivist judge makes decisions based on a wide range of "contingent considerations": relevant stakes, possible alternatives, probable outcomes, historical evidence and judicial precedent, broader communal interests and goals and her own general values, beliefs and prior experiences (1994:303). There is an ongoing dialogue with continual modification and conclusions are "only contingently and contestably identifiable as best" (1994:308).

A 'non-objectivist' approach supports the local construction of judgements and a concern for temporary, co-operative decision-making. Herrnstein Smith not only promotes action based on non-objectivist analysis but highlights the advantages over objective authoritarianism. Our analysis has shown that strong, objective claims are often temporary but also that persuasive narratives are needed to bring off such claims. Clearly, non-objectivist analysis cannot be free of rhetorical and narrative moves and it is hard to see how non-objectivist debate might proceed. Perhaps the recognition of rhetorical moves might encourage a debate in which positions are exchanged and the rhetorical moves recognised and appreciated. Like Roe, it suggests reaching local and temporary agreements, without falling back on the power of objectivist rhetoric. Herrnstein Smith makes much of the role of the judge. The problem for social workers and others is what kind of judge will be persuaded by non-objectivist rhetoric?

Postmodern stories

We noted in chapter 1 that postmodernism has developed out of a distrust of metanarratives and promotes a concern for little stories ('petit recits'). Does seeking little stories suggest a way forward? Richard Harvey Brown considers that postmodernism has done much to uncover hidden voices and criticise assumptions, but it also "makes something happen" (1994:24). He supports the search for truth as invention and process, and an orientation to communication. He considers that both the social sciences and civic discourse require a language "built from the rhetorical model itself" (1994:31).

> ... a text that is self conscious about its own rhetorical structure is the exemplar of a non-delusional mode of writing for social scientists and, by extension, for citizens as well. (1994:32)

As such, a postmodern social science is empowering and enabling. We can now see that truth is socially constructed and can be judged in terms of how such claims are adequate to their respective purposes and practices.

> To pursue such questions is to be knights in search of a Holy Grail, only now we do so ironically, knowing that the quest itself is our telos, our truth, our communication. (1994:33)

For Brown such self reflection requires a community in which 'critic', 'social scientist' and 'citizen' become interchangeable (1994:25). Other postmodern writers suggest social science should get amongst the people to hear their stories (Seidman 1992:70, Huyssen 1986). There is a search for a new morality based on tolerance, democracy and seeking out unheard stories.

> As general or global analyses of [social problems] give way to densely contextual, local narratives, it would be likely that such studies would be respectful of the complex experiences of the people under study. Discourses of victimisation or heroism would give way to more morally ambiguous accounts. Local narratives are more likely to articulate the viewpoints and concerns of their subjects. In this way, social analysis could function as an important vehicle by which socially marginal or disempowered people gain a public voice. (Seidman 1992:21)

These suggestions for action are relatively new and not well debated. However, there are the seeds of an approach to policy and politics based on little narratives. Postmodernism, relativism and reflexivity have created a world in which objective science and foundational theory are no longer an answer to our complex social problems, if they ever were. What is required instead is an open dialogue between social scientists and citizens in which positions are subjected to rhetorical analysis and local and temporary agreements, negotiated in an atmosphere of scepticism and compromise. There is, of course, the question of power behind all this since some stories are more powerful than others and some judges have greater access to narrative closure, the police and imprisonment. But here the power of postmodern criticism is at its most formidable,[5] and by making alliances between citizens, the establishment can be taken on, in little ways at first. The suggestion, then, is that social workers should look away from the power of the scientific professional towards alliances with social scientists and clients, and the persuasion, deception and empowering of the storyteller.

NOTES

[1] There have been 43 social work documents and conversations displayed, concerning 28 children and their families. 5 major cases have been analysed, accounting for 16 documents. 12 documents are the journal articles in chapter 4, and 9 other fragments of documents have been analysed in some detail. A further 6 documents have been displayed as illustrations. Of the 25 documents considered in detail, 13 were from research interviews, 11 from reports and case notes and 1 radio programme. Compared to other micro-analytic studies this is a large corpus of data (Potter and Wetherell 1987:161).

[2] Gill (1995) has pointed out that 'new literary forms', such as dialogues, do not challenge authorial authority but reinforce it. By raising objections and then rebutting them, the author can appear to have successfully resisted opposition, thereby maintaining the strength of the text.

[3] The conference 'Discourse and Professions' at Uppsala in 1992 included researchers from sociolinguistics, sociology, psychology, social policy, communication studies, media studies, conversation analysis, literary theory, anthropology and educational studies. However, few papers made use of narrative theory, an exception being Hyden (1997).

[4] Knorr-Cetina and Mulkay (1983:6) note that recognising the relativity of science does not mean that it should not be deployed at particular times for specific goals.

[5] Perhaps at this late stage I am suggesting a turn towards Foucault, and a view of power as enabling and interactive (Brown 1994:30).

Bibliography

Ackroyd, P. (1991) *English Music*, London: Hamish Hamilton.
Agar, M and Hobbs, J. (1985) 'Interpreting Discourse', *Discourse Processes*,5. 1-32.
Ashmore, M. (1989) *The Reflexive Thesis: Wrighting the Sociology of Scientific Knowledge*, Chicago: Chicago University Press.
Atkinson, J.M. and Drew, P. (1979) *Order in Court*, London: Macmillan.
Atkinson, P. (1990) *The Ethnographic Imagination: Textual constructions of reality*, London: Routledge.
Atkinson, P. (1995) *Medical Talk and Medical Work*, London: Sage.
Austin, J. (1962) *How to do things with words*, Oxford: Oxford University Press.
Bakhtin, M. (1981) *The Dialogic Imagination*, Austin: University of Texas Press.
Bakhtin, M. (1984) *Problems of Dostovesky's Poetics*, Manchester: Manchester University Press.
Bakhtin, M. (1986) *Speech Genres and Other Late Essays*, Austin: University of Texas Press.
Bal, M. (1994), *Narratology: Introduction to the Theory of Narrative*, Toronto: University of Toronto Press.
Barkin, S.M. (1984) 'The Journalist as Storyteller: an interdisciplinary perspective', *American Journalism*, 1(2), 27-33.
Barthes, R. (1975) *S/Z*, London: Jonathan Cape.
Barthes, R. (1976) *The Pleasure of the Text*, London: Jonathan Cape.
Barthes, R. (1977) *Image-Music-Text*, Heath, S. (ed.), London: Fontana.
Barthes, R. (1981) 'The Discourse of History', in Schaffin, E.S. (ed.), *Comparative Criticism: a Yearbook Volume 3*, Cambridge: Cambridge University Press.
Barthes, R. (1982) *A Barthes Reader*, (ed.) Sontag, S. London: Jonathan Cape.
Batchelor, J. and Kerslake, A. (1990) *Failure to Find Failure to Thrive*, London: Whiting and Birch.
Bauman, R. (1986) *Story, Performance and Event: Contextual Studies of Oral Narrative*, Cambridge: Cambridge University Press.
Bauman, R. and Briggs, C. (1990) Poetics and Performance as Critical Perspective on Language and Social Life, *Annual Review of Anthropology*, 1990 19: 59-88.
Beckford Report (1985) *A Child in Trust: Report of the Panel of Inquiry into the Circumstances surrounding the Death of Jasmine Beckford*, London: London Borough of Brent.

Bennett, W. and Feldman, M. (1981) *Reconstructing Reality in the Courtroom*, London: Tavistock.

Bennett, T. and Woollacott, J. (1987) *Bond and Beyond: The Political Career of a Popular Hero*, Basingstoke: Macmillan.

Best, J. (1987). 'On Last Resorts', *American Journal of Sociology*, 87.1: 1-22.

Best, J. (1989), *Images of Issues: Typifing Contemporary Social Problems*, Hawthorne NY: Aldine de Gruyter.

Best, J. (1993), 'But Seriously Folks: the Limitations of the Strict Constructionist Interpretation of Social Problems', in Holstein and Miller (eds), *Reconsidering Social Constructionism: Debates in Social Problems Theory*, Hawthorne NY: Aldine de Grutyer.

Billig, M. (1985) 'Prejudice, Categorisation and Particularisation: from a Perceptual to a Rhetorical approach,' *European Journal of Social Psychology*, 15: 79-103.

Bird, E.S. and Dardenne, R.W. (1988) 'Myth, Chronicle and Story: exploring the Narrative Qualities of News', in Carey, J.W. (ed.), *Media, Myths and Narratives: Television and the Press*, London: Sage.

Blum, A. and McHugh, P. (1971) 'The Social Ascription of Motive', *American Sociological Review*, 36: 98-109.

Bourdieu, P. (1992) *Invitation to Reflexive Sociology*, London: Polity Press.

Bogen, D. and Lynch, M. (1993), ' Do We Need a General theory of Social Problems', in Holstein and Miller (eds.), *Reconsidering Social Constructionism: Debates in Social Problems Theory*, Hawthorne, NY: Aldine de Grutyer.

Brieland, D. (1959) *An Experimental study of the Selection of Adoptive Parents*, New York: Child League of America.

Brown, R Harvey. (1994), 'Reconstructing Social Theory after the Postmdoern Critique', in Simons, H and Billig, M. (eds.) *After Postmodernism: Reconstructing Ideology Critique*, Newbury Park: Sage.

Bruner, E.M. (1986) 'Ethnography as Narrative', in Turner, V. and Bruner, E.M. (eds.) *The Anthroplogy of Experience*, Chicago: University of Illnois.

Bruner, J. (1991) 'The Narrative Construction of Reality', *Critical Studies*, 18: 1-21.

Burgess, R. (ed.) (1982) *Field Research: A Sourcebook and Field Manual*, London: Allen and Unwin.

Butler, L. (1990) 'The Imaginary Present or What Isn't Literature', *Parlance*, 2.(2): 5-15.

Callon, M. (1986) 'The Sociology of an Actor Network', in Callon, M., Law, J. and Rip, A. (eds.) *Mapping the Dynamics of Science and Technology*, Basingstoke: Macmillan.

Carlile Inquiry (1987) *A Child in Mind: Protection of Children in a Responsible Society*, London: London Borough of Greenwich.
Carr, D. (1986) 'Narrative and the Real World: An Argument for Continuity', *History and Theory*, 25(2): 117-131.
Carroll, D. (1983) 'The Alterity of Discourse: Form, History and the Question of the Political in M. M. Bakhtin', *Diacritics*, 13: 65-83.
Chatman, S. (1978) *Story and Discourse: Narrative Structure in Fiction and Film*, London: Cornell University Press.
Chatman, S. (1980) 'What novels can do that films can't', *Critical Inquiry*, 7:121-140.
Chomsky, N. (1965) *Aspects of a Theory of Syntax*, The Hague: Mouton.
Cicourel, A. (1973) *Cognitive Sociology*, Harmondsworth: Penguin.
Cicourel, A. (1976) *The Social Organisation of Juvenile Justice*, London: Heinemann.
Clegg, S. (1994) 'Studying Child Sexual Abuse: Morality or Science', in *Radical Philosophy*, 66: 31-39.
Cleveland Inquiry (1988) *Report of the Inquiry into Child Abuse in Cleveland*, Cmnd 412. London: HMSO.
Clifford, J. (1988) *The Predicament of Culture: Twentieth Century Ethnography, Literature and Art*, London: Harvard University Press.
Clifford, J. and Marcus, G. (eds.) (1986) *Writing Culture: The Poetics and Politics of Ethnography*, Berkeley: University of California Press.
Cockcroft, R. and Cockcroft, S. (1992) *Persuading People: An Introduction to Rhetoric*, Basingstoke: Macmillan.
Code, L. (1994), 'Who Cares? The Poverty of Objectivism for a Moral Epistemology', in Megill, A. (ed.) *Rethinking Objectivity*, Durham, NC: Duke University Press.
Creighton, S. and Noyes, P. (1989) *Child Abuse Trends in England and Wales 1983-1987*, London: NSPCC.
Cuff, E.C.(1980) *Some Issues in Studying the Problem of Versions in Everyday Situations*, Manchester University Occasional Papers No. 3.
Culler, J. (1980) 'Fabula and Sjuzhet in the Analysis of Narrative', *Poetics Today* 1: 27-38.
Culler, J. (1981) *The Pursuit of Signs*, London: Routledge & Kegan Paul.
Dale, P. Davies, M. Morrison, T. and Waters, J. (1986) *Dangerous Families: Assessment and Treatment of Child Abuse*, London: Tavistock.
Dant, T. (1991) *Knowledge, Ideology and Discourse: A Sociological Perspective*, London: Routledge.
Department of Health (1995) *Child Protection: Messages from Research*, London: HMSO.

van Dijk, T. (1987) *Communicating Racism: Ethnic Prejudice in Thought and Talk*, London: Sage.
Dingwall, R., Eekelaar, J. & Murray, T. (1983) *The Protection Of Children: State Interventions and Family Life*, Oxford: Blackwell.
Dreyfus, H. and Rabinow, P. (1982) *Michel Foucault: Beyond Structuralism and Hermeneutics*, Hemel Hempstead: Harvester.
Eagleton, T. (1983) *Literary Theory: An Introduction*, Oxford: Blackwell.
Eco, U.(1983) *The Name of the Rose*, London: Picador.
Edwards, D., Ashmore, M. and Potter, J. (1992) 'Death and Furniture: The Rhetoric, Politics and Theology of Bottom Line Arguments against Relativism', in Pickering, A. *Science as Practice and Culture*, Chicago: University of Chicago Press.
Emerson, R.M. (1969) *Judging Delinquents*, Chicago: Aldine.
Emerson, R.M. (1987) 'On Last Resorts', *American Journal of Sociology*, 87(1): 1-22.
Fairclough, N. (1992) *Discourse and Social Change*, Cambridge: Polity.
Fish, S. (1980) *Is There a Text in this Class? the Authority of Interpretive Communities*, Cambridge, Mass: Harvard University Press.
Forster, E.M. (1974) *Aspects of the Novel*, London: Edward Arnold.
Foucault, M. (1970) *The Order of Things: An Archaeology of the Human Sciences*, London: Tavistock.
Foucault, M. (1972) *The Archaeology of Knowledge*, London: Tavistock.
Foucault, M. (1981) 'Questions of Method', *Ideology and Consciousness*, 8, 3-14.
Fox, L (1982) 'Two Value Positions in Recent Child Care Law and Practice', *British Journal of Social Work*, 12, 265-290.
Franklin, B. and Parton, N. (eds.) (1991) *Social Work, the Media and Public Relations*, London: Routledge.
Friedson, E. (1986) *Professional Powers: A Study of Institutional of Formal Knowledge*, Chicago: University of Chicago Press.
Fuhrman, E., and Oehler, K., (1986) 'Discourse Analysis and Reflexivity', *Social Studies of Science* 16: 293-307.
Game, A. (1991) *Undoing the Social: Towards a Deconstructive Sociology*, Milton Keynes: Open University Press.
Garfinkel, H. (1967) *Studies in Ethnomethodology*, Cambridge: Polity Press.
Gelles, R. (1975) 'The social construction of child abuse', *American Journal of Orthopsychiatry*, 43: 363-71.
Giddens, A. (1976) *New Rules in Sociological Methods*, London: Hutchinson.
Gidley, M (ed.) *Representing Others: White Views of Indigenous Peoples*, Exeter: Exeter University Press.
Gilbert, G. and Mulkay, M. (1984) *Opening Pandora's Box*, Cambridge: Cambridge University Press.

Gill, R. (1995) 'Relativism, Reflexivity and Politics: Interrogating Discourse Analysis from a Feminist Perspective', in Wilkinson, S. and Kitzinger, C. (eds), *Feminism and Discourse*, Newbury Park: Sage.

Gilmore, A. (1988) *Innocent Victims*, London: Michael Joseph,

Goffman, E. (1959) *The Presentation of Self in Everyday Life*. New York: Doubleday Anchor.

Goffman, E. (1981) *Forms of Talk*, Oxford: Basil Blackwell.

Goodwin, C. (1984) 'Notes on Story Structure and the Organisation of Participation', in Atkinson, J.M. and Heritage, J. (eds.) *Structures of Social Action: Studies in Conversation Analysis*, Cambridge: Cambridge University Press.

Goodwin, C. and Goodwin, M.H. (1997) 'Contested Vision: the discursvie consitution of Rodney King', in Gunnarson. B., Linell, P. and Nordberg. B. (eds.) *The Construction of Professional Discourse*, London: Longman.

Goodwin, M.H. (1990) 'He-said-she said: formal cultural procedures for the construction of a gossip dispute activity', *American Ethnologist*, 9: 76-96.

Goodman, N. (1980) 'Twisted Tales or Story, Study and Symphony', *Critical Inquiry*, 7: 103-119.

Grint, K. and Woolgar, S. (1992) 'Computers, Guns and Roses: What's Social about Being Shot', *Science Technology and Human Values*, 17: 366-380.

Gubrium, J. (1992) *Out of Control: Family Therapy and Domestic Disorder*, Newbury Park: Sage.

Gubrium, J. (1993) 'For a Cautious Naturalism', in Holstein, J.A. and Miller, G. (eds.) (1993) *Reconsidering Social Constructionism: Debates in Social Problems Theory*, Hawthorne, NY: Aldine de Gruyter.

Hacking, I. (1991) 'The Making and Molding of Child Abuse', *Critical Inquiry* 17: 253-288.

Hak, T. (1989) 'Constructing A Psychiatric Case' in Torode, B. (ed.) *Text and Talk as Social Practice,* Dordrecht: Fons.

Hall, C., Sarangi, S. and Slembrouck, S. (1995), *Narrative Transformation in Child Abuse Reporting*, Paper to the Cardiff Roundtable on Media Discourse, 6-8 July 1995.

Hall, C., Sarangi, S. and Slembrouck, S. (1997 a) 'Moral Construction in Social Work Discourse', in Gunnarson. B., Linell, P. and Nordberg. B. (eds.), *The Construction of Professional Discourse*, London: Longman.

Hall, C., Sarangi, S. and Slembrouck. (1997 b) 'Silent and Silenced Voices: Interactional Construction of Audience in Social Work Talk', in Jarowski, A. (ed.) *Silence: Interdisciplinary Perspectives*, Berlin: Mouton de Gruyter.

Hanks, W.F. (1989) 'Text and Textuality', *Annual Review of Anthropology*, 18: 95-127.
Hardiker, P. and Barker, M. (1980) *Theories of Practice in Social Work*, London: Academic.
Harre, R and Secord, P.F. (1972) *The Explanation of Social Behaviour*, Oxford: Blackwell.
Hartley, P. (1985) *Child Abuse, Social Work and the Press: Towards a History of a Moral Panic*, University of Warwick Department of Applied Social Studies.
Hawkins, K. (1983) *Environment and Enforcement: Regulation and the Social Definition of Pollution*, Oxford: Oxford University Press.
Henry Report (1987) *Whose Child? the Report of the Panel Appointed to Inquire into the Death of Tyra Henry*, London: London Borough of Lambeth.
Heritage, J. (1984) *Garfinkel and Ethnomethodology*, Cambridge: Polity Press.
Heritage, J. (1988) 'Explanations as Accounts', in Antaki,C. (ed.) *Analysing Everyday Explanation*, London: Sage.
Heritage, J. and Greatbatch, D. (1986) 'Generating Applause: A Study of Rhetoric and Response at Party Political Conferences', *American Sociological Review*, 92: 110-157.
Herndl, C. Fennell, B. and Miller, C. (1991) 'Understanding Failures in Organisational Discourse: The Accident at Three Mile Island and the shuttle Challenger Disaster', in Bazerman, C. and Paradis, J. (eds.) *The Textual Dynamics of the Professions*, Madison: University of Wisconsin Press.
Hodge, B. (1989) 'Discourse in Time: Some Notes on Method', in Torode, B (ed.) *Text and Talk as Social Practice*, Dordrecht: Fons.
Holquist, M. (1990) *Dialogism: Bakhtin and his World*, London: Routledge.
Holstein, J.A. and Miller, G. (eds.) (1993) *Reconsidering Social Constructionism: Debates in Social Problems Theory*, Hawthorne, NY: Aldine de Gruyter.
Holt, E. (1992) *Journalistic Quoting Practices*, Paper to Discourse and the Professions' Conference, Uppsala: Sweden.
Huyssen, A. (1986), *After the Great Divide: Modern, Mass culture and Post Modernism*, London: Macmillan.
Hyden, L. (1997) 'The Institutional Narrative as Drama', in Gunnarson, B., Linell, P. and Nordberg, B. (eds.) *The Construction of Professional Discourse*, London: Longman.
Illich, I., Zola, I.K., McKnight, J., Caplan, J. and Shaiken, H. (1977) *Disabling Professions*, New York: Marian Boyers.
Iser, W. (1974) *The Implied Reader*, Baltimore: John Hopkins University Press.
Iser, W. (1989) 'The Reading Process: A Phenomenological Approach', in Rice and Waugh (eds.) *Modern Literary Theory*, London: Edward Arnold.

Jacobs, J. (1982) *In the Best Interests of the Child: an Evaluation of Assessment Centres*, Oxford: Pergamon Press.
Jameson, F. (1981) *The Political Unconscious: Narrative as a Socially Symbolic Act*, London: Methuen.
Jefferson, G. (1990) 'List Construction as a Task and Resource', in Psathas, G. (ed.) *Interactional Competence*, Washington: University of American Press.
Johnson, J.M. (1989) 'Horror Stories and the Construction of Child Abuse', in Best, J. (ed.) *Images of Issues: Typifying Contemporary Social Problems*, Hawthorne, NY: Aldine de Gruyter.
Jonsson, L. and Linell, P. (1991) 'Story Generations: From Dialogical Interviews to Written Reports in Police Interrogations', *Text*, 11.3 : 419-440.
Kauffmann, R. (1990) 'The Other In Question: Dialogical Experiments in Montaigne, Kafka and Cortazar', in Maranhao, T.(ed.) *The Interpretation Of Dialogue*, Chicago: University of Chicago Press.
Knorr-Cetina, K. and Mulkay, M. (eds.) (1983), *Science of Observed: Perspectives on the Social study of Science*, London: Sage.
Kuipers, J. (1989) 'Medical Discourse in Anthropological Context: Views of Power and Language', *Medical Anthropology Quarterly*, 3.2: 99-123.
Labov, W. (1972) *Language in the Inner City*, Philadelphia: Philadelphia University Press.
Labov, W. and Fanshel, D. *Therapeutic Discourse*, London: Academic.
Labov, W. and Waletsky, J. (1967) 'Narrative Analysis: Oral Versions of Personal Experience', in Helms, J. (ed.) *Essays in the Verbal and Visual Arts*, Seattle: University of Washington Press.
Landau, M. (1984) 'Human Evolution as Narrative', *American Scientist*, 72: 262-8.
Latour, B.(1987) *Science in Action*, Milton Keynes: Open University Press.
Latour, B. (1983), 'Give Me a Laboratory and I will Raise the World', in Knorr-Cetina, K. and Mulkay, M. (eds.) *Science of Observed: Perspectives on the Social study of Science*, London: Sage.
Latour, B. and Woolgar, S. (1986) *Laboratory Life: the Social Construction of Scientific Facts*, Princeton: Princeton University Press.
Latour, B. and Bastide, F. (1986) Writing Science - Fact or Fiction, in Callon. M., Law, J. and Rip, A. *Mapping the Dynamics of Science and Technology*, Basingstoke: Macmillan.
Law, J. (1986) The Heterogeneity of Texts, in Callon, M., Law, J. and Rip, A. *Mapping the Dynamics of Science and Technology*, Basingstoke: Macmillan.
Lawson, H. (1985) *Reflexivity: the post-modern predicament*, London: Hutchinson.

Levinson, S. (1983) *Pragmatics*, Cambridge: Cambridge University Press.
London, B. (1990) *The Appropriated Voice: Narrative Authority in Conrad, Forster and Woolf*, Ann Arbor: University of Michigan Press.
Loseke, D. (1989) 'Violence is Violence .. Or Is It? The Social Construction of Wife Abuse and Public Policy', in Best, J. (ed.) *Images of Issues: Typifying Contemporary Social Problems*, Hawthorne, NY: Aldine de Gruyter.
Lyons, J. (1977) *Semantics*, Cambridge: Cambridge University Press.
Lyotard, J-F. (1984) *The Postmodern Condition: A report on Knowledge* Manchester: Manchester University Press.
McIntyre, A. (1984) *After Virtue*, London: Duckworth.
MacLean, M. (1988) *Narrative as Performance: The Baudelaire Experiment*, London: Routledge.
Maluccio, A. Fein, E. and Olmstead, K. (1986) *Permanency Planning for Children*, London: Tavistock.
Manning, P.K. (1986) 'Texts as Organisational Echoes', *Human Studies* 9: 287-302.
Marcus, J. (1987) *Virginia Woolf and the Languages of Patriarchy*, Bloomington: Indiana University Press.
Mecke, J. (1990) 'Dialogue in Narration', in Maranhao, T. (ed.) *The Interpretation Of Dialogue*, Chicago: University of Chicago Press.
Miller, G. (1993) 'New Challenges to Social Constructionism: Alternative Perspectives on Social Problems Theory', in Holstein, J.A. and Miller, G. (eds.) *Reconsidering Social Constructionism: Debates in Social Problems Theory*, Hawthorne, NY: Aldine de Gruyter.
Miller, L. (1993) 'Claims-Making from the Underside', in Holstein, J.A. and Miller, G. (eds.) *Reconsidering Social Constructionism: Debates in Social Problems Theory*, Hawthorne, NY: Aldine de Gruyter.
Mink, L. (1978) 'Narrative Form as a Cognitive Instrument', in Canary and Kozichi (eds.) *The Writing of History*, Madison: University of Wisconsin.
Mishler, E. (1986) *Research Interviewing*, London: Harvard University Press.
Morson, G, and Emerson, C. (1990) *Mikhail Bakhtin: the Creation of a Prosaics*, Stanford: Stanford University Press.
Mulkay, M. (1985) 'Conversations and Texts', *Human Studies*, 9: 303-321.
Myers, G. (1990) 'Making a Discovery: Narrative of Split Genes' in Nash, C. (ed.) *Narrative in Culture*, London: Routledge.
Norman, A.P. (1991) 'Telling It Like It Was: Historical Narratives on their own Terms', *History and Theory*, 30.2:119-135.
Orkney Report (1992) *The Report of the Inquiry into the Removal of Children From Orkney In February 1992*, Edinburgh: HMSO.
Packman, J. and Hall, C. (1997) *From Care to Accommodation: Support, Protection and Control in Child Care Services*, London, The Stationery Office.

Palmer, F. (1986) *Mood and Modality*, Cambridge: Cambridge University Press.
Parton, N. (1985) *The Politics of Child Abuse*, London: Macmillan.
Parton, N. (1991), *Governing the Family: Child Care, Child Protection and the State*, London: Macmillan.
Parton, N. (1996) 'Child Protection, family support and social work: a critical appraisal of the Department of Health research in child protection', *Child and Family Social Work*, 1: 3-11.
Pfohl, S. (1977) 'The Discovery of Child Abuse', *Social Problems*', 24: 310-23.
Phillips, N. (1995) 'Telling Organisational Tales: On the Role of Narrative Fiction in the Study of Organisations', *Organisational Studies* 16(4): 625-649.
Philpot, T. (1991) *The Professional Press: social work talking to itself*, in Franklin, R. and Parton, N. (eds.) *Social Work, the Media and Public Relations*, London: Routledge.
Pithouse, A. (1987) *Social Work: The Organisation of an Invisible Trade*, Aldershot: Gower.
Pithouse, A. and Atkinson, P. (1988) 'Telling the Case: Occupational Narrative in a Social Work Office', in Coupland, N. (ed.) *Styles of Discourse*, London: Croom Helm.
Poggi, G. (1990) 'Anthony Giddens and the Classics', in Clark, J. Modgil, C. and Modgil, S. (eds) *Anthony Giddens: Consensus and Controversy*, London: Falmer Press.
Polanyi, L. (1985) 'Conversational Storytelling', in Van Dijk, T. (ed.) *Handbook of Discourse Analysis, Vol.3*, London: Academic Press.
Pomerantz, A. (1986) 'Extreme Case Formulations: A New Way of Legitimating Claims', *Human Studies* 9: 291-30.
Potter, J. and Mulkay, M. (1985) 'Scientists Interview Talk', in Brenner, M. Brown, J. and Canter, D.(eds.) *The Research Interview*, London: Academic Press.
Potter, J. and Wetherell, M. (1987) *Discourse and Social Psychology: Beyond Attitudes and Behaviour*, London: Sage.
Pratt, M.L. (1986) 'Field work in Common Places', in Clifford, J. and Marcus, G. (eds.) *Writing Culture: The Poetics and Politics of Ethnography*, Berkeley: University of California Press.
Prince, G. (1973) *A Grammar of Stories*, The Hague: Mouton.
Propp, V. (1968) *The Morphology of the Folk Tale*, Austin: University of Texas Press.
Rice, P. and Waugh, P. (eds.) (1989) *Modern Literary Theory: A Reader*, London: Edward Arnold.
Rip. A. (1986) *Mobilising Resources through Texts*, in Callon, M., Law, J. and Rip, A. *Mapping the Dynamics of Science and Technology*, Basingstoke: Macmillan.

Rochdale (1990) Judgment discussed in Wattam, C. (1992) *Making a Case in Child Protection*, London: Longman.
Roe, E., (1994) *Narrative Policy Analysis: Theory and Practice*, Durham, NC: Duke University Press.
Rose, N. (1990) *Governing the Soul: The Shaping of the Private Self*, London: Routledge.
Rosenau, P.M. (1992) *Post-Modernism and the Social Sciences*, Princeton: Princeton University Press.
Rostila, I. (1994) 'The Treatment of Client Responsibility in Encounters between Social Workers and Clients,' in Gunnarson, B., Linell, P. and Nordberg, B. (eds.) *Texts and Talk in Professional Contexts*, Uppsala: ASLA.
Rumelhart, D.(1980) 'On Everyday Story Grammars', *Cognitive Science*, 4: 313-316
Sacks, H. (1972) 'On the Analyzability of Stories by Children', in Gumperz, J. and Hymes, D. (eds.) *Directions in Sociolinguistics: the ethnography of communication*, New York: Holt, Rinehart and Winston.
Sacks, H. (1992) *Lectures on Conversation. Volume 2*, (ed.) Jefferson,G. Oxford: Blackwell.
Said, E. (1978) *Orientalism*, New York: Pantheon.
Said, E. (1983), *'The World, the Text and the Critic*, London: Vintage.
Sapir, E. (1929) 'The status of linguistics as a science,' *Language*, 5: 209.
Scheff, T. (1966) *Being Mentally Ill*, London: Weidenfeld and Nicholson.
Schiffrin, D. (1987) *Discourse Markers*, Cambridge: Cambridge University Press.
Schneider, J. (1985) 'Defining the Definitional Perspective on Social Problems', *Social Problems*, 32: 236-8.
Schneider, J. (1993) 'Members Only: Reading the Constructionist Text', in Holstein, J.A. and Miller, G. (eds.) *Reconsidering Social Constructionism: Debates in Social Problems Theory*, Hawthorne, NY: Aldine de Gruyter.
Scott, M. and Lyman, S. (1968) 'Accounts', *American Sociological Review*, 33: 46-62.
Seidman, S. (1992) 'Postmodern Social Theory as Narrative with a Moral Intent', in Seidman, S. and Wagner, D. (eds.) *Postmodernism and Social Theory: The Debate over General Theory*, Oxford: Blackwell.
Semin, G. and Manstead, A. (1983) *The Accountability of Conduct: a Social Psychological Analysis*, London: Academic Press.
Sharrock, W. and Watson, D.R. (1984) 'What's the point of 'rescuing motives?', *British Journal of Sociology*, 25, 3: 435-51.
Shepherd, D. (1989) 'Bakhtin and the Reader', in Hirschkop, K. and Shepherd, D. (eds.) *Bakhtin and Cultural Theory*, Manchester: Manchester University Press.

Shuman, A. (1986) *Storytelling Rights: The Use of Oral and Written Texts by Urban Adolescents*, Cambridge: Cambridge University Press.
Silverman, D. (1973) 'Interview Talk: Bringing off a Research Instrument', *Sociology*, 7(1): 32-48.
Silverman, D. (1985) *Qualitative Methodology and Sociology*, Aldershot: Gower.
Silverman, D. (1987) *Communication and Medical Practice: Social Relations in the Clinic*, London: Sage.
Silverman, D. (1990) *Sociology and the Community: A Dialogue of the Deaf?*, An Inaugural Lecture, Goldsmith's College, University of London.
Smith, B. Herrnstein (1978) *On the Margins of Discourse*, Chicago: Chicago University Press.
Smith, B. Herrnstein (1980) 'Narrative Versions, Narrative Theories', *Critical Inquiry* 7: 212-236'
Smith, B. Herrnstein. (1987) *Contingencies of Value: Alternative Perspectives for Critical Theory*, Cambridge, Mass: Harvard University Press.
Smith, B. Herrnstein (1994) 'The Unquiet Judge: Activism without Objectivism', in Law and Politics', in Megill, A. (ed.) *Re-thinking Objectivity*, Durham, NC: Duke University Press.
Smith, D. (1993) *Texts, Facts and Femininity: Exploring the Relations of Ruling*, London: Routledge.
Spector, M. and Kitsuse, J. (1977) *Constructing Social Problems*, Hawthorne, NY: Aldine De Gruyter.
Spencer, J. (1988) 'The Role of Text in the Processing of People in Organisations', *Discourse Processes* 11: 61-78.
Stanley, S. (1991) 'Studying Talk in Probation Interviews', in Davies, M.(ed.) *The Sociology of Social Work*, London: Routledge.
Stenson, K. (1988) *Social Work Discourse and the Social Work Interview*, Unpublished Ph.D Thesis, Department of Human Sciences, Brunel University.
Stewart, A.H. (1991) 'The Role of Narrative Structure in the Transfer of Ideas', in Bazerman, C. and Paradis, J. (eds.) *The Textual Dynamics of the Professions*, Wisconsin: Wisconsin University Press.
Stocking, G.W. (ed.) (1983) *The Observers Observed: Essays on Ethnographic Fieldwork*, Madison: University of Wisconsin Press.
Strong, P. and Dingwall, R. (1983) 'The Limits of Negotiation in Formal Organisations', in Gilbert, G.N. and Abel, P. (eds.) *Accounts and Action*, Aldershot: Gower.
Thibault, P. (1989) 'Semantic Variation, Social Heteroglossia, Intertextuality: Thematic and Axiological Meaning in Spoken Discourse', *Critical Studies* 1(2): 181-209.
Tiryakian, E. (1979) 'Emile Durkheim', in Bottomore, T and Nisbet, R. (eds.) *A History of Sociological Analysis*, London: Heinemann.
Todorov, T. (1977) *The Poetics of Prose*, Oxford: Blackwell.

Todorov, T. (1984) *Mikhail Bakhtin: the Dialogical Principle*, Manchester: Manchester University Press.
Toulmin, S. (1958) *The Uses of Argument*, Cambridge: Cambridge University Press.
Tyler, S. (1990) 'Ode to Dialog on the Occasion of the Un-for-seen', in Maranhao, T.(ed.) *The Interpretation Of Dialogue*, Chicago: University of Chicago Press.
Vernon, J. and Fruin, D. (1986) *In Care: a Study of Social Work Decision Making*, London: National Children's Bureau.
Voloshinov, V.N. (1973) *Marxism and the Philosophy of Language*, New York: Seminar Press.
Watson, R. (1978) 'Categorisation, Authorisation and Blame Negotiation in Conversation', *Sociology*, 12: 105-13.
Watson, R. and Weinberg, T. (1982) 'Interviews and the Interactional Construction of Accounts of Homomsexual Identity', *Social Analysis*, 11: 56-77.
White, H. (1980) 'The Value of Narrativity in the Representation of Reality', *Critical Inquiry*, 7: 5-27.
White, H. (1987) *The Content of Form: Narrative Discourse and Historical Representation*, Baltimore: The John Hopkins University Press.
Wilensky, R. (1982) 'Story Grammars versus Story Points', *Behavioural and Brain Sciences*, 6: 579-623.
Wooffitt, R. (1992) *Telling Tales of the Unexpected: The Organisation of Factual Discourse*, Hemel Hempstead: Harvester.
Woolgar, S. (1976) 'Writing an Intellectual History of Scientific Development: The Use of Discovery Accounts', *Social Studies Of Science* 6: 395-422.
Woolgar, S. (1980) 'Discovery: Logic and Sequence in a Scientific Text', in Knorr, K. Krohn, R. and Whitley, R. (eds.) *The Social Process Of Scientific Investigation*, Dordrecht: Reidel.
Woolgar, S. (1983) 'Irony in the Social Study of Science', in Knorr-Cetina, K.D. and Mulkay, M. (eds.) *Science Observed: Perspectives in the Social Study of Science*, London: Sage.
Woolgar, S. (1986) 'On the Alleged Distinction Between Discourse and Praxis', *Social Studies of Science*, 16:.309-17.
Woolgar, S. and Ashmore, M. (1988) 'The Next Step: An Introduction to the Reflexive Project' in Woolgar, S. (ed.) *Knowledge and Reflexivity: New Frontiers in the Sociology of Knowledge*, London: Sage.
Woolgar, S. and Pawluch, D. (1985) 'Ontological Gerrymandering: the Anatomy of Social Problems Explanations', *Social Problems* 32(3): 214-227.
Wootton, B. (1959) *Social Science and Social Pathology*, London: George Allen and Unwin.

Zimmerman, D. (1969) 'Record-keeping and the intake process in a public welfare agency', in Wheeler, S. (ed.) *On Record: File and Dossiers in American Life*, New York: Russell Sage Foundation.

Author Index

Ackroyd, P., 225
Agar, M., 36
Ashmore, M., 38-9, 101, 234, 240
Atkinson, J.M., 67, 82-3
Atkinson, P., 5, 19, 37-8, 73, 102-3, 121, 134, 140, 152, 167, 234, 235
Austin, J., 25

Bakhtin, M., 16, 29-34, 35, 42, 43, 57-8, 61, 123, 181, 184, 190-1, 194, 198, 199, 202-4
Bal, M., 5, 33, 43
Barker, M., 22
Barkin, S.M., 91
Barthes, R., 5, 12, 29, 35, 39, 42, 55, 144, 204
Batchelor, J., 104
Bauman. R., 13, 24, 147-9, 165
Bennett, T., 145
Bennett, W., 41
Best, J., 94, 104, 237-8
Billig, M., 206
Bird, E.S., 43
Blum, A., 80
Bogen, D., 237-8
Bourdieu, P., 38
Brieland, D., 235
Briggs, C.13, 24
Brown, R Harvey., 247-8, 249
Bruner, E.M., 14
Bruner, J., 42
Burgess, R., 21
Butler, L., 41, 237

Callon, M., 92, 179
Carr, D., 31, 43
Carroll, D., 180

Chatman, S., 29-30, 33, 34, 92, 162, 204-5
Chomsky, N., 35
Cicourel, A., 36, 82, 134
Clegg, S., 81-2
Clifford, J., 38, 182
Cockcroft, R., 12
Cockcroft, S., 12
Code, L., 102
Creighton, S., 93
Cuff, E.C., 82-3, 88, 203, 207, 224, 225
Culler, J., 26, 42, 177
Dale, P., 82
Dant, T., 13
Dardenne, R.W., 43
Davies, M., 82
Department of Health., 2, 81, 91
van Dijk, T., 42
Dingwall, R., 22, 38, 73, 82, 89, 90, 93, 104
Drew, P., 67, 82-3
Dreyfus, H., 14-15

Eagleton, T., 179, 180
Eco, U., 34
Edwards, D., 101
Eekelaar, J., 22, 73, 82, 89, 90, 93, 104
Emerson, C., 31-3, 59, 183-4, 199, 203
Emerson, R.M., 95-6

Fairclough, N., 15
Fanshel, D., 25
Fein, E., 168
Feldman, M., 41
Fennell, B., 94
Fish, S., 56
Forster, E.M., 205

Foucault, M., 14-16, 18, 34, 38, 93, 165, 243, 249
Fox, L., 199
Franklin, B., 1, 84
Friedson, E., 2
Fruin, D., 9-10
Fuhrman, E., 19

Game, A.., 12
Garfinkel, H., 11-12, 37, 39, 42, 51, 52, 58, 67-8, 80-1, 89, 104, 195, 219, 235
Gelles, R., 79, 82
Giddens, A., 11
Gidley, M., 182
Gilbert, G., 3, 10, 22, 35, 84, 219
Gill, R., 249
Gilmore, A., 104
Goffman, E., 58, 64, 72, 202
Goodman, N., 58, 135
Goodwin, C., 27-8, 73
Goodwin, M.H., 73, 167
Greatbatch, D., 94, 133
Grint. K., 23, 125-6
Gubrium, J., 3, 206, 207, 236, 237

Hacking, I., 81, 102, 104, 239
Hak, T., 165-6
Hall, C., 72, 104, 167, 245
Hanks, W.F., 13
Hardiker, P., 22
Harre, R., 36
Hartley, P., 34
Hawkins, K., 82
Heritage, J., 11, 18, 83, 94, 104, 133
Herndl, C., 94
Hobbs, J., 36
Hodge, B., 165-6
Holquist, M., 202

Holstein, J.A., 237
Holt, E. 183, 186, 188
Huyssen, A. 248
Illich, I., 2
Iser, W., 56, 58

Jacobs, J., 61
Jameson, F., 5, 16
Jefferson, G., 63, 94
Jonsson, L., 73

Kauffmann, R., 182
Kerslake, A., 104
Kitsuse, J., 125, 237
Knorr-Cetina, K., 249
Kuipers, J., 15

Labov, W., 5, 25-8, 30, 40, 42, 130, 135, 148, 149
Landau, M., 5
Latour, B., 6, 71, 118-20, 138, 143, 146-7, 178, 203, 219, 240
Law, J., 71, 72, 163
Lawson, H., 38
Levinson, S., 22
Linell, P., 73
London, B., 179, 182
Loseke, D., 102, 240
Lyman, S., 11
Lynch, M., 237-8
Lyons, J., 193
Lyotard, J-F., 14, 16, 42, 180-1

McHugh, P., 80
McIntyre, A., 39
MacLean, M., 23, 104
Maluccio, A., 168
Manning, P.K., 37
Manstead, A., 11
Marcus, J., 38, 181

Mecke, J., 58
Medvedev, P.N., 30-1, 43
Miller, C., 94
Miller, G., 237, 240
Miller, L., 237
Mink, L., 37, 41
Mishler, E., 46, 53
Morrison, T., 82
Morson, G., 31-3, 59, 183-4, 199, 203
Mulkay, M., 3, 10, 17, 22, 35, 39, 84, 219, 249
Murray, T., 22, 73, 82, 89, 90, 93, 104
Myers, G., 41

Norman, A.P., 39
Noyes, P., 93

Oehler, K., 19
Olmstead, K., 168

Packman, J, 167
Palmer, F., 198
Parton, N., 1, 81-2, 84, 239
Pawluch, D., 238-9
Pfohl, S., 81, 239
Philips, N., 41
Philpot, T., 104
Pithouse, A., 2, 5, 37-8, 134, 167
Poggi, G., 80
Polanyi, L., 26, 42
Pomerantz, A., 96
Potter, J., 10, 17, 82, 96, 101, 249
Pratt, M.L. 24
Prince, G., 42, 51-2, 135
Propp, V., 42, 204

Rabinow, P., 14-15
Rice, P., 16, 29

Rip. A., 71, 72
Roe, E, 55, 244-7
Rose, N., 16
Rosenau, P.M., 24
Rostila, I., 19
Rumelhart, D., 5, 42

Sacks, H., 25, 27-9, 33, 42, 46-7, 60, 120, 225
Said, E., 14-16
Sapir, E., 236
Sarangi, S., 72, 104, 105, 245
Scheff, T., 236
Schegloff, E. A., 25
Schiffrin, D., 36, 61, 63
Schneider, J., 102, 238
Scott, M., 11
Secord, P.F., 36
Seidman, S., 248
Semin, G., 11
Sharrock, W., 35
Shepherd, D., 56
Shuman, A.., 26, 37, 118, 120-1, 123-4, 126, 140, 147-50, 165, 167, 183-4, 199
Silverman, D., 9, 12, 29, 82-3, 225, 244-6
Slembrouck., S., 72, 104, 245
Smith, B. Herrnstein., 29-30, 34, 41, 102, 237, 244, 246-7
Smith, D., 12-13, 33-4, 42, 60, 61-2, 84, 117-8, 120, 122, 129, 131, 133, 134, 140, 155, 160, 201, 206, 214
Spector, M., 125, 237
Spencer, J., 22, 226
Stanley, S., 19
Stenson, K., 16, 19
Stewart, A.H., 26, 42
Stocking, G.W., 182

Strong, P., 38

Thibault, P., 144
Tiryakian, E., 80
Todorov, T., 42, 43, 159, 199, 204
Toulmin, S., 53, 94, 130, 225
Tyler, S., 179

Vernon, J., 9-10
Voloshinov, V.N., 30-1, 43, 183

Waletsky, J., 25, 42, 46, 130, 135, 148, 189
Waters, J., 82
Watson, R., 10, 35, 42, 82-3, 225
Waugh, P., 16, 29
Weinberg, T., 10, 42
Wetherell, M., 82, 96, 249
White, H., 33, 37, 41, 42, 43, 51-2, 70, 86, 93
Wilensky, R., 5, 42
Wooffitt, R., 22, 121, 183, 186, 187-8, 196-7
Woolgar, S., 19, 23, 35, 38-9, 84, 102, 118-120, 121, 125-6, 138 160, 212, 234, 238-9
Woollacott, J., 145
Wootton, B., 2

Zimmerman, D., 82

Subject Index

Accounts, accounting, 10, 29, 35, 37, 53, 80, 82, 89, 102, 121-2, 204, 207
  accountable, 11-12, 17, 26, 224
Agency, 120-1
Appropriation, 181-2, 185, 191
Assessment, 131-8, 145, 150-1, 210, 220, 222
Audience(s), 4, 6, 7, 24, 26, 30, 34, 53, 55, 57, 58, 63, 65, 68, 71, 82, 84, 97, 124, 144, 148-49, 152, 154, 156, 162, 214, 216-8, 221, 233, 245
Authority, 2, 6, 37, 43, 83, 93, 123, 140, 181
  authorisation, 33
  authoritative discourse, 61, 191

Beckford Report, 89, 91
Binding instructions, 63-6
Blackboxes, blackboxing, 144, 146-7, 149-50, 152-3, 160, 162-3, 165
Blame, blamings, 79-80, 82-84, 86, 88-92, 94, 96, 152, 162, 215, 217

Care proceedings, 189-90
Case conference, 119, 123, 150-3, 208-10
Case file notes, 51-2, 67-72, 99, 190, 219-221, 223
Categorical assertions, 147, 192-4
Categories, categorization, 60-1, 100, 122, 126, 129, 131-4, 204-14, 216-8, 220, 226
Character(s), 33-4, 46, 48, 50, 68, 70, 79, 85-7, 88-90, 128-30, 132-4, 144-7, 148-9, 150-51, 154-5, 157-61, 163, 181, 186, 195, 201-14, 219-225
  ambiguous, 214,
  in Dostoevsky, 184, 195, 202-3
  round and flat, 205-6, 211, 224
  unfinalised, 34, 202-3, 211, 216
Child abuse, 2, 12, 18, 45, 54, 68, 72, 73, 104, 121-2, 125-6, 134, 208-10, 224, 239-40, 243
  as media construction, 83-91
  as moral category, 79-82, 102-3
Children Act 1989, 2, 21, 167
Claims, 38, 96-7, 102-3, 104, 119, 134, 135-7, 143, 147, 162, 181-3, 219, 222, 225, 237-8, 240, 246
Cleveland report, 2
Coherence, 36
Community, 13, 35, 37, 51, 52-3, 54, 56, 57, 60-5, 68-9, 78, 84, 92, 119, 145, 146, 224, 248
  interpretative community, 56-7, 60
Competence, 10, 35-6, 52, 63, 102
Contextualisation, 123
Contrasts, 18, 50-1, 61-2, 66, 95-8, 128, 210, 216, 222, 242
Conversation, 13, 48, 57, 68, 72, 83
Conversation analysis, 22, 24, 37, 183
Counselling, 4, 161, 236, 244
Cross examination, 67, 83

Deception, 180, 189
Dialogue(s), 30-1, 37, 57, 58, 67, 187, 203, 249
Discourse, 13-15, 30, 57
  analysis, 15-16, 19
  types, 184

Discursive formations, 14-16, 18, 93
Documentary method, 39, 89, 98, 101, 139

Effects, 34
Emplotment, 86-7, 93
Entitlement, 26, 36-8, 49, 52, 58, 81, 118, 123, 132-4, 148, 150, 183, 195, 209, 211
Evaluation, 10, 64, 68, 80, 149, 151, 158, 191
Events, 10, 25, 27, 29, 33, 37, 39, 46, 48-9, 51, 53, 57, 68, 70, 85-7, 100, 102, 130-1, 144-5, 148-53, 157-66, 214, 219, 221
Excuses, 11, 82, 87-9, 212
Extreme case formulation, 96-7, 128, 136, 213, 216

Facts, 39, 50, 55, 67, 68-9, 70-71, 102, 119-121, 122, 137, 139, 146-7, 149, 155, 165, 191, 214
  fact construction, 37, 117-120, 132-4
  interview data as facts, 9-11, 17-18
Failure to thrive, 91-5, 97, 104
Family therapy, 3, 236
Floor-seeking, 28, 46, 49,
Formal method, 33, 43, 165-6, 204
Fostering, 155, 167, 188, 213
Function, 35-6

Gaps and slippage, 178, 182, 185, 195, 201, 224

Heteroglossia, 32, 181

Inquiries, 2, 83-91

Intertextuality, 144-6
Invitation, 25

Language, 5, 12, 16, 25, 31-2, 34, 35, 38, 57, 65, 235-7
Last resort, 95-7, 105, 212
Literary theory, 5, 29, 32, 35, 40, 42, 55-6, 144, 181, 202-6

Media, 104,
  reporting of social work, 1-2
  reporting child abuse, 83-91
Medical evidence, 37, 67, 69, 93
Medical records, 12, 43, 58, 67, 88
Mental illness, 14, 117-8, 121-2, 134, 206
Modalities, 147, 155
Morals, 79-80, 101, 134, 139
  moral character, 89-90, 91-100, 134
  moral assessment, 37, 47, 82

Narrative, narratives, 5-6, 13-17, 25, 29-33, 34, 41-3, 46, 52, 66, 135-7, 236-7, 240, 246
  a-psychological and psychological, 43, 159
  grand and little, 5, 14-16, 24, 247
  historical, 33-4, 36, 39, 41, 43, 51
  institutional, 151
  interactional, 16, 18, 19, 27, 29-30, 32, 38, 40, 42, 46,
  metanarrative, 14, 16, 246
  non- narrative, 137
  occupational, 37-8
  personal, 120
  policy, 245-6
Narrative analysis, 26, 33, 101

Narrative features, 29, 41-2, 51, 136, 242, 246
Nomination, 204
Non-objectivism, 246-7

Orkney report, 2
The Other, 180-5, 194, 198-9, 201, 207, 223
Out-there-ness, 118, 120-1

Parody, 184
Particularisation, 206, 221
Pathing devices, 120, 121, 136
Pattern, 87-9, 93-4
Performance(s), 3, 16, 17, 23-5, 29, 31-3, 35, 37, 55, 61, 95, 100-4, 123, 131, 135, 148, 162, 183, 202, 207, 234, 245
Persuasion, persuasive devices, 10, 12, 24, 54, 101, 138, 177-80, 191, 235, 245, 249
Planning, 10
Plot, 33-4, 48, 51-2, 70-1, 121, 148-50, 204-5, 224
Point of view, 34, 69-70, 84-5, 92-3, 100, 185
Policy, 17, 243-9
Postmodernism, 236, 246, 247-9
Poststructuralism, 240, 245
Predisposition, 86-7, 93-4
Principled position of doubt, 203, 207, 224
Professional(s), 2-3, 11, 35-6, 59, 68-70, 80, 86, 91, 92, 236
Pronouns, 63-4, 199
Prostitution, 134, 137, 150, 158
Puzzle, 27, 60, 155
  narrative puzzle, 137-8, 140, 143, 149-153, 155, 157-165
Rational decision-making, 71, 235

Reader(s), reading, 6, 23, 26, 29, 31, 33, 36-7, 41-2, 55-71
  critical, 55, 71, 149-50, 178, 180, 186, 194, 201, 205, 207, 208, 213-4, 223, 224, 234, 245
  entitled, 52, 58, 68, 219
  first-time, 154, 159
  ideal, 125-6
  implied, 58, 234
  informed, 149-52, 156, 162, 186, 207
  occasions, 13, 30, 55, 57, 132, 145, 177, 197, 207, 221
  passive, 178-9, 184
  ratified, 58-71, 85, 91, 101, 131-2, 145, 147, 151, 159, 179, 184, 186, 202, 206, 207, 223, 234
  relations, 51-2, 55, 70, 100, 135, 145, 164, 202-3, 207,
  role of, 42, 55-6
Recontextualisation, 186
Reflexive, reflexivity, 36, 38-41, 238, 240, 243, 248
Relativist, relativism, 102, 239, 243-4, 246-7, 248
Reported speech, 31, 48, 61, 66-7, 123, 142, 157, 183-8, 194-7, 199
  and described speech, 183-5
  double voiced discourse, 184, 191
  indirect speech 187, 191
Reports,
  case history, 131, 133,
  court, 48-57, 65-7, 72, 186, 221-3
  social work, 13, 23, 131-8, 150-8, 212-4
Representation, 12, 27, 39, 181-2, 195, 240, 243

adequacy of, 202-3, 208
Research interviews, 17-18, 42, 53
  analysis of, 91-100, 126-30,
    156-63, 185-192, 211, 214-9
  as data, 9-11, 46
  as invited stories, 42
Residential care, 154-8, 160, 163
Rhetoric, rhetorical features, 12,
  17, 53, 94-5, 100-1, 104, 160,
  165, 177, 179, 185, 195, 210, 223,
  242, 245, 246, 248
Serious situations, 129-130
Silenced, 146, 152, 163, 191
Social construction, 3, 81, 102-3,
  125-6, 237-40
  of medicine 102
  of social work, 3
Social work, 2-4, 35, 91, 85-6,
  101-2, 117, 124, 130, 242
  as accounts, 11-12
  as performance, 3, 55
  as narrative, 13-14
  as storytelling, 122
  as text 12-13, 55
  criticism of, 2, 194
  intervention, 61-2, 88-91, 95-6,
    99-100, 132, 147, 153, 161,
    185, 190, 204
  use of phrases, 60-2, 73
Sociology of science, 6, 35, 37,
  146, 240, 249
Speech acts 24-5,
  serious speech acts, 15
Speech genre, 31-2
State of affairs, 42, 47-51, 61-2,
  130, 136, 151, 155-8, 162, 191,
  193-4,
Stories,
  autonomous and interactional,
    29-30

cameo, 157-8
conversational 24-9, 46, 48, 167
fight, 148-9
low risks, 126-9
mediate storytelling, 124, 136
news, 43, 91, 104, 183
paranormal, 183
psychological and a-psychological, 43, 159, 204
tall, 147-8
Story evaluation, 26, 48, 50, 63,
  130, 135-6, 149, 156, 189, 193,
  200, 209
Story structure, 25-30, 37, 40, 42,
  46-51, 53-4, 61, 135, 213, 242
Subversion, 16, 40, 180, 184-5,
  207
Superaddressee, 58, 65-8, 89, 103,
  234
Synecdoche, 152, 162

Tale world, 148-50, 153-4, 156,
  158, 163
Tenses, 136
Texts, 12-13, 23-4, 26, 36, 38, 41,
  55, 144-5, 179
  dialogic texts, 57
  literary texts, 13, 23, 29-30, 35,
    56
  monologic, 181, 191, 203-4,
    210-1, 221, 224
Three line lists, 130, 133, 137,
  191, 211, 212, 242
Three stage feature, 94-7, 105
Trusted teller, 84, 118, 133
Turn-taking, 29

Unfinalised, 32, 34
Unheard stories, versions, 43, 100,
  104, 134, 188, 191, 215-6, 223-4
Utterance, 31-2

Verisimilitude, 177
Versions, 10, 12, 34-5, 82, 84, 102,
    137-8, 145, 148-50, 160-6, 180,
    182, 206-7
  dispreferred, 59, 61, 132
Voices, 63, 92-3, 180-2, 184-5,
    197, 203, 245
  of the client, 19, 185, 189, 191,
    194, 198
Warrant, 94-7, 130
Witnesses, 27, 83, 122, 132-3,
    216-7

X but not X, 216-9, 220-1

Y'know, 62-5